The Socialist
Economies
in Transition

The Socialist Economies in Transition

A PRIMER ON SEMI-REFORMED SYSTEMS

Robert W. Campbell

INDIANA UNIVERSITY PRESS
Bloomington & Indianapolis

Library of Congress Cataloging-in-Publication Data

Campbell, Robert Wellington.
    The socialist economies in transition : a primer on semi-reformed
systems / Robert W. Campbell.
        p.   cm.
    Includes bibliographical references and index.
    ISBN 0-253-31301-5. — ISBN 0-253-20670-7 (pbk.)
    1. Europe, Eastern—Economic conditions—1989–   2. Europe,
Eastern—Economic conditions—1945–1989.   3. Soviet Union—Economic
conditions—1985–   I. Title.
HC244.C35   1991
338.947—dc20   91-8653

1 2 3 4 5   95 94 93 92 91

Contents

Figures

Tables

Preface

This book originated in a series of lectures the author was invited to give in China on the economies and public finance of the countries of Eastern Europe. That invitation reflected the great attention that financial problems had attracted in China's own experience with economic reform. As I began to try to systematize my thoughts on how economic reform, finance, money, and macroequilibrium interact in the process of reform, I came to see how this theme could help me deal with an increasingly worrisome problem of my own: finding a new framework for the survey course I teach on Soviet-type economies. It is obviously too early to drop the idea of the Soviet-type economy, pretending that the socialist economies work just like any market economy and can best be understood by mastering introductory economics. At the same time, though the classic centrally planned economy model may be exotically fascinating, it no longer exists in the socialist world, and the issue that is relevant today is the problem of the transitional stage between the two cases. In this transitional, semi-reformed economy, issues of macroeconomics, finance, and prices emerge from the irrelevancy they had in the traditional administrative-command system to become central issues of economic policy. That is the idea I have tried to realize in this book.

In keeping with the theme of transition, it is necessary that we look backward at the system that is being abandoned, to understand what it was and why it must be abandoned, as well as forward to the kind of market economy it will eventually become. So this book devotes several chapters to explaining how the administrative-command system functioned. In addition to its *transitional* character, the semi-reformed socialist economy is also a *heterogeneous* phenomenon, exhibiting considerable variation across the countries of the socialist world. The solution to the problem of handling this intercountry and intertemporal variation is to focus on themes and experiences common to all countries and stages, even at the risk of ignoring variations in sequence, and the peculiar conditions of individual cases such as Poland, the USSR, or China. An emphasis on fundamentals is also motivated by a desire to avoid being overtaken by events and to provide an interpretation that will be relevant and helpful for some time to come. This aim also implies extensive resort to standard economics as taught in the West, both as a norm against which to interpret the past, and as increasingly relevant to these economies as they move toward the market institutions which much of standard economics assumes.

In writing the book the target audience I have had most clearly in mind has been students studying the Soviet-type economies, or comparative economic systems. But it is my hope that it can also serve as supplemental reading in two other kinds of courses. In introductory economics courses, it can offer more detail on a matter of great current interest, in a way that helps to reinforce students' understanding of value and allocation, and the way in which markets solve this problem. In survey courses on the socialist world or individual socialist countries, it can provide material for the economic dimension of such surveys that is analytical enough to be useful long past the time when the details of this or next year's happenings have faded. Some parts of the book may seem somewhat technical for the latter purposes, and for the reader who has minimal background in economics, certain sections, such as that on linear programming, may be omitted without undermining the more general flow of the exposition.

The Socialist
Economies
in Transition

1.
Introduction

The Russian Revolution created a kind of social and economic order new to the world. In this socialist society, under the leadership of the Communist party, the means of production were taken over by the state and the economic activity of the society was subjected to a system of central planning. For many years this new system was advertised by the Soviet Union as the historically inevitable successor to capitalism, whose injustices and wastes it would cure. The Soviet planned socialist economy would eliminate unemployment, do away with exploitation, achieve economic justice, supersede the chaos of the market, and direct production for the sake of people rather than for the sake of profit. Although Marx's view of socialism was that it would be adopted in the most economically advanced countries where capitalist development had already prepared the way through industrialization and modernization, the leaders of the Soviet Union created their version of a socialist society under conditions of underdevelopment. In their external propaganda they directed their advocacy of Soviet-style planning with special intensity to the underdeveloped countries where a majority of the world's population lived in poverty and misery. They claimed that this new Soviet economic model was the path to escaping colonial exploitation, overcoming poverty, developing the productive forces of society, and unleashing human creative potential to achieve socialist abundance. Such was the promise of the Russian revolutionary leaders both to their own people and to the workers of all lands.

The Soviet economic model and the development strategy that went with it functioned in the USSR for half a century, with few changes in its fundamental principles. The system spread from the USSR to a considerable number of other countries—all of Eastern Europe, China, and a long list of emulators in the underdeveloped world, such as North Korea,

Cuba, Vietnam, and Nicaragua. In many of those cases adoption of the Soviet model resulted from a conspiratorial movement inside the country, or Soviet pressure and the use of force, rather than from a willing embrace of the system by the population. Nevertheless, during the 40 years after the end of the Second World War, economic systems of the Soviet type were established and functioned in a large number of countries.

Today, it is widely acknowledged that the promises of this distinctive economic model have been very imperfectly fulfilled. In the Soviet Union and its imitators, the system does *not* serve the people, but rather its bureaucratic masters. The centrally planned economy (CPE) does *not* give workers control over their workplace lives, let alone over the functioning of the economy and the polity. In those cases where workers tried to assert their right to control the conditions of their lives, as in Poland in the seventies and in Czechoslovakia in 1968, the system denounced and crushed them. The USSR established a system of socialized free medical care for all, but the health care delivered by that system is frightful, with high infant mortality, widespread mortality from diseases that have been more or less conquered in the rest of the world, and relatively short life expectancy. This economic system has proved so sluggish in generating innovation that in its present form it seems eternally doomed to a role as technological follower. It has been able to benefit from successive rounds of new technology that drive up productivity elsewhere in the world, such as petrochemicals or the computer, only by technology transfer from the market economies.

It was in the realm of economic growth that the socialist economic system showed itself to best advantage, but it lost its dynamism in this respect sometime in the seventies. At various points in the seventies and eighties, different for different countries, this economic system stopped delivering even on growth. It never did as well as its sponsors claimed, as we know from careful reconstruction of the growth record by western scholars. Today some economists within the USSR itself assert that even western reconstructions of Soviet growth rates are overgenerous in evaluating its past performance. That proposition should perhaps be taken with some cautious allowance for the need of Gorbachev and his reform supporters to blacken the record of the previous leadership. In *all* the socialist countries output growth virtually stopped in the seventies, and in some, output actually fell in the eighties. China was the one bright spot with respect to economic growth under socialism, largely on the basis of significant reforms in the seventies and eighties, especially in agriculture. After the Tienanmen Square repression of 1989 and the leaders' subsequent backtracking regarding economic reform, the Chinese economy seemed destined to fall back to its earlier economic turmoil and stagnation.

By the early eighties it had become transparently obvious that as long as the USSR stuck with its traditional economic system it would never achieve the goal Stalin had proclaimed for it—to catch up with and surpass the capitalist countries in output and productivity. The centrally planned economy in all these societies had lost the loyalty of its own citizens, and whatever attraction it once had had for potential emulators in underdeveloped countries. The time had clearly come for the Soviet-style, centrally planned economic model to "be cast into the dustbin of history," in an ironic reversal of the prediction Marxist dogma had announced for capitalism.

At the end of the eighties, and especially dramatically in the upheavals in Eastern Europe in 1989, virtually the whole socialist world turned seriously toward a course of economic and political reform. This process had been building for a long time. The Soviet economic model has always had serious defects, and experiments with reform of its institutions in the hope of better performance go back a couple of decades, first in Eastern Europe, later in China. Declarations of the *need* to undertake serious reform in the USSR began during the Khrushchev period, but only with Gorbachev did the process begin in earnest there. At the beginning of the nineties, economic reform had progressed quite unevenly among the nations of the socialist world, with some countries, notably Poland, having essentially abandoned the main features of the planned economy, while others such as Romania and Cuba had barely started. Reform seems also to be characterized by the phenomenon of "two steps forward, one step backward." The mixture and sequence of political and economic reform in the *perestroika* recipe has been highly varied among countries. But by the beginning of the nineties, it began to appear that far-reaching transformations were inevitable. Although reform effort was proceeding against many obstacles, and it was possible that progress toward reform might be blocked at various points, the reform leaders were trying to make the process irreversible.

As we survey this broad range of experience and experimentation, it is clear that the first steps reformers typically take to modify the central institutions of planning do not seem to lead to much improvement in the functioning of the economy. Performance may improve marginally in particular respects—the agricultural sector may respond to decentralization, the supply of services may improve, or better pricing may help remove disequilibrium in consumer-goods markets. These were the positive effects of the Hungarian New Economic Mechanism, for example. But much of the old waste, sluggishness, and structural distortion remains. Moreover, new problems arise as reform progresses. These commonly include inflation, balance-of-payments problems, threats to job security, and a disruption of the formerly egalitarian income distribution. Yugoslavia, one of the pioneers in economic reform, was suffering inflation rates of 20 percent *per month* toward the end of the eighties. The Polish and Hungarian economies were unable to solve long-standing balance-of-payments crises and output stagnation. Their people had come to identify "reform" with futility and austerity. After a decade of success with economic reform, the Chinese economy began at the end of the eighties to experience accelerating inflation and a rapidly growing disparity between those who secured rapid increases in income by taking advantage of the new conditions for entrepreneurial activity, and those whose fixed incomes from employment in the still-planned state economy pushed them into poverty. After the first four years of active *perestroika*, Gorbachev ended up with complete chaos in the consumer-goods market. The black Soviet joke was that *perestroika* had at least eliminated lines in shops; with nothing on the shelves, there was no point in forming lines in the first place!

Reform programs in communist countries do not start out being advertised as the abandonment of socialism and the restoration of capitalism. Even when the reformers introduce market relations they are usually careful to say that their aim is a special blend of "plan and market," a kind of "socialist-market" system. The ideological biases of the system and the political interests of the elites make some dissimulation inevitable. The reformers usually begin by tinkering with the system, perhaps decentralizing some decisions and functions to give enterprises more freedom, or substituting "economic levers" for direct commands as the planners' instruments for influencing enterprise behavior. They may also introduce price "reform" that brings the fixed administered prices that are part of the system closer to actual costs, and may even allow some degree of market influence on pricing. The bolder efforts may include experimenting with some exceptions to the principle of state ownership of capital through allowing the formation of cooperatives, leasing, and other forms of privatization. However, such limited programs of "administrative tinkering" help but little, and in the end are unsuccessful in reviving performance. It is the author's view that those who would reform the centrally planned economy must make a clean break with some of the principal features of the old system, and make market institutions the defining basis of a new system, if reform is to be effective. The socialist economies in their present state are a long way from constituting a definitively reformed system.

What has emerged is a phenomenon that might be called the "semi-reformed economy," a "halfway house" between the old "administrative-command" system and a market-driven, price-regulated, private-property system. More ambitious transformations began to be attempted after the dramatic political changes of 1989 in which several countries decided to throw off Soviet suzerainty, abolish the communist monopoly of political power internally, and democratize the political system. Whether the Polish reform, to take an example, will succeed or will have to be abandoned in the face of popular opposition to the disruption accompanying marketization is unclear. But even as these reform programs move forward, there will be a multiyear transition period in which the new system will still retain features from the old.

It is the thesis of this book, based on the experience of socialist economic reform so far, that the semi-reformed economy is unstable. The semi-reformed economies that existed in Hungary and Poland in the eighties and the economic reform that Gorbachev was trying to introduce in the USSR (especially in the fuzzy blueprints of 1989 and 1990) did not go far enough toward abandoning the instruments of central control and turning firms loose to interact via markets to radically improve performance. In addition, the halfway measures typical of reform in all socialist countries lead to a hybrid system that has distinctive new problems of its own. In the author's view (and many voices from among both the leadership and the opposition groups in the socialist countries are openly declaring the same view) the reformers *must* move on to more radical transformation and the creation of new institutions. A full reform can work only if accompanied by anti-monopoly measures, creation of a new system of banks and financial institutions, a more sophisticated fiscal system, and a considerable degree of privatization. It will be a slow process in *any* country, and some countries will resist powerfully. But the process is underway. Most significant, the USSR—the most important country in the socialist world—is today embarked on it along with the others.

The aim of this book is to provide an interpretation of the economic functioning of these semi-reformed systems, and of the process of further change made necessary by the instability of the half-reformed model. It begins by explaining how the old economy functioned, what its weaknesses and strengths were, and why its viability has permanently evaporated. It then shifts to the question of what reformers typically do, and the kind of halfway house that results. In the course of the argument, I want to develop the proposition stated above that this transitional model has its own distinctive problems, and to explain what additional reforms must be undertaken to solve the continuing systemic deficiencies. In this approach, it is appropriate to focus a great deal more on financial mechanisms and institutions, prices, and issues of macroeconomics in the basic planned-economy model than has been customary in past analyses. In the traditional CPE, financial institutions and policy tools are undeveloped and unimportant, compared to the method of micromanaging the economy by manipulating physical quantities. The semi-reformed economy implicitly depends on a better understanding of financial processes and institutions and better policy in their use. The reforms alter the system in a way such that it is no longer productive for economic policymakers to concentrate on the "real" magnitudes (i.e., the physical amounts of resources and outputs) and ignore the "financial" magnitudes (which may be thought of as the q's of the real magnitudes multiplied by prices). The problem is that there is a protracted lag in making this shift.

A second major organizing theme in the book is identification of reform with marketization, which I consider the high road to reform. The degree to which marketization has proceeded differs among the various socialist countries, but in general, it is still incomplete. Beyond explaining how marketization works, I want to focus on several different *kinds* of markets, what a *set* of markets is, and how they are interconnected. Most discussions of reform talk about the markets for goods and for labor services, but if we take a clue from history and from the nature of other market economies or from the literature on development, we realize that a complete system also has to have a foreign-exchange market, markets for real assets (what the Russians would call the means of production), financial-asset markets, capital markets, markets for land and other natural resources, and so on. When a market is missing, or where it is impossible to make a market (as in the case of environmental goods or the equity rights to an individual's earning power), efficiency and equity are infringed. One big question is whether the socialist reformers can "create" these markets, or whether they must grow organically.

Reform is unlikely to be completed for a long time. For the USSR twenty-five years might be a reasonable horizon for the transition to a really different kind of economy. After all, the Hungarians began serious reform in 1969, and only twenty years later, in 1989, arrived on the threshold of a definitive shift to reliance on markets, profit, and an incentive system that includes private-property rights. So this book deals with issues and problems that will be in dispute for some time. Given that there are likely to be many ups and downs, and perhaps stunning political events such as the dissolution of the USSR, I have tried to back off from the most detailed concrete current developments, to concentrate on more fundamental explanations of problems and mechanisms.

The dilemma for anyone who seeks to understand the socialist economic world today is how to juggle the contradictions inherent in its halfway-house status. Since the classical system is on its way out, one may ask, why waste time trying to understand how it worked—what can that tell us about how the Soviet economy operates today? But the system is still saturated with remnants of the old principles, so that we cannot understand what its current problems are without understanding the old. Nor can we dismiss the old system as of no interest on the grounds that since these economies are beginning to marketize, they can be analyzed in terms of the market principles explained in the introductory economics textbook.

These economies are still a long way from that stage. This book tries to walk that schizophrenic line between describing the caterpillar and describing the butterfly, to guess at what is happening in the chrysalis. Chapters 2–5 begin the analysis by explaining how the old system functioned. The second half of the book will turn to the problem of how reform has begun to modify the system of resource allocation, the new problems that come with reform, and what still needs to be done.

2.
A Perfect-Administration Interpretation of the Soviet-type Economy

The best way to understand the classic Soviet-type, centrally planned economy is as an "administered economy." It is an economy in which the basic mechanism for making decisions about resource allocation is administration instead of the institutions of the market and price signaling. (As will be explained later, not *all* decisions in this economy are covered by administration, and there is some room for the operation of markets.) Just what "administration" is will be explained more fully below. This label, with all it implies, has by now been widely accepted even among the indigenous socialist analysts of the system—in the USSR the standard epithet for the old system is the "administrative-command economy."[1]

It is possible to develop a model, or at least a concept, of "perfect administration," analogous to the model of "perfect competition" that is used as a basis for understanding the market economy. This will give us an idea of how the administered economy is expected to work, a background for interpreting its failings, and some insights into what limitations there may be on improving its performance.

One of the main points that will emerge is that in the classic version of the administered economy, money, public finance, fiscal policy, and

1. Over the years a wide variety of summary labels have come to be used to describe this distinctive economy. These include the centrally planned economy (often abbreviated as CPE), the socialist economy, the command economy, the Soviet-type economy, the administered economy, and now the Soviet term the *administrative-command economy*. Each is useful in capturing some aspect of the system, and for the sake of variety I will use them all interchangeably.

macroeconomic equilibrium are not matters of great operational importance. I stress this point, because as later chapters take up economic reform in the socialist world, one of my main theses will be that the reformers have not yet understood or given enough attention to the importance of developing new institutions and mechanisms in fiscal and monetary affairs, and of devising instruments for macroeconomic stabilization.

Actors, Sectoring, Administration, and Markets in the Classic CPE

Let us start by developing an overall scheme of the major actors and linkages in the classic centrally planned economy as it evolved in the USSR. The major institution of this economy is the "state production establishment" (SPE hereafter), which combines the normal functions of government with the task of running the economy. The Soviet economy is sometimes described as analogous to a single corporation in charge of all production in the society: "USSR, Inc." It is this entity which owns and administers the means of production—i.e., all natural resources, and most of its capital—on behalf of society. The SPE is managed by a process of administration much like that of a western business corporation. Calling this body the *state* production establishment is intended to draw attention to a special feature that differentiates it from the usual business corporation, however large, in market economies. In the classic system, the SPE takes on in addition to running the economy all the traditional functions of the state—administration of the legal system, exercise of coercive state power, conduct of foreign and national security affairs, and so on.

To operate this production establishment, the services of households as a source of labor are needed. The socialist state has socialized the means of production, but the means of production does not include workers. Households are linked to the SPE through two kinds of markets, indicated by the arrows in figure 2-1, namely, a consumer-goods market and a labor market. The allocation of consumer goods among individual households and the assignment of individual members of the labor force to various production activities are *not* handled by the process of administration.

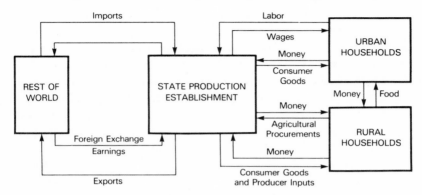

Figure 2-1. Sectors of the Administered Economy

Within the SPE, enterprises are told how much steel to produce, and to whom to ship it. But by and large the bureaucrats of the SPE do not directly tell individuals (members of households) where to work and do not tell them how much of each consumer good they are to receive. These functions of allocating labor and allocating consumer goods among households are taken care of by markets.

An important consideration in this connection is that in its relationships with households, the SPE has a great deal of market power. As the only supplier of consumer goods it is a monopolist, and in hiring labor it is a monopsonist (the only buyer). This market power means that it can manipulate the prices in these two markets to turn the terms of trade in its own favor. It is a ''pricemaker.''

Figure 2-1 distinguishes two kinds of households, those which are located in cities and whose members work in the modern, nonagricultural sector of the economy, versus households located in rural areas whose activity is primarily in agriculture. They might be peasant households carrying on a combination of subsistence and commercial agriculture, or they might be households organized into the collective farms typical of the Soviet-type economy. This rural household sector might be more or less coterminous with agriculture, but in the usual CPE, some part of agricultural activity is usually organized in the form of state farms. State farms are very similar in character and in the way they are managed to industrial enterprises, and we should probably consider the state-farm sector of agriculture as a sector of the SPE. The rationale for distinguishing agricultural households from urban households is that the SPE's exchange relationship with agricultural households differs somewhat from its inter-action with urban households. The latter exchange their *labor* for *consumer goods*, while rural households, either individually or organized in collec-tive farms, sell the SPE agricultural *outputs* rather than their labor, and buy from it not only consumer goods but also *production inputs* such as fuel and fertilizer. Unlike urban households, rural households have fairly direct access to the means of production (i.e., the land) and are engaged in production as well as consumption. In most socialist societies rural households, even when grouped into collective farms, have been allowed to carry on production on their own account on small private plots.

In its relations with other nations, the administered economy also relies on market links. If the administrators of the SPE (such as the planners of the Soviet economy) want a foreign firm to supply steel pipe with which to build a gas pipeline, or if they want a foreign firm to take some of the USSR's output of oil, they cannot get that result by administrative orders or by commands, as they do in analogous domestic transactions. Rather, they must deal with the foreign firm through the market. In *this* link, however, the SPE is a "pricetaker" rather than a "pricemaker," as in its relationship with households. As long as a socialist country is a relatively small player in the world market, those who administer its SPE must accept the prices set by the impersonal forces of supply and demand arising from the actions of many buyers and sellers in that market. Without monopoly power, the SPE can do business with firms in other countries only at the going world-market price.

One other market that is a standard part of this system is the "collective-farm market" linking urban and rural households. This market, in which collective-farm households may sell some of the produce of their private plots to urban households, is basically a free market in which prices are determined by supply and demand rather than by administrative decisions of SPE officials.

So the classic Soviet-type economy combines an administrative ap-proach within the SPE with some market-type links to actors outside it.

What Is Administration or Management?

What does it mean to say that the USSR has an "administered economy," or that the SPE is "managed" as if it were a single capitalist corporation on the model of "USSR, Inc."? There is a large body of thought dealing with administration, drawing on many disciplines. In answering "what is administration?" here I want only to summarize and generalize some major points from that literature.

A central idea in all the literature on administration is that administration is closely connected with the concept of an "organization," so that we must talk about organizations as well as about administration. Organizations exist to achieve goals that the individuals participating in their activity cannot achieve by themselves. That is, organizations have "organizational goals" that may differ from and extend beyond the goals of the participants in their activity. The question "what is administration?" can also be formulated as "how do organizations work?"

In most of this literature one can find a definition of management (or administration) to the effect that "management is working through people to achieve the goals of the organization." As one explores how management achieves this purpose, most discussions explicitly or implicitly break down the task of administration into several "functions" of management.

Functions of Management

1. One function is "planning," by which is meant choosing *goals* for the organization and *strategies* to achieve those goals. In most areas of purposive action, for organizations as well as individuals, it is possible to construct a hierarchy of goals and means. At the apex are very general goals—profit for a corporation, for example, or protecting the environment for the EPA. The next level down in the hierarchy shows a variety of means by which these goals can be pursued. For example, the corporate goal of maximizing profit might be achieved by keeping costs low, by monopolizing the market for the firm's product, or by introducing new

products. But usually these ideas about means are themselves rather general, and at a more detailed level we can think of a variety of ways of carrying out those means. The means on the second level can thus be thought of as proximate goals for a more detailed set of means, instruments, or policies on the next level down in the hierarchy. This disaggregation can usually be continued for many steps. The planning function in administration is not confined to choosing the ultimate goals of the organization, but also devotes major attention to the selection of intermediate-level means to achieve them. That is what is meant by saying that the planning function includes devising strategies for achieving the goals of the organization.

2. The second function of administration is "coordination," which involves disaggregating the overall goals and strategies of the organization into responsibilities and tasks for each of the units within it. It could be described as making an operational plan and handing out individual assignments. Coordination sets concrete targets, assignments, and responsibilities for the various participants. The major problem in defining and quantifying all these separate tasks and responsibilities is the need to do so in such a way that the activities of all participants taken together are coherent, and efficient in the pursuit of the goals of the organization.

3. A third function is "control." It is not enough merely to communicate to units and individuals what is expected of them. Once an organization achieves any significant size, it is necessary to follow up by collecting information on performance, evaluating performance, and passing out rewards (or imposing sanctions) in accordance with performance. It is this *reward structure* that most powerfully harnesses individuals to organizational goals. Many kinds of rewards and sanctions can serve as incentives, but the most powerful and universal are material rewards. Bonuses and salary increases are familiar examples of material rewards, while promotions, honors, and status symbols are examples of nonmaterial rewards.

4. A fourth function is called by many names, such as leadership or command. It could be described in a general way as the "personal element" in administration. It is necessary that members of the organization identify with its leadership and goals, and be inspired to participate in achieving those goals. The essence of this function is to legitimate the

goals of the organization and to socialize its participants in those goals, that is, to get the participants to internalize them.

These four functions constitute the basic "paradigm of administration" common to all organizations, and to all administrative systems. There is one additional aspect of any organization that needs to be mentioned, i.e., structure.

5. By structure I mean what is represented by the familiar organization chart. Fundamentally, it is the structure of authority relationships and information flows, specifying who is subordinate to whom, who reports to whom, who is empowered to issue orders downward and ask for reports upward. Structure thus provides a framework within which each participant works. It is important to add that there is formal and informal organization. We all know situations in which the true channels in which information and authority flow are informal ones not indicated on the formal organization chart.

Thinking about any organization, one can quickly identify these functions and see that they are indeed what is needed to get every unit and every participant to do his or her individual bit in the total effort to advance the goals of the organization. Consider the capitalist corporation, for example.

Capitalist corporations have a board of directors whose job is to set general goals and strategies for the organization. Goals may include various combinations of growth, profits, market share, public trust, and so on. To accomplish these adopted goals, most corporations engage in strategic planning. The strategies chosen may involve different mixes of innovation, monopolization, service, quality of product, expansion of foreign sales, or focus on cost reduction to provide a competitive edge. To actually implement these strategies and achieve these goals, someone has to work out a much more detailed operational plan which will direct the different participants in the corporation—the production people, the sales division, the advertising group, the quality-control office, the R&D division—as to what their activities should be to contribute to this goal. This coordination process usually generates detailed production schedules, cost budgets, sales targets, and goals for profit centers, extending down to the smallest managerial units within the corporation. To motivate people to strive to adhere to planned budget assignments or to increase sales, there is an elaborate process of reporting, evaluation of performance, and incentive payments or sanctions. Most capitalist corporations put large resources into socializing the important participants in their operation in the goals of the corporation through such devices as training and indoctrination programs for managers, company social events, stock ownership plans for middle management, creating a distinctive corporate image, and so on.

A nation's military establishment engages in all the same functions. Its mission is the preservation of national security, and in pursuing that goal it must have in mind some strategy. There must also be a much more detailed set of assignments for the members of the organization (missions for the individual services, detailed operations plans in case of war, allocation of responsibility for supply, training, and other such functions, and so on). In the national security case, the control mechanism is likely to include some strong *negative* sanctions which reinforce whatever positive inducements are offered for good performance in meeting the goals of the armed forces.

You can think for yourself about how this paradigm works in its application to a university, a government bureau, the institutions of organized religion, and the many other kinds of organizations that operate in a society.

It is easy to see how this paradigm applies to the Soviet-type economy. The function of *goal setting and strategy* is in the hands of the political leadership. The Communist party and its leading organs always saw themselves as the "vanguard of the working class" armed with a special wisdom in the form of dialectical materialism, Marxism-Leninism, or Maoist thought, enabling them to choose wisely the directions of social-economic development, and strategies for achieving those goals. Every five-year plan ever promulgated in a socialist country begins with a preamble listing these goals and strategies.

Coordination is essentially the task of making the plan. Although the Five-Year Plan is a widely propagated image of what constitutes this document, the truly operational expression of the coordination function in Soviet-type economies is actually found in the annual plan. It tells every institutional actor within the SPE—each ministry, each enterprise, each hospital, each R&D organization and its managers—what to do, i.e., what it is to produce, what inputs it should use to do so, what its cost, revenue, and profit should be, etc. Note, however, that the plan does *not* tell each *household* what to do.

The nature of the *control* process is obvious in these systems. Any Soviet textbook on planning contains a chapter on "control of plan fulfillment." There is a huge reporting system, on which rests an elaborate system of auditing and evaluation of enterprise performance. The Russians call this *analiz khoziaistvennoi deiatel'nosti*—the analysis of managerial performance. Rewards and sanctions are dealt out in accordance with performance. An important feature of the administrative paradigm is that the control function needs to be "isomorphic" with the coordination function. That is, the control process should match exactly the coordination process in its structure, definition of assignments, and detail. One cannot expect that enterprises will do the things they are told to do unless the system checks up on precisely those orders. Similarly, there is no point in checking up on whether managers achieve some particular goal, and then punishing them for not doing so, if it was not indicated in the plan that they were assigned responsibility for that goal, defined in exactly the same way as they are now being held to account.

When the administrative process under consideration is the job of running a national economy—especially one the size of the Soviet economy, but even much smaller ones such as those of Eastern Europe—the functions of coordination and control become extremely complex. They are extremely information-intensive. One essential feature of an economy is that "everything depends on everything else," which means that the number of interactions that must be foreseen in the coordination phase and monitored in the control phase is immense. The amount of data that must be collected, processed, and communicated to carry out the coordination function has swamped the data-processing capacity of the system. The isomorphic control function requires an equally mind-boggling volume of data gathering and processing. Many of the breakdowns of the administered economy come from the inability of the administrative process to cope with the information requirements of coordination and control in a modern economy, especially one the size of the USSR.

As for the *leadership* function, all these societies devote great attention to enlisting the loyalty and enthusiasm of the participants in the economy. Many instruments are used for socializing the participants in the legitimacy and worth of the leaders' goals—propaganda, training, party guidance, and so on. The most concentrated expression of this function is the *"nomenklatura* system" which controls the careers of managers by checking on their political reliability and their loyalty to the goals of the system, as well as on the effectiveness of their performance as managers, at each point in the progress of their careers. The role assigned to the little red book of Mao's thoughts is an extreme example of the process of socializing cadres in the goals of the organization and its leaders.

If the leadership function is badly carried out, the system will not work. In recent years the societies of the USSR and Eastern Europe have had trouble with this function. One of the greatest threats to energetic service to the goals of the economic leaders is apathy and cynicism, and the Czechs tried to revive dedication to the system by creating "socialism with a human face." Nationalism may sometimes serve as an important element in this legitimation process, as has been the case in Romania. Ceausescu skillfully appealed to chauvinistic and xenophobic prejudices to retain the loyalty of his cadres. But the main point is that the functioning of a Soviet-type society or economy requires a legitimizing ideology, and a socialization process that can instill loyalty in those entrusted with managing the system at lower levels. Because the organizational goals are so often at odds with individual values in the Soviet-type system, this general principle applies there with special force. When the dedication of the supporting actors goes, the system cannot function.

Finally, of course, these economies operate with an elaborate bureaucratic structure in the form of an organizational pyramid, with a hierarchical arrangement of bosses and subordinates and a pattern of information flow and authority.

It might also be mentioned that the basic administrative paradigm is reinforced with various kinds of auxiliary mechanisms—law, policy, and custom. These are all devices for settling choices, resolving conflicts, achieving coordinations not fully taken care of by the basic paradigm. If an enterprise has authorization to acquire inputs but does not receive the deliveries that the plan ordered some other enterprise to make, the "state arbitrage'' system provides a way for the two enterprises to interact directly without going all the way back up the hierarchy. Similarly, the plan directives may not have settled some technical issue—e.g., how an enterprise director should be guided in some fuel-use decision not fully covered by the plan. One approach is to have an announced *policy* stating that in an ambiguous situation, the director should remember that one of the goals is to conserve energy. This is a kind of broadcast message rather than the ''addressed'' message characteristic of the administrative approach. These mechanisms operating outside the basic administrative paradigm have always been underdeveloped in the Soviet-type administered economy compared to the role they play in other kinds of systems.

Is Perfect Administration Possible?

In approaching the administrative economy, one might reasonably wonder whether there is a set of ideas that could provide a normative model of how economic administration ought to be conducted. If there were such a ''theory,'' it might then be useful in understanding the failures of the real-world Soviet-type system, and in suggesting how to make it work better. Maybe we could develop a theory or model of ''perfect administration,'' which could be used in analyzing the Soviet-type economy just as the model of ''perfect competition'' is used to analyze the real-world market economy and prescribe remedies for its failures.

Unfortunately, there is no well-developed theory of economic administration. Although there is a large literature on administration, it is amorphous rather than coherent and integrated. It comes from many disciplines, such as cybernetics, sociology, business administration, public administration, economics, engineering, biology, information theory, communications theory, and operations research. All these disciplines provide useful insights regarding organization and administration. There is a broad-ranging set of ideas called general systems theory, but it is rather abstract. There are even specifically Soviet attempts to develop a general theory of administration, beginning with Bogdanov's *tektologiia*, which he considered a ''universal theory of organization'' (the *vseobshchaia organi-*

zatsionnaia nauka),[2] and continuing today with cybernetics and general systems theory.

But although a theory of perfect administration in application to economic management has not been worked out in the same detail that perfect competition for the market economy has been, the literature on administration does contain many suggestive insights about the correct principles for designing an administrative system for the planned economy. It concerns itself with things that are important to our understanding of the Soviet-type economy, as can be seen in a few examples.

The literature of administration emphasizes that organizations operate in environments, and that one of the crucial functions of any organization is to be able to respond to changes in environmental conditions. When an organization's environment changes, the organization may have a hard time adapting to the new environment. Examples sometimes cited are small liberal-arts schools in the United States and oil companies, which may have to think of themselves as "energy companies" rather than oil companies if they want to endure in an era of oil scarcity. The dinosaur is an example of an organism that did not evolve fast enough to remain adapted to its changing environment. Environmental sensitivity may conflict with internal rationality. The more precisely and carefully the basic functions of administration are effected—the more fully goals and strategies are elaborated and internalized in participants—the more difficult it becomes to change direction. Organization theorists are thus likely to talk about environmental sensitivity versus internal rationality, with associated ideas about the possible constructive uses of goal ambiguity, overlapping authority, and uncertainty in specifying success criteria.

Another important concept is the distinction between consensus organizations and coercive organizations. In the former an identity of interest among participants eases the problems of coordination. In large, highly structured, and perhaps "coercive" organizations, coordination of individual and organizational goals may be much more difficult because of a conflict between the leaders' and the participants' goals.

---

2. Originally published in the twenties, this work has recently been republished by the Institute of Economics of the Academy of Sciences (A. A. Bogdanov, *Tektologiia*, 2 vols., Moscow: Ekonomika, 1989) as the Russians struggle to understand better the nature of their own system.

There is a large body of writing on the pathology of organizations, describing such ideas as the "Peter Principle." This principle states that all positions in an organization will eventually be filled by persons unqualified for their jobs. Another is C. Northcote Parkinson's axiom that the first law of organizations is that the work to be done will always expand to fill the time available. Organizations often lose sight of goals, and shift from constructive work to mere "organizational maintenance." As the Russians look at their bureaucracy in the *glasnost'* of the Gorbachev era, they are much impressed with how large ministries such as Minenergo (the electric company) or Minvodkhoz (the ministry in charge of water resource management) keep their organizations going by dreaming up grandiose projects requiring massive resources whether or not they have any economic justification.

It is common for breakdowns to occur in the coordination function as a result of growth. A standard scenario for a small innovative firm is rapid growth based on daring and flexibility, followed by breakdown and failure when problems of marketing and finance outgrow the capabilities of the original informal style of management, and call for the more bureaucratic controls of a big organization. At the opposite pole is the huge organization that develops excessive formality and becomes so routinized in its daily operation that it is inefficient and antithetic to risk, imagination, and novelty.

"Suboptimization" is another defect in which the missions assigned to units within an organization become too "partialized," or when these assignments are not defined in a flexible way to take account of interactions among various parts of the organization. In this situation the effective pursuit by each element of its prescribed mission does not lead to a *global* optimum for the organization as a whole. In the USSR exploration for oil involves the coordination of seismic surveying, general geological mapping, and drilling exploratory wells, and these responsibilities are assigned to specialized organizations. Each is given a success criterion for measuring performance in fulfilling its task. But as the seismic people strive to accumulate more miles of seismic profile, and the drillers seek to get rewarded by drilling more footage, they may do so in a way that contributes little to the joint effort to find oil. For example, it may be more advantageous for the drillers to continue drilling wells with rigs set up in one area, even after it is pretty clear there is no oil there, than to move else-where.

All these pathologies are glaringly evident in the socialist planned econo-mies. The literature of administration often suggests approaches for work-ing on them, but alas, it also suggests that to some extent they are inherent in administration itself.

Approaching the Soviet-type economy from an administrative perspec-tive, one might ask whether its functioning could be improved by making organizational improvements within the framework of administration rather than undertaking the more fundamental change of marketization. If the problem is inadequate communications capacity or insufficient data-processing capabilities, more computers and better telecommunications might be the answer. One of the propositions for effective administration is that authority must be congruent with responsibility. When one finds it is not, perhaps the organization chart could be redrawn. As an example one might suggest that the reason innovation is handled so badly in the Soviet and East European economies is that there is no node in the ad-ministrative structure that has both responsibility and authority to perform this function. The units that have the major responsibility for it, i.e., high-level bodies within the ministry, do not have authority to continue the process beyond R&D, while enterprises, whose behavior determines whether innovations finally are implemented in production, operate under an incentive system that does not in practice make them responsible for it. We will return to this issue at the end of the chapter.

Soviet-type Economic Bureaucracies

The actual administrative structure of any of the real-world Soviet-type economies is too complicated to describe in an easily comprehensible way. There are a bewildering variety of choices to be made about how to set up the organizational chart of the economy, and one of the interesting features of the administered economies is how frequently they are reor-ganized. The best way to convey some idea of these bureaucratic structures will be to describe in a brief and generic way the Soviet case as it existed in its mature form, and then go on to review some major issues in the design of this hierarchy.

First, in the Soviet-type economy, management of the economy as the major task of government is fused with the normal functions of government. An important feature of the Soviet-type system is the role of the Communist party. Although the society, and within it the economy, is nominally run by the government, behind it lies a shadow government— the Communist party, which is the real source of power. The party structure parallels the official government structure rather closely so that party influence can be exerted at all levels and in all the corners of economic administration. The basic priorities embodied in economic plans are decided on by the party leadership, and plans are issued in the name of the Central Committee of the party as well as the state organ nominally in charge, the Council of Ministers. In short, the "planning" function of the administrative paradigm is actually exercised by the party. The party has important economic functions in the day-to-day administration of the economy as well, serving as a communication channel, as the final arbiter in personnel evaluation and advancement via the *nomenklatura* system. It has an expediting role on the local level, ambivalently trying to guide and control local economic activity in light of the priorities of the party leadership, but also trying to assist local economic actors to cut through the tangles of the bureaucratic jungle. In what follows, the focus is on the formal governmental structure through which the economy is administered, but it should always be understood that behind this state administrative structure stands the party as the real source of power.

The economic-administrative hierarchy charged with administering the economy has a tripartite structure, with executive, reporting, and planning functions, as indicated in figure 2-2. At the top of this pyramidal structure are a number of central bodies. At the lower level are the primary production units of the system—factories, stores, hospitals, universities, railroad operating divisions, power stations, and the little old ladies who sell ice cream on the streets. Line authority lies with the executive chain of command, but at each level these officials are assisted by offices that perform the staff functions of information gathering and planning. In

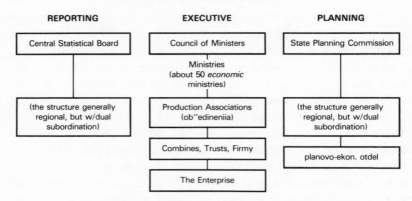

Figure 2-2. The Soviet Administrative Hierarchy

between, the rest of the structure consists of a great variety of intermediate bodies. Starting from the *top*, we can imagine the structure as one in which the aggregate national economy is subdivided further and further and responsibility for its various parts is allocated among successively smaller units. Starting from the *bottom*, the structure can be thought of as being put together by grouping primary production units into collections of related activities for supervision and coordination at various levels of aggregation.

Topmost of the intermediate levels is the ministry. In the USSR at the end of the eighties there were 50–60 production ministries and a number of similar, but smaller, units called state committees, such as those for radio and TV and for cinematography. The ministry has traditionally been divided into "chief administrations" (*glavnye upravleniia* or "*glavki*"). The next level is some kind of intermediate organ, of which there is great variety—associations, trusts, combines, and "firms." In most of the Soviet-type economies administrative reform in the sixties and seventies worked in the direction of enlarging and strengthening the organs at this intermediate level, with a heavy emphasis on what the Russians call associations (*ob''edineniia*). There have been corresponding bodies in the other planned economies. In creating these "large economic organiza-ns," as they were called in Poland, the designers of the administrative structure were trying to develop something like the western corporation in size, range of activities, and position in the market. Other intermediate forms include *firmy*, NPOs (science-production associations that contain both R&D and production units), and a great variety of others.

The government structure, and the economic administrative bureaucracy within it, also has a territorial hierarchy. At lower levels of this territorial hierarchy the national governmental structure is replicated in simpler form. The USSR, for example, is divided into republics, and below these lie bodies somewhat like states in the U.S. structure, mostly called *oblasti* in the case of the USSR. Under these come city and *raion* governments. Some primary production units are directly subordinated to these territorial units at various levels, or are dually subordinated both to the central ministerial structure and to the territorial body. At one point, for example, there was a Ministry of the Oil Industry of the USSR, and also a Ministry of the Oil Industry of Azerbaidzhan, the latter dually subordinated to its own republican government and the Moscow ministry.

This structure is so complex that it is a very ambitious task to describe it in detail. Moreover, just when one thinks one is getting a good idea of how it works—which bodies have what function, who is responsible for what to whom, etc.—it is likely to be changed. The most useful approach we can take here is to describe some of the main issues in the constant effort to improve the design of this managerial bureaucracy.

1. As a basis for splitting and aggregating functions and responsibilities there is a choice among the *sectoral*, *territorial*, and *functional* principles. When the focus is on the sector or branch because of its production and technical homogeneity, territorial connections get ignored. The best-known illustration in the USSR was Khrushchev's attempt to overcome the narrowness of the branch perspective (which forestalled interenterprise cooperation in such activities as foundry production) by creating *regional* economic councils. But the regional organization form undermined attention to such desiderata as common R&D and technological policy across all the plants of an industrial branch, which might be scattered over many regions. Personnel policy is an example of an issue that might be handled in a uniform way across all industries and regions by a single specialized functional organization.

2. A more general form of the problem is how to partition broad areas of responsibility, or alternatively how to combine primary units into larger units, as can be illustrated by some examples from the energy sector. Both the Ministry of the Oil Industry and the Ministry of the Gas Industry drill wells. The oil industry is much bigger than the gas industry and has a drilling program several times larger than that of the gas industry. Should the gas ministry do its own drilling, or would it be better to assign responsibility for all drilling to the oil industry to take advantage of economies of scale and experience? In electric power there was a debate over the point at which responsibility for developing the breeder reactor should pass from the State Committee for the Utilization of Nuclear Energy (which did the R&D) to the Ministry of Power (Minenergo, responsible for commercial operation). These tasks require different perspectives, but the problem is not to let one perspective control too much of the process. As a final case, Minenergo was originally responsible for both conventional and nuclear power generation, but after the Chernobyl accident, it was concluded that the problems of safety in nuclear power generation were so different from those in conventional power stations that a new Ministry of the Nuclear Power Industry should be split off from Minenergo.

The basic principle, when one thinks about all these cases, is that the pyramidal structure should be designed to shorten communication links, and to concentrate in the same portion of the pyramid those units that have close interactions with each other.

3. At what level should the line between budget and *khozraschet* organs be drawn? Budget organizations are financed directly from the budget—e.g., ministries and *glavki*. *Khozraschet* organizations are organized as financially separate entities with their own balance sheets, operating statements, and bank accounts. They are supposed to meet their outlays out of their incomes, and their managers are supposed to act in an economizing and independent way to cut costs and increase output. In the Soviet hierarchy the distinction between budget and *khozraschet* status has generally been drawn just above the enterprise level—all the supervisory bodies above the enterprise are state-budget-financed, rather than earning their own way. There has been some experimentation with making *glavki* into *khozraschet* organizations—with the incomes that finance their costs dependent on the incomes of the organizations subordinate to them. The

argument is that this would make them materially interested in the success of their subordinates in a way they are not now, and hence likely to do a more responsible job of planning and supervising.

4. How many levels should there be in the hierarchy? Here we have a complicated interaction among the total size of the organization, the "span of control," and the problem of "noise," about which the communications engineers have useful ideas. They think in terms of the capacity of a communication channel, the noise on the channel, and the signal-to-noise ratio. The more links through which information has to pass, the more noise is introduced. For an organization of a given size, too few levels means that each boss has to supervise too many subordinates, thus weakening control. Introducing more levels generates more noise and less assurance that information passed upward will reach the top, or that orders issued at the top will reach the bottom ungarbled. As an organization increases in size, the problem intensifies.

It is characteristic of Soviet-type systems to alternate between the two horns of the dilemma. The bosses try to simplify administration by eliminating layers, but then find that some issues, and some interactions, get ignored for lack of supervision, and so they reintroduce layers. An example is the creation under Gorbachev of superministries such as Gosagroprom and, within the Council of Ministers, "bureaus" for machine building, for energy, and for other sectors that are spread over several ministries. But the introduction of another layer makes the communication process more noisy, and the cycle starts once again.

5. At what level of the hierarchy should responsibility for a given function be lodged? The inventory-control problem is to balance the danger that production may be stopped because of a lack of supplies versus the costs of storage, spoilage, and the opportunity cost of capital connected with holding large inventories. Should this function be the responsibility of the enterprise or some higher-level organ? In the market economy, this is the responsibility of the firm, though in recent years it has moved upward in organizations such as retail chains under the influence of improved data systems that permit decisions on resupply to be made at headquarters rather than by the local store manager.

In the Soviet economy, inventory control has always been located at a level well *above* the enterprise. The incentive system for Soviet enterprises and the uncertainty of supply make them tend to worry more about disruptions in supply than about the costs of large inventories, so that concern for restraining inventory accumulation needs to be in the hands of the higher-level organs. The difficulty is that the higher-level bureaucrats lack the detailed information needed to do this job well.

To conclude, it will be useful to emphasize a few central features of the administrative hierarchy the designers of the Soviet-type economy have built, and to point out some of the implications of those features for its performance.

1. The pathways of communication and the direction of authority and subordination have been vertical rather than horizontal. This means that if two organizations want to deal with each other, say in a conflict over the quality of goods one is shipping to the other, it is often a long way to a common boss who can resolve the conflict and issue the associated directives. Drillers in the oil industry waste a lot of resources because of the low quality of steel pipe and tool joints they use in drilling. But the only way they can put pressure on the suppliers is to pass up their own chain of command a message that spending some more resources on pipe quality would be recouped manifold by savings in drilling. But only at the very top of the hierarchy, i.e., in the Council of Ministers, is there a decisionmaker who could evaluate this tradeoff and adjudicate the conflict.

2. It is a long way from the top to the bottom of the pyramid. Because the managers at the top cannot *directly* control units at the bottom, there *must* be many layers in this hierarchy. That means a great deal of opportunity for noise to be generated in the channels of communication, and great danger that messages will be garbled, statements of priorities will be misread, and important messages will die on the way upward. This implies a need for a high signal-to-noise ratio, to borrow an idea from the communications engineers, through "redundancy." Messages are embodied in more than one indicator and are sent via multiple channels. The enterprise is given a target for output, one for labor input, and one for output per worker. Much use has traditionally been made of the party hierarchy as a back channel for passing information up and down. Party members within an enterprise are expected to report to party organs at their level on the true state of affairs in their enterprises, providing an alternative set of messages for top party organs to use as a check on the story they get from ministries.

3. This hierarchy has grown to immense size. It is reported that in the USSR at the end of the eighties, there were 18 million people employed in the administrative apparatus. Some of these are in traditional state functions rather than in economic administration, and many of them are at the enterprise level. But the number in the supervisory levels of the economic bureaucracy is appallingly large, and represents both a waste of resources and one of the biggest vested interests in maintaining the old system.

4. There is a huge flow of information by the time all the choices at issue, all the indicators of performance, all the potentials to be explored are brought to the attention of people at the top. There is an acute dilemma in trading off the cost saving from aggregating information (which simplifies but *discards* information) against the need to see all the complexities and details if one is really to know what is going on. In the author's view, intelligent, subtle, flexible administration requires more information than the Soviet-type economies could ever handle even if they had computer capabilities far beyond the actual level.

5. Among organizations, the Soviet administrative-command economy is a fairly coercive, rather than a consensus, organization. Because it is comprehensive in its scope, participants in the economy do not have much option as to whether or not to participate. There is a considerable conflict between very ambitious organizational goals and individual participants' goals, leading to complexities in controlling agents' behavior.

6. The leaders of the SPE in the various socialized countries have traditionally tried to insulate the system from the environment. These economies are characterized by secrecy toward their people and the rest of the world, and by economic autarky vis-à-vis the world economy. They are inner-directed in their preoccupations. This has helped the system to survive, but like the cockroach whose racial survival also depends on a wonderful ability to reject the poisons we push at it via the environment, it survives at a cockroach level of performance. If the economies of the socialist world are to achieve better performance they must adapt, and this depends in part on submitting themselves to the stimulus of competitive exposure to the world economy.

7. Finally, the designers and reformers of the system have tried all the alternatives that exist in the domain of administrative tinkering. They have rung all the changes in experimenting with different principles for par-

titioning, adjusting the incentive formulas, defining the variables used in the orders of the coordination plan. After the best job they can do, they are left with an irreducible amount of conflict, noise, and administrative confusion, and this irreducible amount is large enough to cause an un-acceptable amount of slack, waste, and lower-level unresponsiveness.

A Possible Model of Perfect Administration

Despite all these real-world cautions about the limitations of improving administration, however, it will be useful to ask if it would be possible to get closer to perfect administration if we could develop a "perfect" plan. Let us abstract a bit from all the problems outlined above, assuming that information flows easily, that it is possible to design a structure to collect, process, and communicate it at negligible cost. To make such a plan, the central planning body—the Gosplan in the case of the USSR—would first have to have an acute sense of what the goals of the leaders were: how strongly they felt about defense versus general economic growth, about improving the welfare of the consumer today versus diverting resources to investment to improve the lot of future generations, and so on. The Gosplan might well have to conduct a continuing interaction and dialogue with the leaders as it explored different variants. Second, it would have to keep constantly in mind an elaborate picture of what resource constraints the economy faced—the capacity of enterprises, the terms on which goods were available to it from outside the SPE, such as the wage rates needed to attract the correct amounts of the various grades of labor, and the relative prices of goods in the world market. It would have to have a clear idea of the technology by which these resources could be converted into in-termediate outputs and ultimately into final goods serving the goals the leaders had decided on. That last simple statement covers an almost un-imaginable variety of tradeoffs growing out of the interdependence of all the economic variables in the system. No one should underestimate what a huge information problem these requirements involve.

With all that knowledge and awareness, however, would not perfect administration then be possible? Perfect administration is certainly easier to envision if we imagine that a perfect plan could be constructed. Such a plan would be *feasible*, since it would be perfectly balanced, and its results would be *optimal*, in the sense that it would allocate the scarce resources available to the society in a way that would maximize attainment of the goals of the leaders. We will return in a later chapter to the question of how such a plan might be derived. But the point for now is that if a perfect plan could be constructed, it is possible to imagine that we might achieve perfect administration. Since the plan would be feasible, there would be no need or latitude for decisionmaking at the level of the enterprise. The enterprise manager would never find that the planners had failed to allocate his enterprise enough inputs to produce its assigned output or that the planned supply was unavailable because the planners had not specified a large enough total output for that commodity. And it seems a reasonable corollary of the assumption that we have the information to make a perfect plan, that we could collect the parallel set of information to check whether it had been fulfilled. In fact, as we will see later, a perfect allocation of resources is reflected in a price system that reveals the true "values" of all resources, i.e., how much any resource, any intermediate or final good, costs to produce and is worth in terms of its contribution toward meeting the organizational goals of the leaders. Although we have to postpone the reasoning on this point until a later chapter, it is one of the insights of the science of economics that perfect allocation (getting all the *quantities* right) and the true values (the correct *prices* for all goods) emerge together. So the creators of a perfect plan would necessarily also know the true value of all economic resources and outputs. This adjunct to a perfect plan would make it easy to evaluate enterprise performance for the control function. As in perfect competition, no firm would make a profit, and none would incur a loss. So all the evidence we would need to identify a bad manager would be a loss in his operations, and he could be fired and replaced with a competent bureaucrat, who would execute the feasible plan assigned to him.

There is something paradoxical in this vision of perfect administration. It would become "perfect" because managers in effect would be turned into automatons, and the central problem of attaining perfect administration—the difficulty of "working through people to attain the goals of the organization"—would be bypassed.

In short, we have to conclude our discussion of perfect administration with a judgment that it is not possible. Perfect administration is a contradiction in terms. But it is still a useful concept like many other scientific constructs, such as a frictionless medium or the profit-driven, perfect-competition model, which, if it *is* perfectly competitive, eliminates profits! It is my view that administrative tinkering, administrative decentralization, administrative reform will not provide a tolerable approximation of perfect administration. The information and computational requirements suggested for a perfect plan seem incapable of being met. The administered economy has outlived whatever usefulness it may once have had. Reform means giving up the administrative system, abolishing the administrative hierarchy that goes along with it, in favor of a market-type economic mechanism. That case will be developed further in a later chapter. But for the moment, it is enough to accept the idea of perfect administration and the allocation and valuations that go along with it as an abstraction, a theoretical construct.

As a final comment, remember that we have been talking about the task of making a plan for all the units within the SPE. As our earlier scheme suggests, the planners of the SPE have to get some information from the outside world. The SPE does not really control the allocation of each household's labor. The notion of how much labor (and, more important, labor effort) is available is not given absolutely, but depends on how effectively the SPE can attract labor through the labor market. And although we expect the leaders to know and formulate in some fairly explicit form their priorities about the tradeoff between investment goods and consumption goods, we cannot expect them to have a detailed set of ideas about tradeoffs within the consumer-goods domain, such as the relative worth of sardines and peanut butter. That information needs, rather, to be generated by an interaction with the households that will consume these goods. And the best way to carry on that interaction is via the consumer-goods market of figure 2-1. The two chapters following will examine how the administered system *actually* works within the SPE, and how the SPE's interrelations with households and other market-linked actors in the system should and do work.

3.
Resource Allocation in the Classic CPE

This chapter takes up the question of how the administrative approach has actually settled the allocation of resources—the basic problem of any economy—in the Soviet-type system. We approach the topic under two main headings, setting output and allocation of goods in the current period (short-run balancing) and longer-term planning of investment and innovation. Chapter 4 will complete the survey by considering market-mediated relationships in the Soviet-type economy.

Short-run Balancing

The biggest task confronting the planners of the real-world SPE is devising a plan that specifies how much of each of the millions of different products of the economy is to be produced each year, and how the output of each is to be allocated among users. In the market economy, this job is taken care of automatically by the market, and we often fail to appreciate how complicated a task it is. In the administered approach to running the economy, however, this "coordination" component of the administrative paradigm absorbs a huge amount of effort on the part of the bureaucrats of the SPE, and even so is done very imperfectly. Briefly, the process works as follows. On the basis of general priorities and guidelines worked out by the political leadership, the Gosplan sets fairly aggregative targets for output levels and makes gross allocations of investment and labor resources among ministries. These "limits and directives," as they are sometimes called, are passed down the hierarchy, and along the way get broken down into more detailed allocations and production assignments for lower-level units. When the enterprise, at the bottom of the chain, receives its output assignment, it proceeds to figure out in detail what inputs it needs to produce it, and sends "requisitions" (*zaiavki*) for these inputs back up the hierarchy. For example, a tractor factory will calculate that to produce the numbers and models of tractors targeted for it, it needs so much steel of various kinds, so much paint, so many tires, a certain volume of electrical components, and so on. These requisitions are assembled at the top in the so-called material balances.

A material balance, as in the schematic example in table 3-1, shows the sources and uses—i.e., the supply and demand—for the product involved. If the output targets set in the first phase of the planning process do not match the demand that emerges from aggregating the *zaiavki*, the planning office must make some adjustments. If the demand for coal is too large, for example, as shown in the coal material balance below, possible ways to make these adjustments might be to increase coal output, or to decrease demand by cutting the output targets for the coal-using industries. Any such changes lead to great complications. Raising coal output, for example, would mean that the requirements of the coal industry for various inputs would increase, requiring adjustments in many other material balances, such as electricity, cable, timbering, and repair parts for machinery. Even if the planmakers were lucky enough to have had perfect equality of supply and demand for each of those products in the first round (as in the electricity material balance shown), the corresponding material balances would now indicate a shortfall. If the planners tried to solve the problem by reducing the demands of coal-*using* industries by cutting *their* levels of output (say, by reducing the planned output of steel), then the material balance for steel, which already showed a shortfall in the example in table 3-1, would be even more in deficit. Planners learn from long experience that many of the requests for inputs are inflated, and so another approach to adjustment is "norm forcing." The planners might try to remedy the deficit in coal by telling the electric power industry that its original target for producing electricity remains unchanged, but that it must produce it with a smaller expenditure of coal than requested. They would be forcing on that sector a lower "norm" for the expenditure of coal per KWH generated than the enterprises in the sector had claimed

Table 3-1. Illustrative Schematic Material Balances

COAL MATERIAL BALANCE (*million tons*)

Sources		Requirements	
Imports	2	For electric power	55
Stocks at Jan. 1	4	For the steel industry	29
Domestic production	94	For the tractor industry	3
		For the auto industry	4
		For construction	1
		For other branches	11
		For export	4
		Stocks at end of year	4
TOTAL	100	TOTAL	111

ELECTRICITY MATERIAL BALANCE (*billion KWH*)

Sources		Requirements	
Domestic production	301	Own consumption	14
Imports	6	For the steel industry	23
		For the coal industry	14
		For automobile production	16
		For the tractor industry	6
		For construction	5
		For other industries	123
		For households	85
		For export	21
TOTAL	307	TOTAL	307

STEEL MATERIAL BALANCE (*million tons*)

Sources		Requirements	
Domestic production	89	For the tractor industry	20
Stocks at Jan. 1	8	For automobile production	19
Imports	0	For construction	26
		For other industries	24
		For export	4
		Stocks at end of year	7
TOTAL	97	TOTAL	100

And so on, through many *thousands* of such balances . . .

they required. Over many rounds of planning, enterprise managers do indeed learn to inflate their requests, since their experience tells them that in allocating inputs to them, Gosplan is likely to cut their requests arbitrarily. The result is a vicious circle of self-fulfilling prophecies in which enterprises inflate requests and Gosplan routinely cuts them, with no assurance that what is cut is fat rather than muscle.

A final possibility is to shift most of the burden of any shortage to low-priority "buffer sectors," such as those that produce consumption goods or inputs for the consumption-goods industries. The shortfall in the balance for coal might be made good by cuts in the allocation to the food industry, accepting that this will probably mean the food-processing output target cannot be met. The defense-industry branches, capital-goods industries, or other high-priority sectors can thus still receive the planned allocation. If the original goals cannot all be fulfilled, it is the sectors producing primarily for consumption that the leaders are most likely to see as expendable.

There are two big deficiencies in the adjustment process. First, the number of material balances used in the USSR in the seventies was on the order of 40–50,000, and when one considers the huge variety of commodities that exist in a modern economy it is clear that these balances must be fairly aggregated. For example, many specific shapes, grades, and specifications of steel must be lumped together under a single heading, such as "sheet steel," rather than having a separate balance for each of thousands of thicknesses, quality grades, degrees of finish, and so on. Second, the planners never manage to carry the adjustments through enough iterations to get everything all balanced, or if they do, the finished plan may reflect extensive norm forcing. Even if the plan looks balanced on paper in terms of aggregate groups of output, it is not balanced in terms of individual kinds of output or in terms of its ability to be fulfilled in reality. As a consequence, once the year's operations begin, Gosplan must spend a great deal of its time trying to correct the original plan, redistributing some commodity when it turns out that its supply is inadequate, ordering enterprises to produce some product that got overlooked, pushing enterprises to produce a specific kind of output that was not distinguished and balanced in detail.

What makes the balancing task so difficult is that all these outputs are interdependent. How much coal should be produced depends on how much electric power, steel, machinery, and so on is to be produced, since the need of these industries for coal depends on their level of output. But how much electric power needs to be produced depends in part on how much coal will be produced, since the coal industry requires electric power in proportion to the amount of coal it produces. It is impossible to plan one sector in isolation from another.

To understand the interdependence problem and how it might be solved, it is helpful to introduce the idea of input-output. We might state the coal material balance above in somewhat different form, as follows: The amount of coal to be produced = coal needed by the coal industry itself + coal needed for electricity generation + coal needed for steel + the amount needed for export + the amount needed for inventory accumulation + the amount needed for the armed forces + the amount needed for household consumption. The "equals" sign indicates that our goal is to have the amount of coal *produced* equal the amount *required* by the various users.

The problem in the material balancing operation on which the earlier discussion was based was that the planners set a target for the amount of coal to be produced early in the process before knowing how much would be needed for all the other uses. The alternative statement above acknowledges that it is not possible to specify in advance the amount of coal needed. The new formulation of the coal balance could be expressed symbolically as the first equation in the array below, in which X_1 is the unknown amount of coal to be produced. The subscript indicates that we are talking about the output of the first commodity; X_2 would stand for output of the second commodity, and so on.[1]

$$X_1 = a_{11}X_1 + a_{12}X_2 + \ldots a_{1n} + I_1 + C_1 + D_1 + X_1$$
$$X_2 = a_{21}X_1 + a_{22}X_2 + \ldots a_{2n} + I_2 + C_2 + D_2 + X_2$$
$$\cdot$$
$$\cdot$$
$$X_n = a_{n1}X_1 + a_{n2}X_2 + \ldots a_{nn} + I_n + C_n + D_n + X_n$$

---

1. A statement is shown for electric power (expressed as X_2, since it is the second commodity) in the same form. Obviously each material balance could be replaced with a statement in this form.

In the coal equation, the first term to the right of the equals sign is the amount that will be needed by the coal industry itself, expressed as the product of the amount of coal consumed per ton of coal it produces (the a_{11} is a technical coefficient showing how much of the first commodity—coal—is needed per unit of output of the first commodity—coal) times however many tons of coal we finally decide are to be produced. The second term is the amount of coal needed for the electric power industry. But since we do not yet know how much electric power will be needed, we express its demand for coal by its still-unknown output (i.e., X_2) times however much coal is needed per KWH of electricity generated, the technical coefficient a_{12} indicating the amount of the first commodity (coal) used per unit of the output of the second commodity (electric power). In discussing coal and electric power, I have assumed output is being measured in physical terms, but for these commodities, or for any others, output could alternatively be measured in terms of its ruble value. In this case, the technical coefficients—a_{34}, for example—would indicate how many rubles' worth of the third output is required per ruble's worth of the fourth output produced. In transforming the material balances to this symbolic form we are acknowledging that it is impossible to know the required output of any of the commodities without considering the amount of all the other commodities to be produced.

If we have such an equation for each product or each industry, the result is a system of n equations, with n unknown outputs. Assume for the moment that we know all the input-output coefficients. Also unknown in the equations above is how much of each commodity is needed for each of the "final" uses, indicated by the symbols for investment, defense, consumption, and exports. If the planners can obtain from the leaders a statement of how much output they would like to see devoted to those final uses, they can solve the set of equations to find the output required of each industry, i.e., the amount sufficient to meet all the demands for its output. In the language of the administrative paradigm, once the leaders have expressed their goals and priorities in terms of final output, the technicians of the Gosplan can use the input-output approach to solve the coordination task.

Unfortunately, mutual consistency among the amounts of these outputs is not enough. Each of them is produced by an industry that may have some capacity limitation. For example, given the number of power plants and the nameplate ratings on the generators working in them, there is an upper limit to how heavy a load the electricity network can bear without overloading the generators. Also, all of these industries require labor, the supply of which is not unlimited. If the consistent set of gross outputs violates any of those constraints, the technicians at the Gosplan will have to go back to the leaders, asking for more guidance as to what final uses should be cut to make the plan *feasible*, i.e., consistent both internally and in relation to the amounts of capacity and labor or other primary inputs available.

Input-output can also be thought of as an accounting framework for recording what actually happened in the economy in some past period. We might show the total amount of coal and every other kind of output produced, and what happened to it. Table 3-2 is an input-output table of this kind for the USSR in 1988. In this table output and its allocation are shown not in physical amounts, but in terms of its value at existing prices; i.e., the output of electricity is measured not in KWH but in millions of rubles' worth of electricity. We have aggregated all kinds of energy into a single sector and have measured its output and use in terms of rubles' worth, rather than in physical terms. Obviously we could recast the equations above in a similar mode, replacing all the separate energy demand-supply equations in physical terms with a single one for demand and supply of all energy, and with energy measured in rubles' worth rather than in tons or KWH.

Referring to this table, we can add some useful terminology. The total output of each commodity (i.e., the 269.751 billion rubles' worth of machinery) is called the "gross output" of that commodity. Gross output gets used in two different ways. Some is consumed as "intermediate output," that is, it gets used up in producing other outputs (the 36.761 billion rubles' worth of metals and chemical products is used up by the machinery industry to produce its output). The other part is "final product" going to the "final uses" of consumption, investment, exports, and "other" (the main element of which in this table is defense uses).

This table also suggests a possible source for the a_{ij} needed for using input-output in a planning mode. Looking at the flows that occurred we can see that 5.948 billion rubles' worth of energy was used in producing

Table 3-2. Input-Output Table for the USSR, 1988 (million rubles)

USER→ PRODUCER	Fuel and Energy	Metals and Chemicals	Machinery and Metalworking	Wood, Construction Materials, and Other	Consumer Goods	Construction	Agriculture and Forestry	Transport and Other	Consumption	Investment	Other End Uses	Export	Subsidy	Total
Fuel and Energy	32,731	13,369	5,948	5,666	2,925	3,265	3,405	5,681	11,281	393	380	9,947	5,289	100,281
Metals and Chemicals	1,320	53,275	36,761	7,194	5,823	8,496	6,723	1,585	10,544	1,646	2,928	9,162	937	146,393
Machinery and Metalworking	2,601	3,998	82,237	3,364	1,949	12,475	9,176	3,382	25,584	87,339	24,730	12,436	483	269,751
Wood, Construction Materials, and Other	1,111	2,653	4,689	24,028	3,526	30,760	16,237	3,438	18,730	2,008	6	3,906	0	111,094
Consumer Goods	267	3,182	2,907	5,394	105,688	960	6,475	1,759	134,300	1,075	637	6,089	4,978	273,710
Construction	0	0	0	0	0	0	0	0	0	165,447	0	0	0	165,447
Agriculture and Forestry	2	58	93	8,002	62,070	68	44,982	711	57,027	9,468	0	248	78,078	260,807
Transport and Other	1,947	1,541	1,973	2,576	2,437	3,194	985	1,554	8,926	436	0	1,221	0	26,789
Imports	595	4,571	5,489	2,247	13,162	3,017	4,393	526	36,371	23,250	3,012	0		96,632
Depreciation	17,071	14,731	20,277	10,013	8,037	11,449	18,989	24,250						
Wages and Social Security	9,660	12,550	50,759	19,964	20,330	51,753	53,494	41,306						
Indirect Tax + Markup	8,513	8,818	8,206	8,033	18,076	10,699	4,159	6,243						
Profits	24,465	27,648	50,413	14,615	29,687	29,310	91,790	44,061						
TOTAL	100,281	146,393	269,751	111,094	273,710	165,447	260,807	134,494						

Note: Components may not add to totals because of rounding errors.

the 269.8 billion rubles' worth of machinery-sector output, implying a coefficient of 5.948/269.8 = .022 rubles' worth of steel per ruble's worth of machinery. The planners might have reason to believe that this particular coefficient could be reduced in the coming year, and so might change it slightly before embarking on calculating next year's output by solving the set of equations described earlier. The same calculation (with possible adjustment of the corresponding coefficients) could be made for each cell in the matrix, generating the whole system of a_{ij} that appears in the earlier set of equations.

We can think of each of the columns in table 3-2 as an accounting statement of the elements that went into creating the value of the output of that sector. The "intermediate consumption" shown in the column for any sector represents the using up of resources produced in other sectors, but all the items below the double line—labor expenditures, imported inputs, depreciation, and other such items—represent elements of "value added" in this sector. The amounts shown in these cells represent expenditures of "primary inputs," or "primary factors of production" such as the labor used in each sector. Unlike steel, labor is not produced by any industry whose output we are planning, and its supply is a separate constraint. According to Marxist theory, it is thought that the only real source of value is these labor inputs, and traditionally the Soviet-type system does not in fact charge for land, or for capital used in production. Thus the column does not show any rental payments for land or interest charges for capital. In setting a price for the product a sector produces, the price setters do add to outlays on intermediate and labor inputs various markups in the form of taxes and profits. So those markups, too, are shown as an element of value added in figuring the total value of output of the sector.

At one point, it was suggested both by outsiders and by some Soviet planners that input-output was a model that could help solve the balancing problem. In most of the centrally planned economies the economists have produced I-O tables over a number of years since the sixties, usually at a fairly aggregative level. In the end, however, none of the planned economies has ever introduced input-output approaches as an operational technique for making the actual plan. The information requirements are great, and it turns out that input-output is not compatible with the administrative structure. Although we have spoken as if the sectors in an input-output table were defined in terms of pure products (coal, steel, etc.), in fact the administrative sectors to which the planners must address orders are not coterminous with the production of a single physical product. In the framework of an administrative structure where the actual steel-industry sector produces many things besides steel, and in which lumber is produced not just in the lumber ministry but in many others as well, the coefficients lose their technical basis. The amount of steel needed per tractor, as determined by the technical specifications of the tractor, might be easy enough to determine and fairly stable. But how much steel is needed for a ruble's worth of output of the Ministry of Tractor and Agricultural Machinery Industry is subject to fairly rapid change depending on the mix of products in a ''ruble's worth of output'' in that ministry.

Used in a more aggregative and research mode, however, I-O has been a significant aid to the planners in improving their understanding of and ability to deal with the interdependence of sectors. It is flexible and can be used in many ways—as in multiperiod planning or in regional planning. One such use, in setting prices, is worth elaborating on.

The problem of setting consistent prices involves the same interdependence as setting outputs. As costs change differentially among sectors, the prices the planners have set get out of line with costs. Some industries will make big profits, others losses, and the price setters want to bring prices back in line with costs. Suppose that only the coal price is too low—covering, say, just 80 percent of its cost of production. Suppose they raise it by 25 percent to eliminate the losses in coal production. They would then find that many industries formerly covering their costs would now have losses because of the higher price they pay for the coal they use. So we have here the same interdependence as in setting quantities. This interdependence could be dealt with by a system of equations similar to those used in balancing output, but based on columns rather than rows. In the system below we specify that the price per unit for any commodity, P_i, be high enough to cover the cost of its purchased materials (amount of coal used per unit of electric power times the price of coal, and so on for each of its purchased inputs) plus the cost of primary inputs and the desired profit markup. The interdependence is expressed basically in the same matrix of technical coefficients as in the output-balancing exercise.

$$P_1 = a_{11}P_1 + a_{21}P_2 + a_{31}P_3, \ldots$$
$$+ a_{n1}P_n + \text{Labor}_1 + \text{Deprec}_1 + \text{Profits/taxes}_1$$
$$P_2 = a_{12}P_1 + a_{22}P_2 + a_{32}P_3, \ldots$$
$$+ a_{n2}P_n + \text{Labor}_2 + \text{Deprec}_2 + \text{Profits/taxes}_2$$

.

.

$$P_n = a_{1n}P_1 + a_{2n}P_2 + a_{3n}P_3, \ldots$$
$$+ a_{nn}P_n + \text{Labor}_n + \text{Deprec}_n + \text{Profits/taxes}_n$$

The solution to this problem is a set of reformed prices in which the interdependence of prices has been fully taken into account. This approach has in fact been used on several occasions in price-reform exercises in the centrally planned economies.

In short, the problem of interdependence makes planning current output a very information-intensive process, whether in the kind of trial-and-error approach the planners have generally used, or in the more computationally sophisticated terms of a formal input-output procedure. It is so far beyond their information-processing capacity that the planners are unable to achieve tolerable equilibrium in supply and demand. The CPE is an economy continually disrupted by shortages of some goods while unwanted surplus goods pile up in other places, and where despite the theoretical possibility of calculating mutually consistent prices, in practice the economy functions under a rigid system of infrequently adjusted prices that are massively out of line with costs.

Control—Evaluating Performance and Passing Out Rewards

Making a plan and addressing it to those who are to carry it out is only the first step. The administrative paradigm always involves control—here "control of plan fulfillment," as the Russians call it. Since in the real-world planned economy the plan is not perfectly balanced, it will be impossible for enterprise managers to fulfill it exactly. In *trying* to fulfill it, they have to make choices—such as overfulfilling the output plan but overexpending the budget, or meeting the *aggregate* output plan but failing to fulfill the *assortment* plan. In making these decisions enterprise managers are guided by what serves their own advantage. In the Soviet-type economies their own advantage is mostly a matter of the bonuses managers receive if they are judged successful, or the misfortunes their careers will suffer if they are seen to be unsuccessful. Bonuses play a large role in managerial rewards, generally amounting to over half the income of managerial personnel. The penalties for failing to fulfill the plan can be deprivation of bonuses, demotion, or worse. The bonus is determined according to some "payoff function" or "bonus function," indicating how managerial bonuses will vary with the various dimensions of performance. This bonus function then becomes for the manager an "objective function," a statement of how what he wants (as big a bonus as possible) is related to the various dimensions of performance. Handling this control function effectively turns out to be beyond the capacity of an administrative approach to running an economy. Many of the defects of the centrally planned economy are a result of failures in the control function.

The difficulty is that the problem of monitoring and evaluating the performance of enterprise management is as information-intensive a process as making the plan in the first place. We might restate the problem of enterprise control in the administered economy as follows. Enterprise managers are charged with a kind of stewardship of society's resources—they are entrusted with some of the resources available to society in the form of production capacities and current inputs, to be used to produce something for society. The enterprise's drain on society's resources takes the form of material inputs, use of the environment, the health hazards to which it exposes its workers, and many other variables. The enterprise's contribution is measured by the amount of output produced, along with the many different attributes of the output—such as its quality, assortment, timeliness of delivery, and adaptation to the desires of customers. Stewardship "effectiveness" can be thought of as the relationship of these two measures. What the enterprise does for society ought to exceed or at least equal what it takes from society. The bigger the contribution for a given drain, or the smaller the drain for a given contribution, the better. The problem is that on each side of this balance there is a bewilderingly large number of dimensions of performance, and it is impossible to specify in detail in the plan assigned to the enterprise all these dimensions, or to measure them all in evaluating its performance. This multitude of aspects gets reduced to a relatively small number of indicators in the plan and in the report on plan fulfillment, *and to still fewer in the actual evaluation of enterprise performance.* A typical payoff function would figure bonuses for enterprise management as a function of profit, output growth over the previous period, and size of the enterprise—which we might express in a somewhat oversimplified way in the following form:

BONUS = (.10 × profit rate + .20 × percent growth in output) WAGE BILL.

An actual payoff function will usually contain some other arguments, and may not be this explicit. But however it is stated, lower-level people learn what the implicit function is, and it becomes the guide for their actions and decisions.

To decide whether an action is worth taking or not, whether the best choice is A or B, the socialist manager looks to this payoff function, just as in a capitalist firm the ultimate criterion for any contemplated action or choice is its impact on the "bottom line"—on profit. *For the manager in the Soviet-type economy the payoff function is the bottom line.* His decision on introducing a quality improvement, replacing an old machine, firing some workers, or changing the plant's output assortment is guided by what will increase the bonus he and his management team receive. Whether this rule will guide him to take actions consistent with the social good depends on how well the tradeoffs embodied in the payoff function (i.e., its coefficients) reflect the multifaceted costs and gains to society resulting from those actions. Because the payoff function is such a crude reduction from the multiple dimensions of burden and benefits to society, the decisions managers make in the CPEs are in fact often contrary to the interests of society. Many different kinds of things can go wrong in this approach. Several are explained below.

First, important aspects of performance may not get measured at all. Because quality is difficult to measure, it tends to be neglected when evaluating performance. This is the major reason product quality is so low in the socialist countries. In a classic example, the engines in trucks produced by a certain Soviet factory served very short lives before requiring expensive overhaul, which put a costly burden on the users of the trucks. Engineers in the plant diagnosed the problem as inadequately cured castings for engines. They suggested several solutions—longer curing, heat treating in special furnaces, and so on. These proposals were always vetoed by the enterprise director on the reasonable grounds that they would have an adverse effect on the payoff function by adding to costs, without improving any positive component measured in the function. The end result would be reduced bonuses for all the managerial and technical staff. Innovation and follow-up service are other dimensions of performance not generally rewarded in the bonus functions, and hence are neglected by enterprises. Contrast the fabled superattentive service IBM gives its customers with the total scorn Soviet computer manufacturers exhibit toward buyers of their product.

What *is* measured may be measured one-dimensionally. The famous *Krokodil* cartoon of a nail plant putting all its effort into producing one big nail when nail output is measured in tons is mirrored in thousands of real-life examples reported in the economic literature of every administered socialist economy. When milk was measured in "liters of milk of standard butterfat content," producers whose milk had a high fat content watered it down to the standard and got credit for more milk than they had actually produced. The builders of apartments who fail to connect plumbing fixtures with outside mains defend themselves by explaining that pipe in small diameters suitable for connecting to outside mains is unavailable. Output of such pipe is measured in tons so that it turns out to be advantageous for the producers to produce only large diameters. Physical measures of output, widely used in the planning and control process, often capture only one or two of numerous dimensions. One example is the Soviet practice of measuring output of batteries in terms of the weight of lead they contain, ignoring all other features of a battery's capacity. To get an idea of how many additional dimensions of battery performance are relevant to users, and thus affect the benefit to society, look in your Consumers Union *Report*, or in a Sears catalogue.

The coefficients by which heterogeneous things are brought to a common denominator may reflect contributions to society very inaccurately. This may be actual prices (by which, say, different models of an electronics plant output are aggregated to total value of output) or a separate set of coefficients. The output of canneries (consisting of some highly processed outputs, others less so, in many sizes of cans and bottles) is all reduced by a set of coefficients to a measure called "standard cans." Varied blast-furnace products—ferroalloys, pig iron for conversion to steel, foundry iron—are reduced to "standard tons of pig iron" by a set of such coefficients. When these ratios differ from cost ratios, the enterprise finds it disadvantageous to produce those which have a high cost in relation to their coefficient in the payoff function, and products urgently needed by customers are simply dropped from production.

What never ceases to amaze an observer of Soviet-type systems is the endless variety of forms this miscuing of behavior can take. Consider the case of pipe for oil and gas pipelines. Its wall thickness might be specified as a nominal 15 mm. But allowance is made for the imprecision of rolling mills by adding a tolerance, say plus or minus 3 mm, specifying how much variance is allowable if the pipe is to be accepted as output. That means the thickness should never exceed 18 mm or be less than 12 mm. Some enterprises with more modern and precise equipment may be capable of staying within tolerances of plus or minus 2 mm. Such enterprises would find it advantageous to adjust their equipment for an *average* thickness of 16 mm. Their pipe, never thicker than 18 mm, never thinner than 14 mm, will meet the specifications. But the result is pipe with walls thicker on average by 1 mm than it needs to be, and a corresponding waste of steel to do the job of moving gas.

For a long time output was measured in terms of gross output (*valovaia produktsiia*), which includes not only the value added by the enterprise but the value of the materials going into the product. As a consequence, enterprises in the administered economies have always been biased toward material-intensive products and designs and are motivated to use the most expensive materials they can obtain. In a project that interviewed the managers of cooperatives, the author came across the following typical case. This particular co-op produced exercise equipment—a kind of poor man's Nautilus. To avoid charges of profiteering and unwelcome attention from the authorities, it sold its output through the state marketing system at state prices. How, then, could it make the impressive profits it reported? Part of the answer was higher labor productivity—the co-ops have been tough-minded about paying according to effort, and so they get effort.

But another source in this case was that the price for the state-produced analog was based on the use of tubing much heavier and more expensive than needed. The co-op used lighter, cheaper tubing, offering it a significant profit margin.

Activities are often measured at an intermediate stage in the production process, and success indicators get fragmented. In oil exploration, drillers are rewarded in proportion to how many meters they drill, seismic prospecting teams on the basis of kilometers of seismic profile. Each of the partners can show good performance on its own indicator without the exploration establishment necessarily finding any oil. What is needed is a *hierarchy* of success indicators to go with the hierarchical structure of the responsibility chain, and the hierarchical structure of the task.

This type of suboptimization and the measurement by gross output mentioned above—the cult of *"val"*—are the basis of the *"zatratnyi mekhanizm,"* the expenditure mechanism that the Soviet reformers have come to see as a major defect of their system. They are both examples of measuring success not by the amount of output that finally emerges but by how much the enterprise *spends*—a sure formula for encouraging waste.

The *form* of the payoff function may be defective. Two special problems are discontinuities and fixed tradeoffs. Discontinuities mean that there is no reward at all if the target is not reached, and it is no better in this respect to fall 1 percent short than 10 percent. A famous case is the taxi driver with a target of so many paid kilometers to meet. As he approaches the end of the month and sees that he will not meet the target, it may pay him to turn on his meter and drive around aimlessly, paying the associated fare out of his own pocket. The resulting bonus, which more than covers the fare he has paid, is a gain to him, but society loses in the form of wasted gasoline and wear and tear on the taxi. This example may seem amusing but trivial, but the same phenomenon works in a thousand forms in the CPEs to waste resources on a massive scale.

Obviously the "reward structure" embodied in the bonus function is a kind of price system, but one that includes not just prices in the usual sense but also the coefficients and the form of the payoff function. In the reduction process, which weights all these dimensions of performance by these coefficients, a divergence between private advantage and the social good creeps in. Some product or some act that is highly desirable from a national economic point of view may have a low price and thus be disadvantageous. Or vice versa—some product or act that is advantageous to the producer (because it is cheap or easy to produce in relation to the price, contributing toward easy fulfillment of output targets) may be useless or even harmful to the national economy.

The evaluation process is cyclic. Because it operates on a short cycle, there is strong pressure to do things that will improve measured performance in the current period, but which may mortgage future potential. Oil-well-drilling teams, under pressure to meet monthly footage goals, find it advantageous to continue drilling more and deeper holes on a given prospect rather than shift to a new one, since a move and setup time would cost them footage. The extra drilling on an already explored site may be totally useless as a contribution to finding or producing more oil. The short time horizon that flows from the brief period of this cyclic process (i.e., basically one year) is disastrous for innovation, which typically is likely to disrupt output in the short run for longer-term benefits. Ideally it would be desirable to establish evaluation cycles of differing periodicity for different aspects of performance. But again to avoid complexity, the designers of the CPE system stick with a uniform time period.

Finally, enterprises are motivated to try to influence the plan to make it easy to fulfill. In such a case overfulfilling the plan does not necessarily mean a corresponding contribution to national economic welfare. Any astute manager in this system will soon realize that if he can get an easy plan, a moderate effort will be seen as good performance leading to big rewards. But if he ends up with a hard plan, dedicated and conscientious work may still be read as poor performance, leading to trouble. So lower-level officials work hard to obtain an easy plan, or to influence the way the general payoff formula is applied to their unit. The nature of this game and possible methods of countering such behavior will be discussed further in chapter 5.

The socialist hope was to get rid of private property, the unbridled chaos of the market, and replace the capitalist driven by the greedy desire for profit by socialist managers who would work "for the good of the working class." But socialist managers, even if they are dedicated to socialist goals, need more operational guidance than an exhortation of that type. In practice the payoff function, which combines actual prices and its own tradeoff coefficients, is the bottom line that guides socialist managers. This reward structure is egregiously more distorted than the price system of *any* market economy. In a market economy most dimensions of performance tend to be evaluated in intimate interaction with customers, and are reflected in prices and in the bottom-line success indicator of profit. When they are not, when the customer is in a poor position to monitor performance of the producer and reward him correctly, the market economy suffers from analogous problems, such as too many heart bypass operations and caesarean sections. But on the whole the bottom line of profit is a better indicator of success in meeting society's needs than is the bottom line of the CPE payoff function.

A wonderful little book by the Soviet aircraft designer Oleg Antonov expresses in its title *Dlia vsekh i dlia sebia* (For Everyone and for Oneself) the goal the reward system should achieve. But its content is a kind of "thousand and one nights" collection of stories describing how the actual incentive system in the USSR drives a wedge between the private and the social interest. Evsei Liberman, a reformer of the Khrushchev era, proclaimed that "in principle, under socialism, what is advantageous for society is also advantageous for the individual production collective," and thought that the principle could be turned into reality more effectively by abandoning the bonus function as the bottom line and substituting profit. Unfortunately, Liberman was a prophet who came along too early, and his idea never got incorporated into reform.

Long experience suggests that there is no solution to this problem of effective monitoring of performance. We cannot expect that over time, by gradual fine-tuning, the designers of the bonus function will eventually get it just perfect. First, there is too much data processing involved, and in any case the situation is always changing. Second, the clash of interests between top and bottom means that one set of players in the game, the managers, have a stake in generating disinformation. These inherent difficulties may not mean such inefficiency that the system actually collapses, but the associated wastes in the Soviet-type economy seem to be on a grander scale than we know in administered organizations elsewhere and certainly exceed those of most market economies. The system lacks signals and tools analogous to those that exist in the market economy for correcting these wastes. If GM falters, the rest of the auto industry can win its customers. If the whole U.S. auto industry falters, the Japanese will run it out of business. There may be a special Russian flavor to administrative inefficiency in the USSR (the famous Russian *khalatnost'*—a richly evocative term for general sloppiness and negligence). But fundamentally, I believe that the problems are mostly inherent in administration per se, whether in the Soviet Union *or* the old East Germany, when it is applied to an excessively complex task.

Investment Decisions

The input-output framework described above suggests two other problems that need to be discussed—projectmaking and innovation. In the short run, choice of output and input proportions is narrowed by the framework of existing plant capacities, technologies, and locations, making the norm-based Gosplan procedures or the fixed coefficients of the input-output matrix not too far from reality. But that raises the issue of how the decisions that create this framework are made—how the capacities of different plants were determined, how the technologies were chosen, where plants were located—i.e., the kind of decisions that determine how much of various inputs are required per unit of output of any given commodity. The answer is found in another sphere of decisionmaking, what the Russians call projectmaking or the design of production facilities. Moreover, in a dynamic economy, the technology embodied in these production facilities should be undergoing improvements through research and development and innovation. So we should also ask how the administered economy handles projectmaking and the creation of new technology.

As suggested, projectmaking can be defined as the ''design of production facilities.'' ''Design'' here covers many dimensions, including the location and size of a plant, the technology—with its implications for capital intensity and input mix—of a factory, a system such as a communication-satellite network, or an individual item of equipment such as a computer. Projectmaking is the responsibility of projectmaking and design offices, usually located at a high level in ministries. They go by a great variety of names, but Giprosviaz', the State Institute for Designing Telecommunications Networks, might be cited as an example.

The starting point is a decision to expand the capacity for producing some product. Without considering the details of how that decision is reached, think of it as coming from Gosplan's forecasting work. Working back from planned growth rates to growth of individual outputs, it derives the new capacities that will be needed to produce those larger outputs in the future. Projectmaking organizations are then charged with designing facilities with the requisite capacities. The goal might be creation of so many megawatts of electric power–generating capacity, or the design of a new generation of locomotives that will handle the expected volume of freight transport in the coming years.

The projectmakers always find that there are a great many possible alternatives for achieving the assigned goal. The designers of new tractor models to meet the needs of agriculture have a choice between wheeled or tracklaying tractors and between gasoline and diesel engines. The designers of a gas pipeline could specify the use of domestically produced or imported pipe and compressors. The broadcasting authority could meet an assignment to design a TV distribution network for the country by using coaxial cable, radio relay, or communication satellites, or various combinations of these transmission media. Within an existing plant, it might be possible to repair and modernize old equipment, or to scrap it and replace it with new. These examples give only a hint of the huge variety of choices that have to be made by projectmakers working in the many branches of the economy.

Despite their variety, all these decisions are approached in the centrally planned economies via what might be called a "generalized effectiveness calculation." The projectmakers specify several variants that will do the job prescribed. The technical specifications for each are worked out, and the variants are then costed out to see which is cheapest. This seems a straightforward, commonsense approach, and indeed is how decision-makers who make these choices in the market economy approach them. In the Soviet context, however, there has been much confusion about how properly to decide "which is cheapest."

First, given the kind of localism characteristic of a partitioned hierarchy of the kind we have described in discussing the organization chart of the administered economy, there is a danger that the projectmakers will refer the choice to too narrow a criterion of what is cheapest or most efficient.

Projectmakers in the steel industry may decide on very large plants, taking advantage of scale economies to cheapen the production cost of steel. From the national economic point of view, however, the savings in production cost may at the margin be overbalanced by excessive transport costs. The larger the plants, the larger the resulting market areas, and the higher the average transport cost of delivering steel to the customer. Such "suboptimization" may also result from the narrowness of view of the Soviet engineers that usually staff these projectmaking organs, who may not be economically sophisticated.

Consider the design of the turbodrill. For a long time the USSR had great difficulty in improving the traditional technology for drilling oil wells. In this technology, a long string of pipe, made up of fairly short sections screwed together, is rotated by equipment at the wellhead to turn a bit at the bottom of the hole. This string is subjected to tremendous strains, and given the low quality of Soviet pipe and of the tool joints with which the string is screwed together, drillers had great trouble with breakages of the string. These breakdowns required stopping drilling to engage in expensive efforts to fish out broken drill pipe and tools, and then starting over. Soviet engineers sidestepped the problem by developing a turbodrill in which the drill string is not rotated but is used to carry fluid down the hole to operate a long, narrow turbine at the bottom. By greatly reducing the stress on the pipe, this innovation led to big improvements in rig productivity. As in any projectmaking situation, the designers of the turbodrill had to make a lot of choices, and they designed the various elements of the system to maximize its *mechanical efficiency*—i.e., they wanted to maximize the amount of work done at the bottom of the hole in relation to the work input at the top of the hole. But in a hydraulic system of this kind, mechanical efficiency requires a high rate of rotation of the bit, which meant that bits wore out rapidly. When actually drilling, they made holes fast, but these periods of drilling were followed by long idle periods spent pulling the string from the well, to replace the bit and then relower it before drilling could recommence. The gain from efficient use of the power at the top of the hole while drilling was lost by excessive idle time devoted to replacing bits. This "engineering bias" often appears in the form of an infatuation with automation, using "the most modern technology," going for big size, or copying foreign experience, even though technological copying may be inappropriate in the Soviet context. For example, the innovation might depend on quality of inputs, skill of operating personnel, or cheapness of capital that is not present in the centrally planned emulator.

A second set of perplexities concern what costs should be included. In a replacement decision projectmakers ignore the insight of western economics that "sunk costs" are irrelevant to current decisions. Rather, following a Marxist prejudice, they have traditionally included the unamortized value of an old asset as part of the cost of the replacement variant. That biases the decision against replacement, one of several factors that have led to far too little replacement of obsolete facilities in Soviet-type economies.

The biggest weakness of all is probably that the prices used for figuring costs are often treacherously misleading indicators of the real cost to society of the resources involved. The price system is badly distorted by a variety of arbitrary markups, taxes, uneven profits, losses, and subsidies. A particularly interesting case is the complete failure to account for some costs that, according to Marxian lights, are not considered costs at all— namely, the opportunity costs of capital and natural resources. This prejudice has led the projectmakers to design hydroelectric facilities that have flooded huge areas of excellent agricultural land without reckoning whether this cost was justified by the gains from the project.

Soviet economists have puzzled over these issues, and have gradually moved toward more sophistication in their effort to find the cheapest way. An issue that has troubled them more than any other, and that illustrates this growing sophistication, is the *capital intensity problem*. We can approach the problem in the classic form in which the Soviet planners originally encountered it. Consider assignments to projectmakers to design new capacity in a number of sectors. These include creating a new power station with a capacity of 10 MW, a new rail link to handle a given amount of freight each year between Omsk and Tomsk, and a new tractor plant. In each case there is more than one way to design the new capacity, as shown by the variants in table 3-3. In power there is a choice between a hydro plant or a coal-fired plant. The railroad can be built with a high or a low "ruling gradient." (The ruling gradient, the steepest segment of a line,

Table 3-3. Illustrative Choices in Projectmaking Decisions

	POWER		RAILROADS		TRACTOR PLANT		
	hydro	*thermal*	*low ruling*	*high gradient*	*low*	*intermediate level of automation*	*high*
INITIAL I	100 MR	50 MR	100 MR	50 MR	75 MR	125 MR	175 MR
ANNUAL OPERATING COST depreciation fuel labor	5 MR	10 MR	8 MR	12 MR	75 MR	68 MR	65 MR
∧ I	50 MR		50 MR			50 MR	50 MR
∧ OP COST	5 MR		4 MR			7 MR	3 MR
PAYOUT PERIOD	10 YRS		12.5 YRS			~7 YRS	~17 YRS

Note: In each case the operating costs include depreciation to cover the cost of replacing the facility, so that we can think of these productive capacities, once built, as capable of being operated forever.

governs important determinants of operating costs such as train weight and speed.) In the tractor plant various degrees of automation are possible. These variants exhibit a common economic phenomenon—the possibility of substituting capital for other inputs. In each case, a larger initial investment makes possible lower operating costs each year to produce the stipulated amount of output.

The puzzle is that in all these cases the variant that is cheapest in terms of initial capital cost is more expensive in terms of annual operating cost. How should these divergent measures of cost be traded off? In a market economy the choice presents no problem. The extra investment in the more capital-intensive variants creates additional annual costs in the form of interest, and the capitalist firm judges which is cheaper by simply taking both kinds of cost into account. But in Marxian ideology, interest is not considered a real cost but rather a form of surplus value extracted by the capitalists, and the designers of the Soviet system rejected interest payments for capital. Capital is made available to investment projects interest-free.

As the electric power projectmakers consider their choices, they could make a case for choosing the hydro variant along the following lines. It will cost more initially, but the cost savings each year will recoup the extra investment within a fairly short number of years, and will continue thereafter in perpetuity. This sounds like too good a deal to be refused! The same logic applies in the other cases as well, and in contrast to the simple two-variant form of our example, in the real world projectmakers find that though substituting capital for current outlays may run into diminishing returns, they could absorb very large amounts of capital to reduce operating costs. Railroads offer special temptations in this respect, having an almost endless set of possibilities for making a straighter and more level roadbed, which will save on costs of operating trains across it. But if all the projectmakers succumb to this beguiling reasoning, the demand for capital is likely to exceed its supply. By "supply of capital" we mean not money but the real resources of steel, bricks, cement, and so on available to build new facilities (i.e., the goods in the investment column in the I-O table). The question is where to put these physical resources to get the biggest effect, the biggest savings of the labor, energy, and other inputs that constitute the operating costs. The calculation is made in rubles just to have a common denominator.

The solution adopted by the Soviet planners finally was to set a limit on how far to carry the substitution of capital for current inputs, in the form of a "normative" payout period, i.e., a stated number of years within which the cost savings must recoup the extra investment. Additional investment in a given project would be justified only if it generated enough cost savings to repay itself within the specified number of years. In the case above, if we set the payout period at 15 years, the electric power planners would choose the hydro over the coal-fired plant, the railroad designers would go for the low-ruling-gradient version, and the designers of the tractor plant would choose the intermediate variant, on the judgment that an extra 50 MR investment over the simpler version was justified, but that the next step upward was not.

Note that although we have talked about capital intensity, this process can also be thought of as the allocation of capital. From the point of view of the projectmaker, this is a capital-intensity decision. But the sum of all these decisions together is a pattern of allocation of the available investment.

On a closer look it is clear that the payout-period approach is equivalent to the use of a rate of interest in the market economy. The payout period for the extra investment is figured by dividing extra investment by the cost savings, but its reciprocal, the cost savings divided by the number of years, is obviously the annual rate of return on the extra investment. And comparing the actual payout period for extra investment with a normative payout period is like comparing the rate of return on the extra investment with the rate of interest one must pay to obtain the extra funds. The payout period, like the rate of interest, is a way to decentralize the decisionmaking process, by providing guidance to reconcile local decisions with a global optimum. If the payout period is really to work like the rate of interest, the normative payout period should reconcile demand and supply of investment resources.

Unfortunately, the use of the payout period as a signal in the administrative approach works much less subtly than does the capital market in reconciling supply and demand for investment resources. The normative payout period is set administratively, not in a market, and has remained unchanged at 8 percent since the sixties. Such a fixed rate obviously cannot do the equilibrating job, and we have to conclude that there is still a great deal of arbitrariness in the allocation of capital in these economies.

The payout-period approach ran into ideological difficulties when its similarity to the rate of interest was recognized. The resulting controversy played an important role in the evolution of Soviet economic understanding through the contribution the Soviet economist V. V. Novozhilov made to the argument. Novozhilov introduced the idea of "inversely related outlays" (*zatraty obratnoi sviazi*), which is equivalent to the notion of "opportunity cost," one of the most powerful ideas of western economics. Novozhilov's idea can be explained in terms of the first two projects in table 3-3. Suppose that these two projects represent the total investment program, and that we have available for investment a total of 150 MR worth of capital resources. If the projectmakers in electric power decide to build the hydro rather than the fossil-fuel-fired station, that means there is only 50 billion rubles left for investment in the railroad sector, and it will not be possible to choose the low-ruling-gradient variant. Choosing the hydro plant thus means sacrificing the possibility of saving 4 MR/year by choosing the low-ruling-gradient version of the railroad. So, says Novozhilov, the real cost to operate the hydro plant each year is not just the out-of-pocket costs of 5 MR, but also 4 MR of forgone savings for a total of 9 MR. That is still better than the 10 MR it would cost to operate the coal-fired plant, and so the best allocation for the economy is to build the hydro plant and the high-ruling-gradient railroad.

We can work the calculation the other way as well. If the low-ruling-gradient variant is chosen in the railroad case, the hydro variant in electric power becomes impossible, sacrificing the opportunity to save 5 MR a year. So the real cost of operating the low-ruling-gradient rail link would be $8 + 5 = 13$ MR, which > 12 MR. *Including opportunity costs*, the low-ruling-gradient variant is more expensive. Novozhilov generalized this insight, and made clear that we need a measure for the opportunity cost of committing capital to a given project that tells every decisionmaker what the actual cost of such a commitment is—i.e., the saving forgone on the best alternative that must be rejected somewhere in the economy. In the sixties and seventies the Soviet planners came to accept the overall logic, and thereafter in the USSR and Eastern Europe a straightforward interest rate was used routinely in all kinds of capital-allocation and capital-intensity decisions. The standard way to make these calculations now is to cost out variants, *including* the opportunity cost of the capital involved in each. The opportunity cost of capital and operating cost are aggregated in the concept of *privedennye zatraty*, the sum of the operating costs and interest (figured at a rate that is the reciprocal of the payout period) on the capital invested in the project.

Unfortunately, this is only a partial solution to the problem of taking account of the opportunity cost of capital, since it fails to communicate it to other people making decisions about using the *outputs* of these facilities. Imagine that the projectmaking process concludes that the optimal choice for new electric power capacity is a hydro plant. Pricing in the Soviet-type economy does not take into account *privedennye zatraty* but has typically been based only on the concept of *sebestoimost'*, i.e., the operating costs in our example above, including depreciation. Suppose these kinds of plants are the norm in the industry. With a load of 5,000 hours a year, the 10 MW capacity generates 50,000,000 KWH, and electricity would be priced at 10 kopecks per KWH. Other projectmakers would use this as the cost of electricity when they make their cost-minimizing calculations. This price fails to tell them the opportunity costs of the electricity they are asking the economy to produce. As we saw, that is really properly measured by *privedennye zatraty* of 26 kopecks/KWR. So throughout the economy people will be making choices about whether to use electric power or some alternative energy source, or how much to spend in capital to save electric power, on the basis of a measure that is well below its actual cost.

A final crudity in this tradition is that the planners may not consider enough variants. Actually capital is more or less continuously substitutable for current inputs, and by choosing only a few variants along this spectrum they may overlook the best. Suppose that in the tractor plant example above, the intermediate variant had been overlooked. That makes the payout period for the extra capital for the most capital-intensive variant of a new tractor plant 10 years. Suppose that the normative payout period is 11 years, and that there is 325 MR available for all projects. We would thus choose the hydro variant of the power station (requiring 100 MR), the high-ruling gradient for the railroad (committing 50 MR), and the fully automated machinery plant, using up 175 MR, and exhausting the supply, with an annual operating cost of 5 + 12 + 65 = 82 MR. But clearly if the intermediate alternative for the tractor plant were also being considered, we would choose hydro (100 MR), the low-ruling-gradient railroad (100 MR), and the intermediate machinery plant (125 MR), again exhausting the capital allocation, but ending up with annual expenditures for operating these facilities of 5 + 8 + 68 = 81 MR.

There is still a great deal of confusion about the relation of the opportunity cost of capital to pricing. One example surfaces in disputes about trade specialization in CMEA, the preferential socialist trade bloc to which until the end of the 1980s the socialist economies directed most of their trade. The Soviets argued, for example, that it was disadvantageous for the USSR to produce minerals and exchange them for machinery from Eastern Europe. Mining is capital-intensive, machinery production less so, and if goods are exchanged at their ''value'' (in the Marxist sense of *sebestoimost'*, without an interest charge) the country producing the capital-intensive item is getting cheated. It will have a lower ratio of output to new investments than the country specializing in machinery, and accordingly will suffer from slower growth. The Soviet negotiators have taken the position that if Eastern Europe wants minerals from them, the East European importers must provide some of the investment for expanding mineral production. This has led to serious squabbles. However, if everything is priced inclusive of the opportunity cost of capital, then there will be no problem.

Research, Development, and Innovation

The second major process shaping the structure of input-output relationships is the rate and direction of technical change. Technological change is constantly renewing the product mix and changing the input coefficients in the direction of reducing the amount of input required per unit of output. Managing technical change is of course a very important function in any society, raising productivity as one way of increasing the economy's output. In general, the Soviet-type administered economy has proved inept at this process of discovering new knowledge and putting it to work to develop new products and new processes that raise productivity. That is paradoxical, because the leaders of the system have consistently emphasized that technical progress is one of their main strategies for catching up with the rest of the world, and have lavished resources on the creation and support of a huge research and development establishment. The discussion that follows will refer mostly to the USSR, but it is generally applicable to all the variants of this model across the socialist world.

Research and development spans a spectrum of activities from basic research through applied research, design, testing, engineering, and innovation. Innovation as the final stage in the process means putting the new products into commercial production and use. It is usually said that the USSR does a better job at the basic-research end of this spectrum than at the innovation end. The bosses of the Soviet system themselves characterize their problem as one of weakness in "introducing the achievements of science and technology into the economy." I would amend that characterization only by adding that the institutional setup of the administered economy is not conducive to moving through the whole series of steps along the spectrum between basic research and successful commercialization. The main difficulty is that the system depends on administrative-command "push" from above rather than on "demand pull" from units at the bottom of the hierarchy strongly motivated to demand and employ new technologies. This centralized approach works better for "science," where the main thing the center has to do is provide resources, and for well-defined, high-priority, mission-oriented projects such as space exploration, than it does for widespread innovation and diffusion of new technologies.

Half of the team that drives the innovation process is the R&D establishment. In the USSR the institutions responsible for research and development constitute a distinct branch employing 4.5 million people. At the apex of this empire is the "academy system," consisting of the multibranch Academy of Sciences of the USSR, academies in each of the republics, and some specialized branch academies. The main responsibility of the academy network is basic research. It is the most prestigious part of the system, staffed with the most able Soviet scientists. A distinguishing feature of the Soviet R&D system is a relatively unimportant role for institutions of higher education in the development of science. In contrast to the United States, where most basic science is performed in the universities, Soviet institutions of higher education conduct very little research, basic or applied.

Quantitatively the most important part of the R&D system is the system of "branch science," consisting of a large network of R&D organizations subordinated to the various ministries. These institutes conduct some basic research oriented to the needs of their branches. Their main responsibility, however, is to carry on the R&D that creates new products and processes relevant to their branch of the economy. Finally, there is a small "enterprise sector" of science, attached to the enterprises at the bottom of the hierarchy. Again, in contrast to most other countries, the labs and institutes of the enterprise sector, which are closest to the people who will actually produce newly developed items, account in the USSR for only a very small share of R&D resources and activity.

The R&D sector works like all the rest of the administrative system.

At the top there is a central planning body (the State Committee for Science and Technology or GKNT), and the system as a whole works according to a centrally approved plan that specifies themes for research, budgets, employment, investment, and so on. There are targets for the creation of specified numbers of new models of machinery. The plans of individual institutes are centrally approved, and funds to support their work come mostly from highly centralized sources. The volume of resources devoted to R&D in the USSR is impressive. Adjusting for differences in definitions, the USSR has about as many scientists and engineers engaged in R&D— 1.5 million—as does the U.S. The puzzle is how this effort can have so little impact on the economy. We can single out several major causes.

Much of Soviet R&D has been, and indeed at the beginning of the nineties still is, devoted to military research. Defense R&D takes the form of work done by nominally civilian institutions on behalf of the military and the defense industries, but most is done in an extensive network of R&D institutes in the defense-industry ministries. These institutes have high priority in access to resources, they are better equipped than the general run of R&D establishments, and the scientists and engineers working in them enjoy higher salaries and better working conditions. When in 1989 the Soviet government released for the first time a figure for its actual defense expenditure (which until that point had been kept secret and blatantly misrepresented in the budget), the total included an expenditure on military research and development of 15.3 billion rubles. Given that total R&D was about 30 billion rubles, the military had commandeered about half the whole enterprise. Given the departmentalism of the system, reinforced in this case by secrecy, spillover from military R&D to civilian needs has also been minimal. Hence the combination of huge expenditure and little apparent impact in the form of technical progress is explainable in part by the distorted *direction* of R&D. (On the other hand the R&D efforts of the other socialist countries have not been as dominated by military demands as in the USSR, and their performance in technical progress has been far from impressive.) The reduction of military expenditures and conversion of the defense industry that has accompanied *perestroika* has important implications for these R&D organizations. Like the defense-industry sector overall they have operated with a degree of priority and on a level of competence well above the average for the economy as a whole. An important task for the reformers is to find a way to keep the competence of these R&D teams alive and shift their experience and potential to improving the technical level of the civilian economy.

A characteristic weakness in Soviet R&D (less so in the military than in the civilian wing) is that it is poorly supported with equipment. Research institutes lack sufficient computers, laboratory equipment, and instrumentation. At the more applied end, the R&D establishment is weak in experimental production facilities in which to test the new designs, produce prototypes, and operate new processes at a pilot-plant level.

The second group of players on the technical progress team are the enterprises who will introduce the new technology into production. Unfortunately, there is a big disjunction at the point where responsibility for new products and processes is transferred from the research and design establishment to production plants. The R&D organizations are driven by their own incentive system, which does not effectively orient them to "commercialization." They do the assigned work, designing a new truck model, say, or creating a new design for a telephone exchange including writing the software that will run it, or developing the specifications for a new model of energy-producing equipment (such as a new turbo-generator block). But the work of the design organizations usually ends with the detailed specifications, or maybe working blueprints. They tend to push these out the door, forget about them, and go on to the next assignment. It is often complained that the designs they deliver are incomplete, are not producible, are not up to world standards, and that the R&D organization is not much help in working out the bugs. If a new product, say a new tractor model, does get into production, new complaints often arise further downstream from those who are supposed to buy the product and begin to use it in *their* operations to improve quality, lower costs, or raise productivity. Like any subunit in USSR, Inc., design organizations are responsive to their own bosses and to central organs such as GKNT rather than to their downstream partners. Their separation from the other half of the team is reinforced by the fact that they are located at a high level in the hierarchy of their ministries and are often geographically distant from the customer—an overwhelming majority are located in Moscow and Leningrad. In this area of the economy the system of vertical communication and authority results all too often in such aberrations as the creation of robots and flexible manufacturing systems that after delivery are ignored by the customers who are supposed to use them. The intended users say that they are not fitted to the conditions of the Soviet economy, demanding a level of quality and reliability in supplies, maintenance services, and worker skills that does not exist.

Textbooks for introductory economics explain that the allocation of resources includes as two major subproblems decisions about *what* goods to produce (including decisions about how much of each) and *how* to produce them, i.e., what mix of inputs (capital vs. labor, aluminum vs. steel) is to be used. This chapter has tried to explain how those aspects of the resource-allocation problem get solved in the administrative-command system. The summary conclusion is that that system is a clumsy substitute for the market. The system is not in equilibrium at an optimum. There is misallocation and wasteful overexpenditure of resources, hoarding, misallocation of effort that produces surpluses of some things, too little of others. The system is deficient in feedback mechanisms that could sense these misallocations and respond to correct them. The forces stimulating innovation are weak, and the system exhibits sluggish technical progress. To some extent this is a failure to follow the rules of good (even if not perfect) administrative practice. The success indicators are defined badly, the administrative hierarchy suffers from faulty design. In the area of innovation, for example, it might be said that the system lacks a node where the information, resources, motivation, and responsibility needed for this function come together in one organization, as they more or less do in the capitalist firm.

Ultimately, however, the explanation of why the system does so poor a job has to do with the burden of *information processing* and *incentives*. It turns out that these two factors are interrelated. The amount of information that needs to be absorbed to prepare balanced and feasible, let alone optimal, plans is beyond the capacity of the system to handle. There is a corresponding information overload in the control task, mirroring the errors of the imperfectly worked out plan. But the information problem in control undergoes added distortions as enterprises seek to escape effective control by concealing information from, or distorting the information they send to, the center.

4.
Market-mediated Relationships

In a number of areas the Soviet-type administered economy relies on markets, specifically in dealing with households, with the rest of the world, and (to some extent) with the farm sector. An important set of economic variables gets settled through the SPE's interaction with others via these markets—the wage structure, the aggregate supply of work effort, real income distribution among households, the foreign-trade pattern. Numerous aspects of the poor performance of the socialist economies— deficits in consumer-goods markets, foreign-trade imbalances, repressed and open inflation—are strongly influenced by the fact that these markets do not function very well. The task of this chapter is to analyze these relationships in more detail. It will help in understanding them if they are discussed in an integrated way, in a framework suitable for understanding how they fit into the problem of reform.

In the input-output flow table presented in chapter 3, the labor row represents the supply of worker effort, the consumption column represents the flow of consumer goods to households. Imports constitute another of the rows, and exports another column. We might also think of peasant and/or collective-farm agriculture as a row and column external to the input-output relationships within the SPE.

Thought about in this way, the structure of prices in the system is determined in part by wage levels and differentials, in part by the way imported inputs are priced, in part by the way agricultural inputs are priced. As explained in the discussion of input-output–based price reform, total outlays for steel production consist of what the steel industry purchases from other sectors (coal, railroad transport, repair parts for equipment, etc.) plus those value-added elements. The cost and price of the inputs purchased from other sectors are in turn built up from what the respective sectors spend for labor, for imports, and for inputs they purchase from other sectors. The whole price structure is thus ultimately built up in a circular fashion by the way prices are set for labor, agricultural outputs, and imported inputs, together with the magnitude of the markups in the form of taxes and profit margins that are added in the various sectors to these input costs.

So let us turn now to an analysis of the relationships of the SPE with households, with the farm sector, and with the rest of the world, devoting special attention to the setting of prices in these relationships.

Market-mediated Relations in the Administrative-Command Economy

What these three cases have in common is that they are market relationships in which decisions are made in response to prices. A first question is why in these areas important allocational variables are turned over to the market, rather than being set by the administrative-command principle. The answer, briefly, is that it is too difficult to make all these decisions by administrative methods, basically because of the very large number of actors to be dealt with, and the heterogeneity among these actors. Even the most overambitious and arrogant central planner in Moscow would not attempt to figure out what job each individual should have to make the greatest contribution to achieving the goals of USSR, Inc., and what volume and composition of consumer goods that individual should be given to best satisfy his or her wants and motivate him or her to do that job well. So in these areas Soviet-type economies let people sort themselves out among jobs as they prefer, and permit them to allocate their incomes any way they like among the possible consumer goods. Given the freedom to make choices, households show the kind of behavior that generates supply curves for labor and demand curves for consumer goods just like those to be seen in an Econ 1 textbook. But these markets are not free competitive markets, since households confront the SPE on the opposite side of each market as a monopolist supplier of consumer goods and as the only buyer to whom they can sell their labor services. As a monopolist-monopsonist the SPE has the power to set the prices in those markets—it is a "pricemaker."

There is a similar phenomenon in agriculture: there are such a large number of individual production units and so much variety among them that the task of planning their productive activity in detail is beyond what the administrative approach can handle. The degree to which the SPE bureaucrats have sought to exercise administrative control over agriculture versus steering it via market methods has varied greatly over time and across countries in the socialist world. In the USSR before collectivization, and for most of socialist Poland's history, market steering was the rule. After collectivization in the USSR, agricultural producers were subjected to a great deal of administrative interference. In the period of the communes Chinese agriculture was subjected to intense administrative interference, but in the reforms of the seventies this was abandoned in favor of price guidance. But even when the SPE directors do try to micromanage the agricultural sector, their ability to control it usually turns out to be far from complete. To a considerable extent agricultural producers do what they want rather than what the bosses tell them to do, and their decisions are much affected by price signals.

If the SPE wants to govern these two domains of economic decisions by markets, it must follow the rules for efficient markets. Markets work through the instrument of price, and the main question is what principles should govern the setting of those prices.

The situation in foreign trade is a bit different. The SPE is not able to direct foreign firms in the same manner it directs domestic firms, and so perforce cannot use the administrative-command system in disposing of exports and acquiring goods from abroad. It does not even have the power to set the prices on the goods it exports and imports, since they are set by the competition of many buyers and sellers in the world market. Generally speaking the USSR, let alone the smaller socialist countries, is too small a player in those markets to be able to influence them—it is a "pricetaker." In the foreign-trade area, accordingly, the question of how to work through markets is not one of what prices to set. Rather, it is how to *react to* the prices the SPE finds in the world market, which represent tradeoff opportunities available by trading exports for imports. Let us consider each of these market-mediated relationships in turn.

Relations with Households

In its relations with households, the goals and considerations that should guide the SPE's setting of prices and the rules for achieving those goals can be characterized as in the following tabulation.

Goal	Consumer-goods Markets		Labor Markets
macrobalance	expenditures	=	incomes
microbalance	marginal utility proportional to prices		marginal disutility proportional to wages
efficiency	prices proportional to cost		wages proportional to productivity

Macrobalance

The macrobalance equation flows from the fact that the labor markets and the consumer-goods markets are related to each other; incomes earned in the labor markets are the source of spending in the consumer-goods markets. The macrobalance condition says that whatever prices are set on individual consumer goods, and however the earnings are determined for each of the millions of jobs in the economy, there is an overarching requirement that when the quantity of each consumer good is multiplied by its respective price and these are summed, this total must be equal to the product of all the individual wage rates times the quantities of the corresponding kinds of labor supplied at those prices. (There are complications of taxes, savings, etc., to which we will return later.)

How satisfactorily do the price setters in the administered economies satisfy this principle? It is easy to satisfy it in the plan. If the plan is balanced in physical terms, then the planned amounts of consumer goods will be delivered and only the planned amounts of labor will be employed.

Macrobalance in financial terms is then only a matter of setting the relative prices of labor and consumer goods correctly, a relationship which can easily be adjusted on the consumer-goods side by adjusting the amount of turnover tax or other markup. In fact they have problems here, because the plan is not balanced in reality. The consumer-goods sectors and the sectors that work mostly to supply them are treated as "buffer sectors," which are starved for inputs when it turns out that it is impossible to fulfill all the targets set by the overambitious planners. As the priority system works to adjust overambitious plans to reality, the result is underfulfillment of consumer-goods production. On the other side of the exchange, labor is the one input enterprises can purchase relatively easily in amounts exceeding the budgeted total. Pressed to fulfill overambitious plans, they are likely to overexpend the planned wage fund by hiring extra workers, paying overtime, or offering premiums for greater effort. This is one illustration of the "soft-budget constraint" characteristic of the Soviet system that will be analyzed in much more detail later. The consequence of excessive wage payments and under-plan consumer-goods production is unspendable money accumulated by households, resulting in repressed inflation of varying intensity.

Performance on this macrobalance condition has varied among socialist countries over the years. In the USSR in early years it was handled poorly, and the result was a long record of inflation. It became necessary to impose rationing in the thirties, and repressed inflation was significant during the Second World War. The Soviet planners got rid of the excess money in 1947 with a currency conversion. Other techniques for soaking up these money holdings have been bond sales and legalization of cooperative housing in which households provide funds for housing construction.

Repressed inflation shows up in upward pressure on prices, in rapid growth of savings deposits, in rising collective-farm market prices, and in the creation of black markets. When the Soviet government tried to curb drunkenness by cutting the production of vodka and other alcoholic beverages, on which very high turnover taxes are collected, the result was a huge budget deficit and a serious case of repressed inflation. In fact, in recent years the excess money problem has been so bad that it has become necessary to reinstitute rationing in many areas of the Soviet Union. All the other socialist countries have had periods of macroimbalance at one time or another.

Microbalance

In the consumer-goods market, the "microbalance" condition can be stated alternatively as a requirement that markets clear, i.e., that supply equal demand for *individual* commodities. If prices are not in proportion to how badly people want various kinds of goods, they will rush to buy the ones that seem cheap, shun those that seem too expensive. If a consumer is willing to accept a dozen oranges in lieu of two dozen apples, we say that the marginal utility of an orange is twice that of an apple ($MU_{or}/MU_{ap} = 2$). If people find in the shops that the price for oranges is only 1.5 times that of apples ($P_{or}/P_{ap} = 1.5$, so that the condition is not satisfied), they will leave the apples on the shelf and take the oranges to the checkout counter. There will thus be long lines and shortages for oranges, and apples will be left to rot.

In labor markets, also, the microbalance condition is the requirement for clearing. Some jobs are more onerous than others, or involve more responsibility or more training, which is costly to the individual in time, money, and effort. The condition that wages be proportional to marginal utility states that if the differences in wages are not sufficient to compensate for the greater disutility of some occupations and jobs, people will not want to take those jobs, and will choose others instead.

Efficiency

The efficiency condition says that in addition to having macrobalance and markets that are individually in equilibrium, the resulting prices for consumer goods must be in proportion to cost and wages in proportion to productivity. For consumer goods this is related to getting the mix of consumer goods right. Suppose that all markets clear, but only because the price office has set very high markups on some goods, resulting in high prices, and in other cases very low markups. That would indicate that the SPE is creating artificial scarcities of some goods, producing too few of them while producing too much of others. If the price of oranges is set at double that of apples to make these markets clear, but in reality the SPE could produce a dozen oranges by cutting apple production by only a dozen and a half (i.e., at the margin the cost of oranges is only 1.5 times that of apples—$MC_{or}/MC_{ap} = 1.5 \neq P_{or}/P_{ap} = 2$), we are frustrating what people would like to have by quoting them a tradeoff that is too high. A fuller demonstration of why this is wasteful will be given in an example below.

How well are the microbalance and efficiency conditions met for consumer goods in the Soviet-type economies? Failure to clear markets is easily observable, and its costs—consumer dissatisfaction, time lost standing in line, creation of conditions for black markets—are obvious. So clear signals are generated when this condition is not met. The instrument for manipulating prices to satisfy the market-clearing condition is the turnover tax. Consumer goods are generally sold at a price well above what they cost to produce, the difference taking the form of an excise tax, called the turnover tax. If it turns out that some good is not selling, the turnover tax can be cut. The price of a good that is always in short supply can be raised by increasing the tax on it. It is probably correct to say that this market-clearing condition is satisfied very imperfectly in the Soviet-type administered economy. There are numerous cases of commodities for which prices are traditionally set below market-clearing levels. Housing is the most glaring example—in the Soviet Union rents have not been raised for 60 years and cover only a small fraction of the real cost of housing. Meat and consumer durables are others. When I spent a semester teaching in Romania, a friend explained to me that buying an automobile there involves not only a many-year waiting list; there are even waiting lists to get on the waiting list! Individuals first have to be accepted on a ministerial list through application at their place of work, on the basis of political reliability and other noneconomic criteria. Only as they move to the top of those lists are they put on a list to actually wait for a car. In the USSR at the end of the eighties about 18 million households had telephones, while there were 15 million households on the waiting list for them. The people who finally get a telephone installed tend to be those with special political influence or those who can offer bribes. In both these cases the official price is far too low to equate supply and demand, and other allocative principles must be invoked.

The efficiency condition is almost universally violated—planners are more clumsy in juggling output to satisfy consumer preferences than in juggling prices to clear markets. Satisfying the efficiency condition requires some interaction with the annual balancing process, which is much more difficult. The procedure would be to raise the output of any good which had to be given a higher than average turnover tax markup to make $S = D$, and to reduce output of those with lower than average markups. But as we have seen, there is a sticky interface between retailing and consumer-goods production—the output of consumer goods responds to the demands of the annual balancing process, not to this rule. If this condition is not fulfilled, there is no obvious signal that something is wrong requiring adjustments. Changing conditions make this failure a more serious problem today, since more variety, quality, etc., are needed to elicit effort in a higher-income society.

In labor markets, the clearing condition is reasonably well satisfied, partly because the firm has some latitude in adjusting earnings to attract the labor it needs. In the USSR a State Committee on Wages (whose name and function have changed over time) tries to establish wage scales for each industry that respond to the condition of differential utility among jobs. The central element is a set of job-classification handbooks (*tarifno-kvalifikatsionnye spravochniki*). Much like a job-classification manual of any western corporation, these describe each of the jobs in an industry and specify the training and experience required to perform it. The *spravochnik* classifies these jobs into something like five to nine skill categories, and specifies earnings differentials among the categories. Even when the centrally fixed scale does not get the differentials just right to clear markets, an individual firm has some flexibility in what it can offer a worker. It can misclassify workers to give them a higher wage than intended. In addition, piecework systems, widely used in the USSR, offer another way to fudge earnings. The centrally determined wage rate is intended to be what a worker will earn if he or his group just fulfills the norm. If the enterprise sets the norm low, it will generally be overfulfilled, and earnings will be above those intended by the central wage scale. Under this system if the coal industry cannot get enough coal miners, the coal-mine managers can fiddle with the piece-rate system to adjust earnings to disutility.

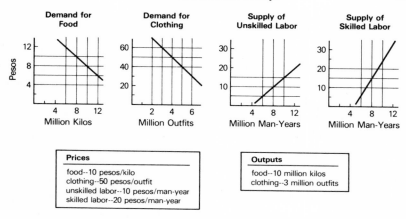

Figure 4-1. **Planning Consumer Goods Equilibrium**

As for the efficiency condition, there is probably a stronger force mo-tivating firms to satisfy it in labor markets than in consumer-goods markets. As long as the enterprise bonus function includes pressure for cost min-imization, management has a motivation to proportion rewards to different categories of workers according to their marginal productivity. In the capital-investment choices analyzed in the discussion of projectmaking in chapter 3, the goal is minimization of cost, including the cost of labor.

The way these three conditions work can best be understood by con-sidering a very simple example. Let us imagine that the Cuban plan for next year sets the prices and quantities indicated in figure 4-1, and that the underlying demand and supply behavior of households is as shown. A quick check shows that neither the macrobalance nor the microbalance condition is satisfied. At the wage rates shown and given the indicated supply behavior, people would earn 260 million pesos, while the value of the consumer goods offered at the official prices adds up to 250 million pesos. In the consumer-goods markets, the prices initially established will not clear the market. At the official price of 50 pesos per outfit for clothing, people will want more than the 3 million outfits offered, while in the case of food, there will be a surplus. Fortunately, we can make some fairly simple changes to correct the problem. Let us lower the price for food to 8 pesos/kilo (by reducing the amount of turnover tax on it), and set the market-clearing price of 60 pesos/outfit for clothing (by raising the turn-over tax charged on it). Fortunately, this then works out also to give us macrobalance; i.e., the 260 million pesos which people earn just matches the 260 million pesos of consumer goods being offered.

Even after these changes have been made, the plan may still not be "optimal," since it may not meet the efficiency condition. Imagine, for example, that the cost of producing an outfit of clothing is 40 pesos, and the cost of producing a kilo of food 4 pesos. Then, $\text{Cost}_{cl}/\text{Cost}_{fo} = 40/4 = 10$, which is different from the price ratio we set in order to get the markets cleared, i.e., $P_{cl}/P_{fo} = 60/8 = 7.5$. Consider the consequences of reducing clothing output by one unit. This would reduce household expenditures by 60 pesos, and to maintain macrobalance an additional 7.5 kilos of food would need to be produced and sold ($7.5 \times 8 = 60$). This switch would cause no change in consumer satisfaction—people have shown by their behavior that as the mix of consumption goods now stands they would be willing to accept 7.5 kilos of food as a fair exchange for an outfit of clothing. (The fact that markets clear means that $MU_{cl}/MU_{fo} = P_{cl}/P_{fo} = 7.5$. When people are offered the choice of getting 7.5 kilos of food or an outfit of clothing, we do not find a long queue in either store.)

The saving in resources to the SPE from producing one less outfit of clothing is 40 pesos' worth of resources, while the cost of producing 7.5 additional kilos of food is $7.5 \times 4 = 30$ pesos' worth of resources. So this switch has generated a net saving of 10 pesos' worth of resources, without reducing satisfaction or incentives. The 10 pesos' worth of resources saved by the SPE in this way could be used either to finance more Cuban assistance to revolutionary movements abroad, to produce an extra 2.5 kilos of food to make people happier, or to satisfy any other of the leaders' goals. As this switch continues, of course, the market-clearing price for clothing will fall, that for food rise. It will turn out that the possibility of improving effectiveness in resource allocation by this route disappears at the point where the cost ratio and the price ratio are identical, i.e., the third condition in our tabulation of the rules for optimal pricing.

Agriculture

Agriculture in the Soviet-type economy is too vast a topic to cover in any great detail in this short description. Rather, the goal here is to provide, in a brief overview, an interpretive approach within which many of the interesting phenomena can be absorbed, and which will prepare the ground for thinking about the treatment of agriculture in a reform program.

The relationship between the modern, nonagricultural, urban sector and the farm sector, often consisting in an underdeveloped country of peasant households, is a serious problem for any development program. Development requires diverting output away from consumption to investment, and in an underdeveloped country most of the nation's income and most of its consumption are concentrated in the rural sector. The development planners would like to turn the terms of trade against agriculture in order to extract a surplus to be directed to investment in industrial growth. The Soviet case, however, was unique in the urgency the leaders felt about diverting large amounts of income to investment to accelerate growth, and unique in its solution to the problem.

The pricing considerations are similar to those in the relationship described above for urban households. To turn the terms of trade against agriculture, the SPE should set the prices on what it sells to the farm sector as high as possible relative to the prices on what it buys from it. It should set relative prices *within* each of these categories in proportion to costs for what it sells to the farm sector, and in proportion to productivities (in terms of ability to contribute to the leaders' goals) for what it gets from agriculture. That would be using its monopoly/monopsony power to "exploit" farm households in the same way it exploits urban households.

It should be noted that the exercise of market power here may be more difficult than against urban households, since rural households are not "alienated from the means of production," to use a Marxist phrase. If the terms set by the SPE are too adverse, there is a danger that the peasants may respond by eating their output—of grain or meat—rather than selling it. This possibility is illustrated in Soviet history in the "scissors crisis," and in the fear that peasants would withhold grain, which led to the collectivization of agriculture. The term *scissors crisis* originated in a situation in the twenties when the supply of grain to the cities diminished. The situation was often explained as the result of an adverse price movement. Under the influence of the industrial trusts the prices charged for goods sold to peasants were rising, while those being paid to peasants were falling, as reflected in the following scissorslike diagram.

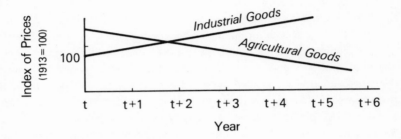

Turning the terms of trade against the peasants means giving up as little as possible in the way of goods delivered to the farm sector for each ton of grain, meat, and so on received from it. We can think of this alternatively as setting high prices for goods sold by the SPE to the agricultural sector, and low prices for the goods bought from it. The relative price is the reciprocal of the physical amounts exchanged. If 10 tons of grain are to be exchanged for 1 ton of fertilizer, macrobalance will be achieved by setting the price per ton of fertilizer at 10 times the price per ton of grain.

The most useful model for analyzing this situation is the idea of "offer curves," drawn from the way economists think about trading between countries. In a sense that is what was happening in the early years of Soviet history—peasant Russia and the urban industrial Russia that the party was organizing as the SPE were almost two different societies, two different countries. Figure 4-2 can help us understand how the SPE can maximize its income. In this diagram we are simplifying the situation by supposing that trade between the urban sector and the agricultural sector involves only two items, the sale of fertilizer by the urban sector to agriculture and the purchase of grain from it.

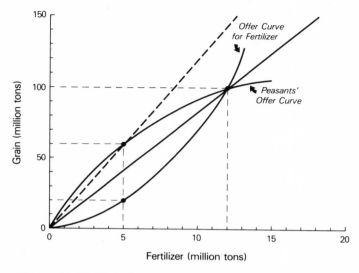

Figure 4-2. Trade between the Urban and Agricultural Sectors

The offer curves of figure 4-2 show the terms on which each side is prepared to deal with the other, *assuming* that each is composed of many producers operating under competitive conditions. Each point on each curve indicates a deal the producers on the respective sides would be willing to make. For example, the diagram indicates that if the peasants see a price for fertilizer such that they could earn enough by selling 12 tons of grain to buy 1 ton of fertilizer, enough would find that attractive enough that a total of 60 million tons of grain would be offered for sale, i.e., point *a* on the graph. Similarly, if fertilizer producers saw prices indicating that they could get 4 tons of grain for 1 ton of fertilizer, enough would find it advantageous that they would turn grain into fertilizer to supply 5 million tons of fertilizer, i.e., point *b* on the graph. What lies behind the peasants' offer curve, obviously, is the possibility of using fertilizer to increase grain output. On the fertilizer side the analogous consideration is converting grain into fertilizer, say by hiring workers and paying them in grain. A straight line from the origin that passes through point *a* indicates relative prices—along that line the relative quantities traded, and hence the grain/fertilizer price, are the same. Under competitive conditions the amount actually exchanged would be point c, where the two offer curves cross, and the relative price (or terms of trade) would be that indicated by the line from the origin to the intersection of the offer curves.[1] The gains from this trade are represented by the space between the curves—i.e., the gains that some peasants get in the form of more fertilizer for a given amount of grain (set by the equilibrium price) than they would settle for if pressed, and vice versa for the intramarginal fertilizer sellers.

But suppose the fertilizer-producing side is organized as a monopoly that can set the price. It can maximize the surplus it receives by setting the price of grain at 1 ruble/ton and the price of fertilizer at 12 rubles/ton. At that relative price it can exchange 5 tons of fertilizer for 60 tons of grain. But as its own offer curve implies, it can produce that much fertilizer using only 20 tons of grain. The gap between the two curves at this point, measured on the vertical axis (i.e., 40 tons of grain), is a "surplus." Obviously the trick is to set the relative price to intersect the grain offer curve at the point where the gap between the two curves is a maximum. We might describe the result as "perfect exploitation" of the peasant sector.

The central feature of the Soviet experience is that Stalin was greedy and not content merely to exploit the agricultural sector. He set a grain procurement target outside the possibility locus defined by the peasants' offer curve. He wanted more than 60 tons of grain in exchange for 5 tons of fertilizer. The implication of that is that peasants were asked to give up more than the additional grain output made possible by the amount of fertilizer received in exchange. The resulting loss came out of their own hides, so to speak. To achieve those terms of trade the SPE had to *coerce*, not just *exploit*, the peasants. Stalin was able to carry out such a confiscatory policy toward agriculture only by the institutional change of collectivization.[2] The collective farm worked by imposing leadership from

---

1. This diagram, since it considers only an exchange of one producer good for each side, need not consider the question of microbalance separately and ignores the fact that peasant households also buy consumer goods. Making the discussion more elaborate to make it more realistic would not, however, change the basic point.

2. For a fuller treatment of the collective farm and its role in the agriculture sector, the reader is referred to the Suggestions for Further Reading; only a brief description can be given here. Agriculture in a centrally planned economy consists basically of three compo-

outside on what was supposed to be a voluntary cooperative. Collection of the state's demand was helped by the creation of the machine-tractor stations (these state agencies rather than the collective farms owned all the agricultural machinery) which imposed planting patterns and took physical control of the harvest to guarantee the state's share. One corollary of this confiscatory approach was the establishment of private plots for collective-farm households. These plots were to provide most of the subsistence of those households, since they could not survive on their income from the collective farm. As time went on, the dynamics of price changes made the relationship truly confiscatory—agricultural procurement prices remained fixed, while the prices of things sold to the agricultural sector went up as the state responded to the inflationary push of the system.

The labor of collective farmers was being coerced, rather than elicited, and decisions were imposed rather than being made by the producers in accordance with their own interests, which was fatal for effort. I once visited a collective farm in circumstances that meant we came to it across the fields unannounced. Under each tree in the apple orchard sat a peasant girl on a box to make sure no one stole the apples, which looked wormy and useless to me. In our discussion with the management, it was explained that though most peasants were paid in proportion to labor days, there were a few especially important jobs that actually carried cash salaries, including that of the head of security. (Probably none of that went to the

---

nents. The state farm, as explained in chapter 2, is much like an industrial enterprise within the SPE, with its workers being paid regular wages. The classic collective farm combined two kinds of activities—the socialized joint activity, and the private plots of the member households of the collective farm (usually consisting of an acre or so per household). Collective-farm members were free to dispose of output from these plots as they wished, though they might be taxed on that income. For their participation in collective operations, the farm members were traditionally paid in "labor days," a notional unit of account rather than strictly a day's work. The members' share in the income in cash and in kind of the collective operations was determined by shares in total labor-day earnings. Until 1958 agricultural machinery was owned by state-controlled machine-tractor stations rather than the farm, and the farm paid for machinery services. Most of the output of collective operations had to be sold to the state at a low price. The important point is that the collective-farm household was a residual claimant against a small and uncertain income. More recently with higher prices, collective-farm members have been paid advances more like a regular wage.

The relative emphasis and encouragement given to these three forms has been one of the variables differentiating individual CPEs and expressing policy change over time. For instance, an important element in the Brezhnev food program was encouragement of private-plot activity relative to collective operations, especially in livestock care.

girls!) In these days of *glasnost'* it is hard to remember how limited our information on the informal realities of Soviet life used to be, but one of the eminent scholars in the field of Soviet economic studies, Alexander Gerschenkron, believed that a great deal could be learned from novels. One of his examples was an agricultural novel in which the collective-farm members operating combines for the machine-tractor station adjusted the threshing mechanism of the combine to discard a high proportion of wheat along with the chaff. The wheat so discarded was then gleaned by hand by their family and friends.

In this situation, it was impossible to hope for any initiative on the part of the collective farmers, and the SPE was drawn ever more deeply into administrative interference to make up for the lack of motivation on the part of the peasants. A huge agricultural bureaucracy was created in both the state and party systems to tell the collective farms not only how much to deliver to the state but what crops to raise, when to plant, how much fertilizer to use, what animals to raise, what to feed the animals, and when to slaughter them. Once this bureaucracy starts to interfere, its meddling expands progressively. Having set procurements, officials then found they needed to set acreage plans to assure fulfillment of the procurement plan. Next came orders about seeding rates, rotations, and on and on. Such detailed orders from the center often were completely at odds with what made sense in local conditions. The erosion of incentive and the clumsiness of administrative interference combined to make agriculture the disaster area of the Soviet economy.

On the whole, the other centrally planned economies have handled the relationship with agriculture somewhat better than the USSR did. The Poles and Yugoslavs virtually abandoned collectives. The Cubans made more extensive use of state farms, a form suitable to the plantation-like sugar production in which they specialized. The Chinese never pushed quite so hard to exploit the peasants. In the Soviet Union itself, an alternative approach had been proposed in the early days—the Bukharinite vision—which it would not be inappropriate to describe as the optimal exploitation policy described above. This was the policy actually followed during the period of the NEP (New Economic Policy), though clumsily enough to lead to disruptions such as the scissors crisis mentioned earlier. This alternative lost out to Stalinist collectivization, but it remains in the

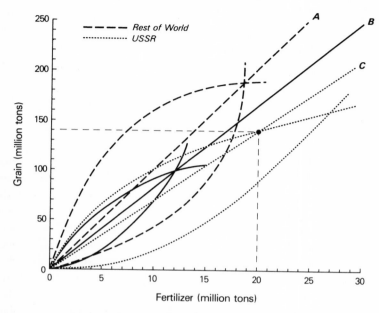

**Figure 4-3. Changing Terms of Trade between
Agriculture and Nonagriculture**

background as an alternative to the classic system. Khrushchev at one
point suggested that his goal for agriculture was to announce prices (for
goods on both sides of the exchange, presumably) and let collective farms
compete with each other for the privilege of doing business with the state.
In the era of *perestroika*, one of the first ideas advanced by Gorbachev
was that reform required organizing relations with the peasants on the
model of the NEP.

Finally, the Stalinist policies had a long-term deleterious effect on agriculture. Facing such adverse terms of trade, agricultural producers had
virtually no incentives or funds to invest for improving their productivity.
Remember that the offer curves represent essentially the possibilities for
turning nonfarm inputs into farm inputs and vice versa. Normally in the
process of development, as productivity grows, both offer curves shift
outward, as in figure 4-3. In the world as a whole, over the years since

the First World War, productivity has grown in both sectors, but much faster in agriculture than in the nonagricultural sector. As a result, the offer curves have shifted as shown by the dashed lines labeled "Rest of World." This implies that the potential magnitude of gains from exploiting agriculture expands enormously. In line with the mechanism explained earlier, the terms of trade have shifted against agriculture; i.e., the price of agricultural goods has fallen relative to nonagricultural goods. Price line *A* involves a reduction in the price of agricultural goods relative to industrial goods compared to the original situation. In the USSR there has been minor productivity increase in agriculture (and hence little shift in the agricultural offer curve), but a large productivity increase in non-agriculture. This situation is indicated by the offer curves shown as dotted lines labeled "USSR." So now, when the leaders want to get more out of agriculture to improve the food supply to nonagricultural households (say that in figure 4-3 they want to increase grain procurements to 20 tons), they have to offer amounts of nonagricultural goods indicated by price line *C* that are quite out of line with the terms of trade existing in the rest of the world. When we take up the issue of comparative advantage below, it will be seen that this is one reason the USSR has a comparative dis-advantage in grain, and must import it on a large scale.

In the fifties, after Stalin died, the treatment of agriculture was reformed considerably. The most important change was to offer improved price incentives and to dismantle some of the machinery of coercive adminis-tration. Procurement prices were tripled over a relatively few years. The machine-tractor stations were abolished in 1958, and their machinery was sold to collective farms. Unfortunately, nevertheless, the effort to ad-minister agriculture rather than to direct it by price continues, and right up to the nineties agriculture has remained a central issue demanding the reformers' attention.

Foreign Trade

In dealing with the rest of the world, the SPE is again only one party to the transaction. But the USSR is only one among many buyers and sellers on the world market, and cannot expect to manipulate the prices to obtain the exploitation gains it did in the other cases. What, then, is the point of foreign trade from the point of view of the leaders of the SPE?

The rationale for specializing and trading with other countries is to obtain the "gains from trade" possible under the principle of comparative advantage. Comparative advantage and the possibility of gains from trade rest on a difference in cost ratios between the domestic economy and the outside world, as in the following illustration.

	Cost in the USSR	Cost in the U.S.	Ruble Is Worth	Dollar Is Worth
Grain	1 R/bu	$4/bu	$4.00	.250 R
Tractors	1,500 R/unit	$9,000/unit	$6.00	.167 R
Bushels of grain needed to equal 1 tractor	1,500	2,250	—	—

Note that the ratio of the tractor cost to the grain cost in the USSR (1,500/1) differs from that on the world market (2,250/1). Given this difference in cost ratios, it is easy to see that there is a potential gain from trade without even considering issues of how many dollars a ruble is worth or how to change one currency for the other. A person could buy 1,500 bushels of grain in the U.S. (costing $6,000), take it to the USSR, and receive 1,500 rubles, since grain sells for 1 ruble/bushel in the USSR. With those rubles, that person could buy one tractor, bring it to the U.S., and sell it at the going market price of $9,000, ending up with a profit of $3,000.

Suppose for the moment that the USSR in the example above is like any market economy, and has a convertible currency. In trade between market economies, there is a foreign-exchange market and an exchange rate, which permits calculation on the part of the individual. If the exchange rate is $5/ruble, then the cost of grain imported from the U.S. would be $4/5 = .80 R/bu, below the grain price in the USSR, and thus offering a profit to the trader. The ruble revenue from an exported tractor is $9,000/5 = 1,800 R per unit, which is above the cost at which it sells in the USSR. As exporters and importers work to take advantage of this potential for profit, prices for tractors rise in the USSR, fall in the U.S., and prices for wheat rise in the U.S. and fall in the USSR, until the ratio is the same in the USSR as in the rest of the world. An equilibrium will emerge in which price and cost structures become similar, and there is an equilibrium exchange rate. In this equilibrium, the U.S. would produce more grain than if there were no trade, and would trade grain for tractors, producing fewer of them itself. The USSR would experience the reverse shift. But the result will be that each country has available for its own use more tractors *and* grain than it did before trade. These gains will be widely diffused among groups and individuals by the reductions in price of imported goods, and the higher incomes earned in the export sector.

CPE Trade with Market Economies

In the *actual* Soviet-type economy, however, the institutions governing foreign trade differ from those of the market nations. The main foreign-trade institution of the SPE is the state monopoly of foreign trade. The ruble and other socialist currencies have not been convertible. There is an artificial exchange rate; individuals and enterprises cannot buy and sell the ruble for foreign currency; foreigners abroad cannot even own rubles. Those conditions define *currency inconvertibility*. More important, however, is *goods inconvertibility*—even if one could go to the bank and trade rubles for dollars and vice versa, it is not possible to just buy any goods you might want. A Soviet citizen who knew that blue jeans sold in the USSR for 100 rubles, heard that they could be bought in the U.S. for only $25, and knew that the official exchange rate is $2 per ruble, could not take 100 rubles to the bank, exchange it for $200, buy 8 pairs of $25 jeans in the U.S., and sell them for 800 rubles. He or she would be a speculator operating outside the law. Similarly impossible is the idea of some U.S. tourist who might dream of buying and taking home a boatload of something that seems cheap in the USSR compared to how expensive it is in the U.S. in light of the existing exchange rate. (Vodka and caviar used to meet these conditions pricewise.)

If the USSR is to obtain the gains from specialization and trade, the planners of the SPE must *mimic the results* arrived at above; i.e., they must adjust the q's of a no-trade plan to produce more tractors and less grain, exporting the extra tractors to cover the deficit between the amount of grain produced in the USSR and the amount they want to make available to the domestic economy. Centrally planned economies have a poor mechanism for reacting to these possibilities and getting gains from comparative advantage. Decisions about exports and imports, like decisions about output and allocation of *all* commodities, are made centrally as part of the annual planmaking process. Recalling how that process works in general, the planning for foreign trade would involve a dialogue between Gosplan and the Foreign Trade Ministry in which Gosplan tasks the foreign-trade sector to "produce" a set of imports, and in which the foreign-trade sector will need some "inputs" allocated to it, i.e., goods for export to finance the imports. The material balance for tradeable goods has the same form as any other, and is one among the whole set of material balances. But it might alternatively be called the foreign-trade plan.

MATERIAL BALANCE FOR FOREIGN TRADE

Outputs	*Inputs*
imports	exports

The planners balancing the annual plan each year find the task of fitting foreign trade into it difficult to handle. There is no capacity constraint here analogous to that for the steel industry that would suggest how high a target should be set for total exports and imports. There is no technological fixity to guide the Foreign Trade Ministry in deciding what combination of goods it should request to export (as the steel industry requests the amount of iron ore and other inputs to produce what it is told to produce). It can sell anything somewhere in the world, just as it can buy anything at some price somewhere in the world. What occurs to a considerable extent is what is called "gap filling," setting imports of various commodities at the amount needed to overcome bottlenecks and imbalances that turn up in the domestic balancing process, and allocating for export such goods as turn up in surplus. Many studies have shown that the CPEs have a kind of "trade aversion"; that is, the volume of foreign trade carried on by these countries has generally been less than would seem warranted by their size. Until recently they did not build production capacity oriented primarily to export.

There has been considerable variation within this general picture over time and among countries. In the earlier years of the USSR trade was extensive, largely of the bottleneck-breaking variety. Imports were sought in those areas where domestic production capacity seemed inadequate to supply demand—in those years this was primarily investment goods. In the late thirties, however, the USSR moved sharply toward autarky. During the Second World War, it received huge amounts of goods from abroad under lend-lease. But the wartime experience was temporary, and there was a deliberate return to autarky after the Second World War.

It is interesting to note how the composition of the Soviets' trade reflects the peculiarities of their economy. The Soviet comparative advantage is largely in commodities that exploit the natural wealth of the USSR— fuels, minerals, and timber—at relatively low levels of technology. Although Soviet apologists have wanted to portray the USSR as a modern industrial country, the USSR has a comparative *dis*advantage in anything with any degree of sophistication, and the Soviet mistreatment of agriculture described in the previous section has made it a sector with a comparative disadvantage.

It should also be added that after the liberation of economic analysis that followed Stalin's death (to be discussed more below), the planners in CPEs turned to more sophisticated approaches and gave growing attention to comparative advantage in deciding what to export and what to import, using various kinds of effectiveness calculations. It is possible for the foreign-trade planners to follow the approach of the gains-from-trade table shown above, arraying all the goods in their purview according to the ratio of a good's ruble price to its world market price. Those with high ruble prices relative to their dollar price would be good candidates for import, those with low ruble/dollar ratios good candidates for export. Various optimizing models based on this idea have been developed, especially in Eastern Europe. But as long as foreign-trade decisions had to be channeled through the balancing process at the center, they were likely to be dominated by considerations other than comparative advantage, and trade volumes were likely to be too small.

A single planned economy facing the world capitalist market typically faces two kinds of problems. It is likely to have a "balance-of-payments" problem, which is the equivalent in the foreign-trade sector of the macrobalance problem with households and agriculture. If the total allocations laid out in the plan exceed what can be produced, then the excess demand will spill over into foreign trade, just as it does into the interaction with households. That balance-of-payments problem may be met by borrowing from foreigners, but more typically it is handled by administrative controls on the micro level—import freezes, denial of permission to import promised goods, and so on. Second, an administered economy may have a "terms-of-trade" problem. That is, it may find that world-market prices move against it, making its imports more costly and its exports less valuable in earning foreign exchange. Fear of this possibility is one reason socialist economies traditionally sought autarky and isolation from the world market.

But this isolated planned economy should encounter no problem in engaging in whatever amount and direction of trade it wants. Whatever it wants to import it can find somewhere; whatever it wants to export can be sold at some price somewhere in the world market. Note also that this one socialist country can balance its trade "multilaterally." If the USSR cannot find enough exports to sell to Germany to pay for the things it wants to import from Germany, it can perhaps sell more in England than it imports from England, selling the extra pounds in world currency markets to get the marks needed to settle the deficit with Germany.

Trade among Socialist Countries

After the Second World War when a number of countries in Eastern Europe shifted to the Soviet-type economic system, Stalin had the idea that there should be a "socialist world market," distinct from the capitalist world market, in which the socialist countries would conduct their trade with one another. In the late forties and the fifties he forced them to shift most of their trade away from western partners toward the USSR. How does the situation change when several centrally planned economies are trading with each other?

Each country develops its foreign-trade plan along the lines described above, trying to import goods that it finds in deficit, and planning to pay for them with exports of goods it can squeeze out in the balancing process. The task of *fulfilling* all these foreign-trade plans simultaneously may present a problem. The export plans of all the countries taken together constitute a supply of goods for trade, the aggregated import plans constitute the demand for these goods. Demand and supply for the whole group taken together are equal in the aggregate. In the foreign-trade plan of each country the value of its exports equals the value of its imports, and this equality will hold when the trade plans are added together. Demand and supply *will not, however, necessarily match for each category of goods*. There is no reason the total number of tractors (or the amount of any other commodity) being offered for export by socialist countries will match the number that other socialist countries desire to import. In such a case it will obviously not be possible for each country to fulfill its foreign-trade plan. It is not acceptable for the minister of foreign trade of Commuslavia to go back to his Gosplan, reporting that tractors are not available, so they should forget about importing them. The reason tractors are in his country's import plan is that they are not available in an adequate number in the domestic economy either. And vice versa for exports. So what kind of behavior is likely to emerge?

The difficulty is the absence of an equilibrating mechanism. In particular, the socialist countries never developed a price mechanism that would assist in equilibrating supply and demand in these markets by raising prices for scarce goods and reducing them on those that are available in excess. Since they have never been able to agree on a way of arriving at special socialist prices for foreign trade, in practice they use the prices on the capitalist world market during some defined period in valuing and settling foreign trade with each other.

In the absence of a price-equilibrating mechanism, over time each country's trade negotiators seek bilateral balancing. No country's trade negotiators are willing to sell to another socialist country more of the goods they have available to offer than they can match in value with goods they have been instructed to import. The Soviet representatives selling to Czechoslovakia must make sure that they get in exchange an equal value of goods needed to fulfill their own import plan. Otherwise they may end up with the socialist equivalent of wooden nickels. If they sell more goods to the Czechs than they buy from them, taking Czech korunas to make up the difference, there is a danger that they would not be able to find another country willing to take those korunas in exchange for the goods the Soviet negotiators have been told to buy. It is a standard proposition in the theory of trade that a regime of bilateral balancing results in less-than-optimal trade, and a failure to obtain the full potential of gains from trade. To the extent bilateral balancing does not solve the problem, an alternative consequence is the phenomenon of hard goods and soft goods. If everybody's import plan is to be fulfilled with respect to goods in which bloc supply is less than bloc demand, the trade representatives of some country will have to resort to the world market, selling on that market (probably at a disadvantage) those goods they did not get rid of in the socialist market.

A significant change in the foreign-trade system of the socialist world came in the seventies. The planners began to develop optimizing models to help them decide what they ought to export and import—ways of calculating comparative advantage centrally. The foreign-trade officials could then have an independent input into the making of the foreign-trade plan. A still more important change was that the CPEs began to turn more to the capitalist world market, reducing the share of their trade conducted within the bloc. The situation changed toward one in which seven countries each dealt with the world market, rather than seven countries having to conduct all their trade with each other in a socialist world market. These countries also tried to use international economic relations in a broader way to stimulate economic development. They undertook extensive technology imports, financed in part by large amounts of borrowing. The rationale was that the technology imports would permit expansion and modernization of domestic industries which would then supply enough exports, saleable on the world market, to service and repay the debt. This was a perfectly reasonable strategy, but in practice the clumsiness of the administrative-command system in innovation and investment meant that even with the advantage of imported equipment the expected modernization and expansion did not occur. Weak or shortsighted leaderships let much of the net inflow of resources go into consumption, corruption, and waste, rather than investment. So in the end they were left with little positive impact and a large debt that had to be serviced.

Backing off from these details, the overall assessment regarding international economic relations is that the administered economies' ability to administer trade to reap the gains from trade has always been limited—

poor trade performance is inherent in the system. They did too little trade, and what there was, whether with socialist countries or with capitalist countries, was not well justified in terms of comparative advantage. Inconvertible currencies prevented an inflow of foreign investment. They have had recurrent balance-of-payments problems. Artificial exchange rates have stood in the way of letting decisions on foreign trade be decentralized. This mechanism also meant that they were unable to let the discipline of world market prices exert a competitive stimulus to domestic producers.

Despite the system-defining dominance of the administrative-command principle in the centrally planned economy, some elements of resource allocation are perforce relinquished in part to market mechanisms. Some domains of decisionmaking, notably allocation of consumer goods and stimulation of effort from households, involve so much detail that they are beyond the ability of the administrative approach to deal with. The foreign firms with whom the SPE must trade are outside its administrative control, and if it wants the advantages of trade it must deal with them through the market.

Unfortunately, the masters of the CPE have generally been intellectually and constitutionally unable to fully understand the logic or accept the discipline of the market and the prices that are its instrument. They have been unwilling to "let markets be markets," even in these areas. In dealing with households, where the SPE is a pricemaker, it has set prices badly, and has frequent resort to administrative interference to supplement the instrument of price. In the Soviet Union during the forties and halfway through the fifties, price incentives in the labor market were often overridden by administratively tying people to particular jobs. There are chronic cases of underpricing of consumer goods that forces resort to rationing (housing always, consumer durables often, and in the inflation-prone half-reformed economy many basic consumer goods). In the case of foreign trade, the SPE has no control over prices, and the task is to absorb and react to market information presented by the outside world. Our conclusion is that it does not do so very well. This illustrates one of the ideas from administrative lore mentioned in chapter 2. Like other organizations that insulate themselves from these external worlds, the Soviet-type economy has suffered severely from this insensitivity.

Agriculture is a kind of hybrid case. The SPE does seek to apply the administrative approach in agriculture, giving detailed orders to the enterprises and actors in this sector. But its success in controlling behavior and eliciting effort by the administrative paradigm in agriculture is far weaker than in other kinds of activities. The supplementary force of correct price signals is therefore crucially important. Indeed, this is an example of a sector that could be separated out of the administered system and ruled wholly by price. But despite some variation in policy in this respect at different times and in different countries, the bosses of the centrally planned economies have usually gone for increasing administrative interference rather than rationalizing prices.

5.
Financial and Macrophenomena in the Administered Economy

In this chapter we turn to value, cost, accounting, and finance in the kind of system we have been describing. We will first consider these topics as they might function in a "perfectly administered system," i.e., when the system functions in a way to achieve optimal allocation of resources. Then, given the practical impossibility of attaining perfect administration, we will consider these topics under a more realistic interpretation.

Allocation, Efficiency, and Value under Perfect Administration

The general idea of making a perfect plan and thus creating the basis for perfect administration was introduced in chapter 2. This idea is that the planners would have to collect and process enough information on goals, constraints, and technology to enable them to reproduce the results of the perfectly competitive market. The process would in some way mimic the actions of market players that lead to optimal allocation and to a set of prices that accurately reflect value—i.e., the worth and cost of any item to society. This process would have to address such questions as whether any given ton of steel had been produced with the least-cost combination of inputs, and, if it were being used to make freight car bodies, say, whether substitution of some other material would save cost and free the steel to be used for a more valuable purpose. For example, it might be possible to use wood in the freight cars, freeing the steel for making a machine that would represent a bigger contribution to maximizing the economy's output. There would have to be some analog of the process in which potential users of each product make offers based on calculations of how valuable the product is to them, in interaction with potential producers who are calculating at what price they can afford to sell. Trying to imagine the workers in Gosplan scurrying about doing all the things that the real economic actors do in a market economy to bring this process to a conclusion makes us realize how improbable perfection in planning is.

But there is one conceptualization of such a process that has tempted planners to think it might be possible, namely, the idea of linear programming. Linear programming is a model of economic interrelationships that the planners could use to direct a computer that would substitute the scurrying of electrons in a microchip for the scurrying of planners, generating quantities and values that would constitute a perfect plan replicating the outcome of perfect competition. A detour here to explain the basic ideas of linear programming will be useful to make concrete the idea of optimality and to show how values are related to the quantities of a perfect plan. Moreover, linear programming also holds a special interest in the history of economic reform of socialism, since its invention by the Soviet mathematician L. V. Kantorovich provided the foundation for a revolution in economic doctrine in the socialist world. Linear programming was at one time thought of as having real potential for enabling the planners to make a perfect plan, but that dream never materialized. In the end its greatest significance was to make it possible for the socialist economists to understand the problem of value and prices, and to understand the concept of running an economy through the decentralized mechanism of the market.

Kantorovich originally worked out the ideas of linear programming in 1939 when asked by the Leningrad Plywood Trust for help in solving a problem in production planning. The trust's responsibility under the plan was to process a given assortment of different kinds of logs on its various machines (these machines peel the logs into thin layers to be laminated into plywood). The plant manager's task was to "fulfill and overfulfill" the plan, i.e., to maximize the throughput of logs in this assortment. Without describing the problem in detail, its essence was that different machines had different productivities depending on the kind of log they worked on. Perhaps the easiest way to understand the point at issue is to

94   *The Socialist Economies in Transition*

think that each machine had a "comparative advantage" in working on particular kinds of logs, and a comparative disadvantage in working on others. The problem was thus to choose how to assign the processing of particular kinds of logs to the machines that could most advantageously handle that kind, and thus maximize output. This would be a simple problem if there were only two kinds of machines and two different types of logs, but the Plywood Trust had five kinds of logs, to be processed on eight different types of machines. One can see why they might go to a mathematician for assistance. The problem, in the form in which it was given to Kantorovich, is more complex than needed to explain the essential ideas of linear programming, and a simpler case will be used here to develop the main ideas. This example is developed in the framework of a firm in the market economy, but we will later extend it to the economy as a whole.

Linear Programming Fundamentals

Imagine a small electronics firm that can produce compact disc players (the output of which we will designate as X_1), TV sets (the output of which we will designate as X_2), or hi-fi amplifiers (the output of which we will designate as X_3). There are prices for each product given by the market, and market-given prices for the components and labor which the firm must purchase to produce them. These inputs are available in any desired quantities. The difference between cost and price constitutes a net revenue, or profit, which can be earned on each product, which we will call P_1 for CD players, P_2 for TV sets, and P_3 for hi-fi amplifiers. This profit is a return to or compensation for what the firm is contributing, i.e., the production facilities in which the purchased inputs are assembled into finished products. The total profit will be the number of units of each product times the profit earned per unit, for all the products together.

Assume that those production facilities consist of two different shops, one in which the units are assembled, the other in which they are aligned and tested. We might express the capacity of each shop in terms of workstation minutes, a total amount of time available at a number of different work stations where the necessary tasks can be performed. We will call these capacities C_1 (the total number of work-station minutes available in the first shop) and C_2 (the work-station minutes available in the second shop).

The firm can hire all the labor and buy all the components it wants, but the number of each of the finished products it can turn out is limited by the capacities of those two shops. Each time it makes a TV set it takes some fixed amount of time in the assembly shop, and some time in the testing shop. These drains can be indicated by a set of coefficients of the type a_{13}, this particular one indicating the number of work-station minutes in the first shop required for the production of one unit of the third output (hi-fi amplifiers). The total work-station minutes available in the first shop committed to the production of hi-fi amplifiers will be the product of the work-station minutes required per amplifier times the number of amplifiers it is decided to produce (i.e., $a_{13}X_3$). Clearly the total number of work-station minutes required for TV sets, CD players, and amplifiers in the first shop cannot exceed the total number available, and likewise for the second shop. We can express the problem as one of choosing a production program (or alternatively as allocating the production capacity of the factory among alternative potential outputs) that will maximize profit. The task is to choose the right values for the choice variables (the X_i or level of output of each product) so that profit is indeed the maximum, and so that the program is feasible, i.e., its drain on the production capacities does not exceed actual capacity, and does not imply that production operate in reverse (it is not possible to create more production capacity by "un-producing" TV tuners). This problem can be expressed symbolically as follows:

$$P_1X_1 + P_2X_2 + P_3X_3 = \text{max}$$

This is the objective function, to maximize profit. It is a linear function of the choice variables, i.e., the levels of output of the various products.

$$a_{11}X_1 + a_{12}X_2 + a_{13}X_3 \leq C_1$$
$$a_{21}X_1 + a_{22}X_2 + a_{23}X_3 \leq C_2$$

These are the constraints imposed by scarce resources.

$$X_1, X_2, X_3 \geq 0$$

These are the nonnegativity constraints on the choice variables.

Once the values for the technical coefficients, the constraints, and the indicators of profit per unit are specified, the job is to find the values of the unknowns—the X_i. These are the choice variables we are trying to settle on to generate the maximum profit. When we find them, they will constitute a plan or "program" of production, and that is why this statement of the allocation problem is called a "programming" model. The solution is found by means of some *algorithm*. For example, we might start by picking some feasible program (one that satisfies the constraints—that does not take more time in the two shops than is available), and then follow a systematic procedure of changing the program in a way that continually increases the profit until it reaches a maximum.

There is a theorem that says that if there is a solution to the problem above, then it will always involve producing only as many outputs (or it is sometimes expressed as carrying on only as many activities) as there are constraints. That is, in the final program the number of X_i with nonzero values will not exceed the number of constraints.

Linear programming problems always come in pairs. Having set up any allocation problem like that above (it is called the primal problem), we can also specify a "dual" to that problem. We create the dual by rearranging the variables of the original problem and adding some new variables, according to a definite pattern. Like the primal, the dual has choice variables, an objective function, nonnegativity conditions, and constraints. The dual to the problem as expressed above is as follows:

Objective function:

$$Y_1 C_1 + Y_2 C_2 = \min$$

Constraints:

$$a_{11}Y_1 + a_{21}Y_2 \geq P_1$$
$$a_{12}Y_1 + a_{22}Y_2 \geq P_2$$
$$a_{13}Y_1 + a_{23}Y_2 \geq P_3$$

Nonnegativity conditions:

$$Y_1, Y_2, Y_3 \geq 0$$

Note that in the dual, the goal is to minimize something rather than to maximize as in the primal, and that the constraints are different in sense, i.e., $\leq$ in the primal but $\geq$ in the dual.

When the primal is an allocation problem as in our present example, the dual can be thought of as an "imputation" problem. That is, its task is to find valuations for the resources constituting the constraints that simultaneously (a) fit within the total value they can create when correctly allocated, and (b) fully impute to the resources the value they jointly create in producing any output that is actually included in the actual program. The solution to the dual, Y_1 and Y_2 in our example, is called "shadow prices." They are a measure of the value these scarce resources can contribute to total value when optimally allocated—Y_1 will be the number of dollars a work-station minute in the first shop is worth, Y_2 the potential of a work-station minute in the second shop for generating profit when it is used to produce the correct output.

If there is a solution to the primal, there is a solution to the dual, and the value of the two objective functions is identical. Remember that the number of different products will not exceed the number of constraints; i.e., in the optimal program one of the three possible products will not be produced. In the dual, that will be the product for which the constraint is satisfied with an inequality: the value of inputs required to produce it would exceed the profit earned. That is why that product is not included in the optimal program as computed in the dual! There is an important computational consequence to duality. If you solve one of the problems, then you know which of the constraints in the other will be satisfied as equalities, and the other problem can be solved as a set of simultaneous equations (a much simpler task than the solution of a linear programming problem itself). If we solve the primal, it is easy to find the shadow prices of the dual.

Thus the linear programming idea corresponds to the general competitive model in choosing how to allocate scarce resources to maximize output. It simultaneously generates prices that impute to scarce resources the value of what they are capable of producing when optimally allocated. Linear programming thus exhibits in microcosm the allocation-valuation duality of the perfectly competitive market model, though in a setting involving linear production functions rather than the more familiar kind in which input substitution is possible. Also as in the competitive model, there is no profit in the final solution—all incomes are imputed to whatever inputs are scarce.[1]

Kantorovich's problem and the description of linear programming above refer to resource allocation within an individual enterprise. But it does not take much imagination to see that one might think of the problem of making a *national* plan in much the same terms. The leaders have an objective function—they want the economy to produce the largest possible amount of consumption goods, defense, investment for growth, R&D, and so on. In the language of the administrative paradigm, these goals are communicated by the leaders to the coordination technicians at Gosplan, and Gosplan's task is to maximize attainment of those goals within the constraints of limited supplies of various kinds of labor, limited capacities for the production of various kinds of output, and so on. Acknowledging how complicated it would be to state this problem in the form of the equations of the linear programming model for the whole economy, we can still accept the idea as a construct of an optimal planning model. The relevance of the shadow prices that would emerge from the dual in this approach merits special mention. These shadow prices indicate the true value of any scarce resource that constitutes a constraint in the problem. Moreover, starting with these values for primary resources, one can figure out the cost of any intermediate or final good produced from them, by adding up the cost of the scarce primary resources that go into producing the down-

---

1. An excellent introduction to linear programming is Dorfman, Samuelson, and Solow, *Linear Programming and Economic Analysis*, which will take a lot of time to study, but which will richly repay the effort. Tjalling Koopmans succeeded in obtaining a copy of Kantorovich's 1939 article sometime in the mid-fifties, and a translation was published in *Management Science*, July 1960. Kantorovich's book was finally published in the USSR in 1959—*Ekonomicheskii raschet nailuchshego ispol'zovaniia resursov*, Moscow, 1959, and is available in English as L. V. Kantorovich, *The Best Use of Economic Resources*, Cambridge: Harvard University Press, 1965. An excellent review of both linear programming and Kantorovich is Roy Gardner, "L. V. Kantorovich: The Price Implications of Optimal Planning," *Journal of Economic Literature* 28 (June 1990), pp. 638–648.

stream goods. There is thus associated with the perfect plan a set of true values, one for each of the resources, products, services, commodities, and so on in the plan—a ton of steel, the time a teacher spends at her job, or the cost to produce a tank. Those values measure the scarcity or worth of all inputs and outputs in terms of their ability to contribute to achievement of the goals of the leaders.

To make things clear for what follows, a couple of additional points are important. Suppose that the objective function for this linear programming problem is to maximize the final output of the economy *other than consumption*, and its constraints are the capacities and supplies of primary resources. As in the example worked through above, some information must come from outside the problem. In that example the prices on purchased inputs and on the various products were given from outside by the market. In the national plan expressed as a linear programming problem, relative priorities for major end uses must be given by the leaders. Also, as explained in chapter 4, relative values for various consumption goods should come from the market interaction with households. And as shown in that chapter, the planners do not face absolute fixed quantities of labor, but rather supply schedules that tell us how the quantity of effort supplied by households will depend on the real wage offered. In foreign trade, there are no constraints on the quantities of goods the SPE can buy or sell abroad, but prices for them are given by the world market.

Thus in the perfect plan there are a variety of prices. For the goods involved in the exchanges of households with the SPE, these prices are the monopoly and monopsony prices. For goods that enter into foreign trade, they are world-market prices (as long as the economy under consideration is a pricetaker). For all internally produced goods, the prices measure the cost of using something and the benefit of producing it, in relation to the goals of the regime. Obviously those values contain valuable information for economic decisionmaking. They enable one to evaluate the desirability of any action that might not have been contemplated in the original plan (producing a new model of a tractor, say) just by looking at the cost to society of the inputs used compared to the benefit to society of what is produced. For any given action being considered, they make it possible to figure out what approach is least costly to society, or for a given expenditure of resources, which among alternative ways of using these resources will provide the biggest benefit. Obviously these prices should be the test for all decisions about resource use made in the economy.

This linear programming model is a concrete example of an approach Gosplan could use to make a perfect plan. If the linear programming approach could indeed be implemented, then, as explained in chapter 2, we could imagine perfect administration based on such a plan, operating via quantity commands. But once we understand the duality of quantities and prices (an insight the socialist planners first gained through Kantorovich's demonstration of linear programming), another possibility dawns on us. If we made the perfect plan using linear programming, the shadow prices implicit in it would make it possible for Gosplan to follow through not by issuing an "addressed" set of targets for *outputs* and their allocation, but by issuing in "broadcast" form the calculated values of all resources and outputs.[2] However the perfect plan might be worked out, implicit in it is a set of price tags for everything that indicates how much that item is worth in relation to the leaders' goals. The accompanying instruction to all actors would be, "Choose how much and what to produce, what and how much to use in producing it according to the rule 'maximize the value of outputs, minimize the cost of inputs.' " These prices would permit perfect administration with decentralized decisionmaking, since it now becomes easy to evaluate whether any enterprise is efficient. If the cost of the resources it uses exceeds the value of what it produces (i.e., if it incurs a loss), it would be doing less well than it could and the manager could be fired as incompetent.

Finance and Money under Perfect Administration

As a basis for understanding the role of finance in the centrally planned economy, think about an accounting system to track activity in it. Like any corporate accounting system, the accounts of USSR, Inc., ought to

---

2. This conclusion is not limited to linear programming. The duality aspect—the notion that implicit in any perfect allocation is a set of perfect prices—would be inherent in *any* system of perfect planning.

show the financial side of all the transactions that take place within the corporation and between it and those it deals with. Figure 5-1 presents a set of accounts that do this. The SPE itself can be thought of as consisting of "headquarters" and operating divisions, i.e., the enterprises. Under *khozraschet* every enterprise has an operating statement, showing its outlays, incomes, and profit or loss. If these are consolidated, we have an operating statement for the enterprise sector as a whole like that shown under IIa in the accounts in figure 5-1. (If this account is compared with the input-output table in chapter 3, it is obvious that the former can be derived by collapsing the multiple sectors of the input-output table into a single row and column.) For headquarters, there is a kind of consolidated income account, showing transfers between headquarters and the enterprise level, interactions with households, and disposition of the income of the corporation. This might alternatively be called the state budget, since the SPE embodies the state as well as the economy. But not all headquarters income goes through the state budget. Some enterprise profits, for example, are spent for investment or for R&D directly by enterprises. Since such uses of enterprise incomes are tightly controlled by headquarters, we should think of the headquarters account as embracing the enterprise profit disposition account as well as the state budget. Since this system operates with money, created by the State Bank, there is also an account for the bank. Adding two more accounts, for relationships with two actors outside the SPE (the foreign-trade sector and households), results in a more or less comprehensive, even if not very detailed, set of social accounts like those shown in figure 5-1.

Note the interconnection of those accounts—each transaction is entered twice, once each in different places. For example, taxes paid by enterprises to the state budget appear both in the state budget and in the consolidated enterprise account. *Sales* of goods by enterprises to other enterprises in the consolidated enterprise account also appear as *purchases* of goods by enterprises from other enterprises. (Since they appear on opposite sides of the same account, we might just let them cancel each other out.)

What is the income of the SPE considered as a corporation? In *real* terms it is deliveries to final demand (remember the input-output accounting framework) other than household consumption. In *financial terms* it can be thought of either as the monetary income collected as state budget

Figure 5-1. The Accounts of an Administered Economy

I. GOVERNMENT BUDGET

Revenues	Expenditures
Turnover tax	Financing the national economy
Taxes on enterprise profits	capital investment
Taxes on households	inventory expansion
	social-cultural measures
	defense
Deficit OR	Surplus

IIa. CONSOLIDATED OPERATING STATEMENTS OF ENTERPRISES

Revenues	Outlays
Sales to other enterprises	Purchases from other enterprises
Sales to investment	Payments to households
Sales to households	Imports
Sales to defense	Turnover tax to budget
Exports	Depreciation charges
	Gross profits

IIb. DISPOSITION OF ENTERPRISE PROFITS

Gross profits	Profit taxes paid to state
	Redistributed to cover losses of other
	enterprises
	Spent for investment
	inventory investment
	fixed investment

III. THE STATE BANK BALANCE SHEET

Assets	Liabilities
capital	cash in circulation
loans	enterprise accounts

IV. HOUSEHOLD INCOMES AND EXPENDITURES

Revenues	Expenditures
Earnings	Consumer-goods purchases
from state	from SPE
from second economy	from second economy
Transfers	Savings
	Taxes paid to state

Figure 5-1. (Continued)

V. THE CURRENT EXTERNAL BALANCE	
Activities generating claims against foreigners	*Activities generating claims by foreigners against the SPE*
Exports of goods and services	Imports of goods and services
Unilateral transfers (either way)	
Borrowing by SPE	Extension of credit to foreign clients

revenues and enterprise-retained profits, or as expenditures from the state budget and from the retained income of the enterprise sector for those final goods.

If we are interested in the income of *society*, rather than of the corporation only, in financial terms we would have to add household incomes as figured in those accounts. In the real product approach we would add the consumption vector of the input-output flow table to investment and defense expenditure. Again, these two measures of society's income will be equal in ruble, zloty, etc., amount.

Important corollaries of the assumption of optimal planning and perfect administration are that (1) the q's are consistent, (2) the plan is feasible and so is fulfilled. In line with the assumption of perfect planning, let us also assume that in evaluating the flows of goods among participants to be entered in these accounts as the perfect plan is perfectly fulfilled, we use the perfect prices associated with the perfect plan, as described earlier. If all flows are priced at true values, then we have another corollary: (3) all the *financial* statements above are in balance.

Now we come to a very important matter. Consider the meaning of price, finance, money, fiscal policy, monetary policy, and macroeconomics in this kind of system. We can interpret prices and finance as features of the internal accounting system of the corporation (except for the prices in household and foreign-trade interactions). What in another society would be market prices become in this system just the internal accounting prices at which goods are transferred between various divisions within the corporation. What in another society would be called the fiscal system or public finance, such as taxes on the incomes of enterprises, is better thought of in this society as a system of collecting and allocating the income of the corporation as between headquarters and the divisions. There *are* financial flows—payments into and from the government budget, enterprises paying others for their purchases, payments to households for their labor, and payments by households for the consumer goods they buy. But all these flows are determined by the administrative system, which sets and controls all the microeconomic *quantities* in the system. Public finance, taxes, profits, prices, etc., are all *passive*, derived from the real instruments that guide activity, i.e., the commands about quantities.

What is usually called taxation is not a separate tool of policy, but only a derivative result of the really operational decisions: quantitative commands and pricing. This price system generates flows that have names similar to the names we use in talking about public finance in other economies—tax on profits, sales tax, and so on. But in fact, there is no fiscal *policy* at all, since it is replaced by internal pricing policy.

Similarly, the shadow prices associated with the optimal plan are used only for accounting; they do not guide decisions. Within the state production establishment, decisionmakers are not influenced by prices. They simply carry out the plans and orders as expressed in q's. Whether or not a firm makes a profit or loss is a secondary matter.

As indicated in the preceding chapter, prices *do* have an impact on the actions of households. Individuals choose occupations, degree of effort on the job and in acquiring new skills, and so on in response to the wage rates or income differentials offered. In spending their incomes to maximize their satisfaction, they are guided by the structure of prices they encounter in the consumer-goods market.

Finally, consider money, which is issued by the State Bank. There is a system of credit creation and money circulation, expressed in the "credit plan" and the "cash plan." The total supply of money consists of the amounts in enterprise accounts plus cash shown as a liability of the bank on its balance sheet. Enterprises pay each other for goods by in effect writing checks on their accounts. The debits to the accounts of payers are just offset by credits to the recipients' accounts so that total enterprise accounts remain unchanged. Enterprises also withdraw cash from the bank to pay households for labor services, and the state pays out cash to households in the form of bureaucrats' salaries, pensions, etc. But households then pay this money back to the state as taxes, or to enterprises in payment for consumer goods. This cash goes back to the bank, and since the income and expenditure sides of the household account are in balance, there is no net expansion or reduction of the cash portion of the money supply. In conditions of growth the bank would extend credit to enterprises, increasing enterprise accounts, but cash in the hands of households would not increase. Households would ultimately find that they had less money than they would like to hold in relation to their incomes and expenditures. So the state could let that amount increase, i.e., it could buy *some* effort from households for money alone without giving anything real in return. That "seigniorage" is one of the incomes of the corporation. In real terms this income might be realized in the form of more investment than it would otherwise be possible to make; in money terms it is an extra item on the income side of total financial balance (in the form of new cash in circulation) to pay for that extra investment.

A bit more explanation is needed about the prices used in transactions with households. On the assumption that the leaders of the corporation want to maximize its income, they want to turn the terms of trade against households, to get as much effort from them as possible for a given flow of consumer goods offered.[3] Taxing households by manipulating the wage rates and prices is *indirect taxation*, and in our earlier explanation of the conditions for balancing we did not allow for any direct taxes at all. The administered economies have always depended primarily on this method of indirect taxation. Is this satisfactory, or might it also make sense to levy direct taxes, such as an income tax, on households, as allowed for in our model set of accounts? Taxation through pricing means identical prices to all consumers, and this ignores one possible source of maximizing the net flow of effort extracted from households. Just as a discriminating monopolist can get extra profit by differentiating prices among segments of the market having different elasticities of demand, a discriminating tax agency can get more income by varying taxes in accordance with "ability to pay." Direct taxes on households would permit targeting groups and extraction of some consumer surplus. Moreover, in the model as so far

---

3. How far the SPE can go in exploiting households was discussed with respect to peasant households in chapter 3. We could discuss optimal exploitation of urban households in somewhat similar terms. The interpretation of households' offer curve for exchanging their labor for real income is a bit more complicated, and let us leave it that households *do* have an offer curve for labor under which smaller real returns to their labor will affect how much they are willing to supply.

described, income distribution among households will be in proportion to labor productivity. If the managers of the SPE are interested not just in the income of the corporation, but in addition have ideas about how they would like income distribution to differ from this efficiency-generated distribution, the way to achieve that is to use public finance in its role as a redistributor of income. They can use transfer payments to add to the income of poorly paid groups, or use taxes differentiated by social groups, etc., to alter the income distribution. In the classic administered economy, however, these considerations and the use of fiscal instruments of this kind are generally downplayed or ignored.

The conclusion to be highlighted here is that in this perfect administration system—in which there is optimal planning and commands are specified in terms of quantities—most prices, public finance, fiscal policy, and issues of macroeconomic equilibrium play no guiding role, and are of no operational importance. With the two exceptions noted above, there is no need for public finance or monetary policy as instruments of policy in either a micro- or a macroeconomic role. Within the SPE everything is administered through the instrument of q's, and households are guided by prices. All the financial magnitudes represented by pxq aggregates— total sales to households, total profits earned by enterprises, etc.—are derivative or passive, and flow from the really important centrally set decisions about p's and q's.

This description of the "perfect administration" model is intended as an ideal normative model. The real-world administered economy as it developed in the USSR, Eastern Europe, and elsewhere has departed from it significantly. We turn in the next section to seeing how reality differs from the model, and to explaining what the implications of these departures are for finance, including public finance, the problem of macro-equilibrium, and the money supply.

Behavior of the Actual System: Microeconomics

In the real world, the plan is not a perfect plan, and the administrative system does not achieve optimality. The plan as promulgated is not even fully balanced, let alone optimal.

The plan may specify too much steel, too small an output of plastics, crawler tractors instead of wheeled tractors that would be more productive in some uses, large trucks instead of small trucks, goods being produced in wrong locations and using the wrong technologies and wrong input mix. Moreover, the q's do not necessarily meet the test of being balanced in the micro sense that demand equals supply for each commodity. This imbalance may exist for any kind of goods—primary resources such as labor, intermediate goods such as steel, and final goods such as clothing. Even the best plan that Gosplan can develop will not be fulfilled because of the imbalances inherent in it, and because the administrative system gives imperfect control over behavior of the lower-level actors. It is weak in motivating such aspects of effective functioning as cost consciousness, innovation, quality improvement, and intensive utilization of capacities. It is universally acknowledged today that the centrally planned economies of the USSR and the rest of the socialist world have typically performed poorly in these respects—the leaders themselves are openly eloquent on this point.

The explanation for this failure is that the administrative approach to trying to run a modern economy is inadequate to the task. There is too much information to handle, and in very large organizations the basic paradigm of motivating by setting goals, offering incentives for performance, breaks down. One of the paradoxes of the system is that the bottom levels have escaped effective control by the center, and are unresponsive to orders, guidance, and rewards from above. The administrative system generates strong noncooperative behavior on the part of the bureaucrats in the managerial hierarchy. This seems a little paradoxical. Since the top levels have power to offer rewards for good performance and to punish bad behavior, why does this incentive system not lead to better response on the part of bureaucrats? To understand the answer we have to think a bit about this as a kind of negotiating game between enterprise managers and their superiors, a game of the type known as the nonzero-sum game, containing elements of conflict and cooperation. The bonus formula is a way of sharing with managers some of the gains to society from effective stewardship. It offers management a share of the winnings, so to speak, but management may not rise to the bait because of the famous "ratchet effect," the practice the Russians call "planning from the achieved level."

Management is likely to find that its superiors' response to good performance is to harden the plan or to change the terms of the bonus formula against it next year in an arbitrary way. The superiors (i.e., the ministry officials) are under pressure to show good performance in their bailiwick as a whole. Never sure just how hard they can push an individual enterprise, they take overfulfillment of the plan as a sign that they can push this one a little harder. With this kind of insecurity in payoffs, managers are reluctant to reveal the true capabilities of the enterprises they control. Strategies in games of conflict and cooperation often involve bluffing, concealing information, probes designed to make the other side reveal its terms, and trying to mislead the other player as to what one's terms are. Management may be able to make its pleas for an easier plan credible by showing mediocre rather than outstanding performance.

We might think of the manager's ability to influence the plan as a defect in the price system. The price system in the sense of a reward structure is not "parametric"; that is, it is not beyond the control of the individual enterprise. In the perfectly competitive market model the price system is parametric. An individual firm has to accept the price determined by the market. It cannot force the price up by withholding output, nor will it force prices down by increasing output, since its contribution to the total supply is too small to have those effects. When competition is absent, however, a monopolist can force up the price by restricting output. The consequence is monopoly profit through an artificial scarcity and a distortion in the allocation of resources. If socialist enterprise management can influence how difficult a plan it is assigned, it has power analogous to that of a monopolist and can cause analogous economic distortions.

One possible cure might be for the bosses to create a "parametric environment," in which the planners announce the rules, the prices, the incentive formulas, and the tax rules unequivocally and respond to special pleading with the message that if you fail, we will let you fail. Each enterprise must sink or swim. The inefficient will be allowed to go bankrupt. At the same time the officials at the top would commit themselves not to change the rules to penalize an enterprise that earned large bonuses under the system. But the bosses of the system are reluctant to bind themselves in this way. It is one of the conceits of the bureaucrats of the central planning apparatus that they are responsible for seeing that no socialist enterprise fails and throws workers out of their jobs. Another is that they must stand guard over the nation's income, making sure that none of it leaks away into anyone's pockets—even to someone who does an unexpectedly good job of cutting costs, increasing output, or raising quality. At the lower levels the bureaucrats engage in all kinds of bargaining behavior in an effort to obtain plans that will be easy to fulfill because they provide easy targets and ample resources. They have a powerful motivation to understate their actual capacity, to hoard resources, and to ask for exceptions from general rules on the basis of what they plead as specially disadvantageous conditions.

The point is that the Soviet-type economies do not have perfect plans, and hence do not have perfect administration. In this situation there is a possibility for enterprise-level managers to make their own decisions, and in doing so, they are influenced by the price system embodied in the bottom line of the payoff formulas, which, as will be remembered, include the prices of outputs and inputs. In the absence of a perfect plan, the actual prices are not the true values that would be associated with a perfect plan, opening a wide gap between what seems profitable to the local decision-maker and what would be good for society, as either headquarters or the population sees it. As a result, microeconomic allocational efficiency, i.e., proper decisions about the use of resources at the microeconomic level, is hopelessly beyond the ability of the central planners to achieve.

Behavior of the Actual System: Macroeconomics

Let us turn now to the *macroeconomic* implications of the failure to achieve perfect administration and optimal allocation.

Plans in the administered economies of the socialist world have tended to be overambitious in a macro sense. The total output planned is not feasible in the light of the primary resource base, sectoral capacities, or behavioral realities of the people in the system. But the planners hope that overambitious targets, even if they cannot be fulfilled, will put pressure on enterprise management to produce more than they would under completely realistic plans. It seems to be an article of faith of the bosses of the SPE that such "taut planning" will keep the lower levels on their toes, and push them to do better than they say they can.

In these conditions of overtaut planning, plans for output and for the many kinds of financial magnitudes in the system must inevitably be underfulfilled. One *sub*aggregative macroimbalance is commonly found in the interaction with households. The value of goods made available for household use does not match the amount of income the households have to spend. The imbalance is a partial expression of the imbalance of the q's already mentioned. The consumer-goods output plan has a low priority in fulfillment, and as the planners reallocate inputs during the fulfillment phase to ensure that higher-priority targets such as defense or investment are met, the quantities of consumer goods produced turn out to be less than indicated in the plan. Also, under pressure to fulfill overambitious targets, enterprises hire more labor and offer higher wages than stipulated in the plan. In this situation the wage level is too high in relation to the level of prices on household goods, leaving households with money they cannot spend.

Another characteristic imbalance arises in investment. The investment process is ineffectively controlled, and costs always exceed estimates. So the funds allocated to pay for investment are inadequate to fund the planned program. Even if the investment plan gets fulfilled in terms of physical amounts, say by diverting inputs from consumption, the higher-than-planned resource inputs mean that the total *financial* expenditure to carry out the investment plan exceeds the amount budgeted for it. The state has to cover these losses of investment organizations somehow, usually by extra expenditure from the state budget. Another area into which excess demand spills over is foreign trade, but we defer discussion of that aspect until later.

Overambitious planning, setting targets above what can be achieved, results in the creation of new money, as can be seen by considering the financial accounts. If an enterprise produces fewer consumer goods than planned but still spends for labor the amount that was set in the plan, its profit is less than intended, and the resource side of the state financial plan is diminished. That shortfall has to be made up if the state is to cover the outlays it has budgeted. The usual way is for the bank to issue money. Similarly, if it was planned for an enterprise to finance inventory accumulation out of its profits, and its profits are less than intended, it will seek bank credit to cover the growth of inventories. The first three accounts in the system laid out above taken together as the "financial plan" (the state budget, the consolidated enterprise account, and the bank) must balance. A budget deficit or a less-than-planned profit figure in the consolidated enterprise account must inevitably result in credit creation by the bank.

Similarly, in the practice of real-world CPEs foreign trade leads to a growth in the domestic money supply. In the perfect plan, with no borrowing and exact fulfillment of the plan and measurement of all flows in terms of true values, the external account is balanced, both in foreign prices and in domestic prices. Hence there is no impact on the domestic money supply. In the real Soviet-type economy, however, the prices of traded goods do *not* adjust to world-market prices, and this leads to a growth in the money supply, as can be seen in the following illustrative example.

Referring back to the comparative-advantage example in chapter 3, imagine that one of the foreign-trade organizations (Traktoroeksport, whose job is to sell Soviet machinery abroad) buys a Soviet tractor for 1,500 R and sells it abroad for $9,000. Further imagine that the State Bank says the exchange rate is .3 R/$. When Traktoroeksport turns in the dollars it earned, it receives 2,700 R. This is more than enough to pay the tractor factory 1,500 R for the tractor, giving Traktoroeksport a profit of 1,200 R, which for purposes of this example we assume gets taxed away by the treasury as a 100 percent tax on profits.

Another foreign-trade organization (misleadingly called *Eksport*khleb, since in the real Soviet Union its business is *importing* grain) imports 2,250 bushels of wheat. It sells this for 2,250 R in the USSR, then goes to the bank to get a check for $9,000 which it needs to remit to Cargill, Inc., from whom it bought the wheat. At the official exchange rate it has to pay 2,700 R for the $9,000 check, and so is left with a loss of 450 R, for which it is reimbursed in the form of a subsidy from the treasury.

Now think what all this means at the end of the day. The bank got $9,000 from Traktoroeksport and paid out that same amount to the grain importer, so that the bank's holdings of foreign exchange have remained unchanged. It has added to the account of the treasury the 1,200 ruble profit of the tractor exporter and taken from it the 450 rubles needed to subsidize the wheat importer. So the budget has an extra income of $750 in the form of "profits from foreign trade." More important, the total liabilities of the Gosbank, as shown in account III in figure 5-1, which, it is important to understand, *constitutes the domestic money supply*, have increased by 750 rubles. Note that this exchange has raised the nominal value of the nation's output by this same 750 rubles. Whether this increase in the money supply is inflationary depends on the "velocity of circulation" of money, i.e., how many times on average a unit of money (in this case each of those 750 rubles) is spent. Normally, each ruble that exists is spent many times during the year. The treasury may spend the 750 rubles to finance construction of a new factory; the factory builder spends the money to pay construction workers, and to buy materials and equipment from other firms. Each of these households or firms will respend this money, and by the end of the year the 750 rubles will result in a total expenditure of many times the original amount. How many times a ruble is spent a year can alternatively be thought of as how long on the average the person or firm through whose hands it passes holds onto it before spending it. Workers in the socialist world usually get paid twice a month. If by the end of the two-week pay period they have spent at an even pace the wages they received at the beginning, the average period they have held their rubles will be seven days. (The rubles that pass through the hands of enterprises may be held for a different length of time.) If *all* rubles experience the same history as they pass through the hands of successive spenders, by the end of the year, each ruble will have been spent $365/7 = \sim 50$ times, and the 750 rubles of extra money will have resulted in $750 \times 50 = 37,500$ rubles of additional demand. Only part of that demand will have been for final goods, but the portion that is will in all likelihood considerably exceed the 750 rubles in total final output the trade generated for the year's output, and so be inflationary.

Given that the exchange rate is arbitrary, it is interesting to work this example through with alternative exchange rates. I leave it to the reader to work through variations on the .3 R/$ rate assumed in the example. The result will be that alternative exchange rates affect the *distribution* of gains and losses among foreign-trade organizations, but there is always a

750 ruble increase in the money supply, as readers can verify for themselves.

The important lesson here is that even if balanced *externally*, the foreign sector can create a macroeffect in the form of a change in the domestic money supply as long as the domestic prices are not equilibrium values. To relate this to the issue of overtaut planning, suppose the foreign-trade plan is underfulfilled. To make it simple, suppose that the foreign-trade ministry is unable to get delivery of one of the tractors it is supposed to export, but does fulfill the plan to import 2,250 bushels of wheat, going into debt externally. The reader can rerun the calculation above, and will find that there is now only one profit or loss to be figured into the "profits from trade," which as we found above is also the amount by which Gosbank's balance sheet has changed at the end of the day, and hence the change in the money supply. But whether this is an increase or a decrease in the money supply depends on the exchange rate.[4]

To reiterate the main point, *disequilibria in the macrobalance with households, or in any of the other relationships in the plan, including the external balance, will lead to a change in the supply of money.* In the usual case, overambitious planning, which can be thought of as similar to excess aggregate demand in a market economy, means that this will be an *increase* in the money supply. The interesting thing is what happens to that new money.

In the unreformed real-world administered economy, money is still relatively restricted in its capacity to command resources. To buy materials it is not enough for an enterprise to have money, it must also have the authorization that is part of the detailed plan assigned to it. This infringe-

---

4. This example could be further developed to show how external disturbances might be transmitted to the internal economy. Suppose that, *ex ante*, exports and imports (q's) evaluated at world-market prices (p's) are balanced in foreign currency, with a corresponding effect on the domestic money supply as just explained. Then imagine that the terms of trade move adversely during the course of the year. If the SPE responds by maintaining the q's, there will be a rise in external indebtedness, but there will be no further impact on the domestic money supply. (The 750 ruble increase in our example came from the difference between the grain equivalents of 1 tractor [the relevant q's] in domestic and external prices.) Alternatively the planners might change the q's to offset the change in terms of trade, to avoid change in external indebtedness. That will change the relevant q's and so alter the amount by which the money supply increases.

ment of the "moneyness" of money (its role as *generalized* means of payment) dilutes enterprises' willingness to hold it, and they will do their best to exchange it for current inputs, or for some more interesting asset. The tendency toward an excess money supply means that they have enough liquidity to indulge in whatever hoarding of real goods they can manage, and in fact, these economies do tend to have excessive inventories. Large stocks of some goods are held idle by some enterprises while there is a shortage of those items elsewhere in the economy. (After a while these goods finally lose their usefulness and value as they become obsolete or deteriorate—another of the characteristic wastes of the administered economy.)

Enterprises might be tempted to get rid of this money by exchanging it for foreign goods. But in the traditional administered economy, the possibilities for getting rid of it in this way are slight. Enterprises cannot turn their money into foreign exchange by bidding up the exchange rate, since that rate is arbitrarily fixed, and there is no market in foreign currency. Moreover, the import side of the foreign-trade balance is so tied up by various kinds of centrally imposed microcontrols that it cannot serve as an outlet for excess liquidity.

The input that is least effectively controlled by microinstruments is labor. Whether we think of the labor supply as number of hours supplied or as hours corrected for effort and productivity, the enterprise manager can usually get more hours by hiring more people, or can get more effort by offering higher wage rates. (As explained earlier, the character of the wage system allows some flexibility in this area.) In short, enterprises try to get rid of money however they can, but whether they do so by buying up other assets or paying it to households directly, it sooner or later ends up as wage payments to households. This prompts the question, What are the consequences of that creation of money?

In a growing economy, some new money can be absorbed. Households and firms have a transactions motive for holding money, and as household incomes and expenditures rise they need a larger stock of money. Most people do not face the kind of asset portfolio choice that is common in other kinds of economies, i.e., the decision as to what extent they should hold their wealth in the form of money and to what extent in the form of other assets. There is nothing like the government securities or stocks and bonds that in the market economy are important alternatives to money. Households could put their money into savings accounts, state bonds, or funds to buy cooperative housing. But the governments of the socialist countries traditionally have not issued large numbers of bonds, and there is no *market* in state bonds. Because of the danger of attracting unwelcome attention from the authorities, or the fear of having their savings partly confiscated in a currency reform like that which took place in the USSR in 1947, households may be reluctant to put cash into state savings banks. The consequence of this excess money is repressed inflation.

Because the prices in the SPE consumer-goods markets are controlled by the state, households cannot turn money into goods by bidding up prices for goods passing through those channels. They can, however, bid up prices in whatever *free markets* exist. That has generally meant the collective-farm market, and excess money causes prices to rise there. But that does not get rid of the money—it simply shifts it out of the hands of urban households into the hands of rural households, who then face the same problem of what to do with the money. They cannot necessarily spend it for consumer goods—the reason the urban households are getting rid of it is that they are unable to find goods in the SPE consumer-goods market on which to spend it. (To some extent the urban population may have turned away from undesired goods to buy food instead, and the spurned goods might be acceptable to the rural population.)

This money can be spent in various kinds of illegal black markets, or it can be spent by buying favors and influence—i.e., for corruption. But even those are not *final* uses for money. We should ask why an official would want to receive money as a bribe. Since it is good to him only if he has some way to convert it into goods, we are back to the problem that there is not much available in the regular market. So the usefulness of money for purposes of bribery presupposes the existence of a second economy that produces real goods, or access to some other source of goods, one of which, at least potentially, is the foreign balance. In fact, some of the income from corruption ends up as expenditure on foreign goods by various illegal ways of getting hold of foreign exchange. The Polish case revealed some truly astounding stories of this kind, including the purchase of vacation homes in Switzerland.

In the end it is very difficult to find outlets for money that cannot be spent on state goods and that will make people willing to hold this amount of money. So administered economies have typically had a monetary overhang—more money than people are willing to hold *voluntarily*. The main effect of this excess money and repressed inflation is to discourage the labor supply. If people cannot spend the money they already hold, their incentive to work hard, to expend effort to obtain more money, is badly undermined. This is a true macroeconomic effect. A major macrovariable (the aggregate labor supply) is affected.

The traditional Stalinist system controlled the scope of black market activity and corruption reasonably well through the imposition of draconian sanctions. But as the systems matured, these controls began to break down, and the "second economy," with its associated corruption of officials bribed to permit it, flourished. The growth of the black economy and corruption has highly undesirable effects on the desired income distribution, and leads to loss of political control. One possibility is for the SPE to legalize these black markets and second-economy efforts as private forms of economic activity. Another is to "socialize" them, that is, to take them over as state enterprises. That has happened to some extent, but let us reserve for the following chapter a more detailed treatment of that solution.

Overall, the macrofailures we have described did not completely subvert the command system. The heavy emphasis on control in physical terms and the weakness of money has meant that the big divisions of the GNP into defense, investment, and consumption have been kept consistent with what the leaders want. Overcommitment has been resolved in the end by cutting consumption. The CPEs have not had terrible problems of external imbalance since the foreign-trade mechanism exercises enough microcontrol to prevent excess demand from spilling over into imbalance in the external accounts. Imbalance in the relationship with households has led to a loss of welfare compared to what could be generated by the resources devoted to consumption, and some withdrawal of effort, but the nature of this loss has typically not been understood or has been within tolerable limits. In short, public finance and monetary policy have not been an *independent* source of trouble, or tools that by themselves could be used to solve the microdistortions or macroimbalances. In the classic real-world model the planners have been content to operate without monetary policy. In the end they are not going to let the economy be hamstrung by failure of the money supply to grow in aggregate, or to let individual firms collapse because of financial stringency.

But it should be emphasized that these macroeffects *did* come to be more and more important as the centrally planned economies matured and as the sanctions of Stalinist terror abated. The growing complexity of price setting as consumption levels rise and as consumer-goods variety increases also makes the consequences of this clumsiness ever more substantial.

The failures at the micro level have been more serious. In the real-world embodiment of the administered economy, the combined system of price formation and financial flows is such that prices depart egregiously from scarcity values. The income of the corporation, which I explained earlier includes, properly speaking, all the rents, returns to capital, monopoly-monopsony profits, and so on, is not collected in that form in the transactions where these incomes are generated. Rather, the corporation's income is collected in the form of arbitrary profit markups, turnover taxes, and various other forms. As a corollary, the prices that generate the financial flows that enter into the income of the corporation do not reflect real values, scarcity, or cost. Something produced via a capital-intensive activity is sold at a price that does not reflect the drain its production puts on society's scarce capital. Prices are not the proper indexes of value that they would be in perfect administration, i.e., not an imputation backward from the leaders' goals indicating how valuable a resource any good is in terms of its potential for contributing to those goals. The failure of prices to reflect scarcities applies to primary inputs and intermediate goods as well. Some goods have zero prices, as, for example, environmental goods. Given the nature of the system, this failure to represent real costs may not generate market disequilibria, but it does have consequences. In a number of decision areas, even within the SPE, decisionmakers do respond to these prices for inputs, and they are led to choose some way of doing something that looks cheaper on paper than alternatives but in terms of real resources is more costly. Even if enterprise managers are not sensitive to costs in current decisions, projectmakers, who make longer-term decisions in designing new production capacities, *are*.

Implications for Reform

Because this administered economy is so inefficient in a micro sense, the leaders are now trying to reform it. The reason reform is on the agenda is that the reformers now realize it is not possible to have even tolerably effective, let alone perfect, administration. The task of reform is focused on changing the microcontrol system. Ultimately that means giving the enterprise independence to make its own decisions in interaction with its partners, facing it with a parametric payoff system, and instituting a single success criterion: whether it meets the profit test. That payoff system must include prices, and those prices too should be parametric, either by coming from outside (world-market prices), by being set in some sophisticated way from above, or by growing out of a market interaction in which the conditions of competition are satisfied. It is difficult to believe that *administered* pricing will ever work, because it takes as much information to generate perfect prices as to do perfect planning. (Remember linear programming and duality.)

As decisionmaking is decentralized, microeconomic decisions become ever more sensitive to price, and at the same time control over macro-equilibrium weakens. More sophisticated public finance systems are needed, and fiscal policy and monetary policy become necessary to control these disequilibria. We will return in a later chapter to analyze the problem of macrocontrol in the half-reformed planned economies and their experience in coping with it.

6.
Growth Strategy and Growth Performance in the Socialist World

The institutional system of the classic administered economy that we have described was combined with a distinctive economic growth strategy, the so-called extensive growth model. This strategy is also sometimes called a "mobilization approach" to economic development.

The *system* and the *strategy* were made for each other. The goal of the Soviet leaders (the organizational goal of USSR, Inc.), once the economy recovered as a result of the New Economic Policy (NEP) in the twenties, was rapid growth. The standard expression of the task in the party's sloganeering was "to catch up with and surpass [*dognat' i peregnat'*] the advanced capitalist countries in a historically short period of time." This goal was treated as a sacred cow, not to be questioned. At the time of the adoption of the Second Five-Year Plan, Stalin answered the question that some comrades had raised, whether it was not possible to slow the rate of growth, by saying, "No, the tempo must not be reduced. . . . To slacken the tempo would mean falling behind. Those who fall behind get beaten." We must not let the USSR ever be in that position again.

Soviet Development Strategy

In describing the strategy adopted to further the aim of growth, we should focus on four major elements—a high rate of investment, technological catchup, mobilization of labor, and wasteful drawdown of a rich endowment of natural (or, more broadly, environmental) resources. The diversion of an unusually high share of the GNP into investment was guaranteed by the dominance of physical allocation at the center over monetary or financial power. In market societies, "money is power and distributes power," and as earnings rise with economic growth, households may use their increased incomes to direct resources toward increased production of consumption goods. Since consumption is a competitor with the investment that expands production capacity, this "eating up the increments" may prevent a rapid growth takeoff. In the administered economy, however, money was made more or less powerless, so that the rate of investment was set not by individual savings decisions but by central fiat. A high share for investment in GNP was also guaranteed by the monopolistic relationship of the SPE with households, as explained earlier. In the pre-industrialization years of the USSR, most households were peasant households, and the power of the SPE to extract a surplus from them was limited. But the bargaining power of the SPE with peasants was transformed by collectivization. By forcing peasants into collective farms, the regime was able to bring agriculture more or less under the sway of the administrative control of the center, and as was explained in chapter 4, after collectivization the terms of trade were turned sharply against rural households. Indeed, the exploitation of the peasants in the collective farms was so great that most collective-farm members were left with too little for even bare subsistence, and they were expected to see to their own subsistence by means of the private plots which the regime permitted them.

A second element in the strategy was technological catchup. When the USSR began its growth drive, it was a technologically backward country compared to advanced industrial countries. But as the economic historian Alexander Gerschenkron has pointed out, this might be considered an "advantage of backwardness." The latecomer can achieve rapid technological progress just by copying the technology the advanced countries have already created. It need not worry so much about the correct technological lines to follow, and it is not burdened with the expensive false starts and experimentation in the development of new technology that the pioneer must bear. Moreover, the 1930s were a propitious time for importing technology embodied in equipment. Because of the depression in the capitalist world, capitalist firms were happy to sell equipment, and to provide engineering advice and services in designing new production facilities.

In the early years of industrialization, the Soviet Union followed a relatively open-economy policy, taking advantage of the possibilities for importing equipment and technology. That policy was intended as a temporary expedient, however. The large-scale imports of the First Five-Year Plan period were intended to permit the USSR to build a comprehensive indigenous industrial base so that it could be independent in providing capital equipment for further growth, and in developing its own technology. It followed an "import-substitution" development policy.

The USSR subsequently received a second infusion of foreign technology through lend-lease from the United States and other western countries during the Second World War. Although the most notable part of that machinery was military equipment proper, lend-lease also included a great deal of civilian equipment for transport and for industrial plants. In the energy industries, for example, the western partners provided the technology to produce higher-quality motor fuels, and that technology became the basis for all the upgrading that took place in the petroleum-refining sector for the next couple of decades.

Technological catchup was carried on in a way consistent with the centralized structure of the economic model. Technological progress was treated as a highly centralized function, under the control of the central administrative organs, performed at the ministerial level by research bureaus and design (or "projectmaking") organs rather than at the enterprise level. This centralization of the technology function was a method of compensating for the thin ranks of a managerial-technical elite at the enterprise level with the experience and knowledge required to innovate on their own.

To man the new productive facilities created by a high rate of investment, the regime intensified the utilization of the society's underemployed and relatively unproductive rural population. The collective-farm system acted as a kind of holding tank from which labor-force increments for the growing nonagricultural economy could be drawn as needed. In fact, during the first several decades of Soviet development, the overall size of the rural population did not shrink appreciably. The new, modern, industrial, nonagricultural economy run by the SPE absorbed the *increments* in the work-ing-age population. It was only later, in the 1960s and beyond, that the increments required by the nonagricultural economy grew faster than the population in the working ages, and the rural population and agricultural employment began to shrink.

Finally, the Soviet development effort drew on a rich patrimony of natural resources, in the form of coal, oil and gas, ores, timber, etc., which had been only lightly tapped at the time Soviet industrialization began. This natural-resource richness was incomplete since the USSR had a relatively poor endowment of good agricultural land, and a relative poverty of water resources generally. When the Soviet mobilization model was copied by the countries of Eastern Europe, they were less advantaged in this respect. This was one reason the Soviet strategy, as we will see below, served their needs less well. The Soviet Union helped the East European countries to compensate for that disadvantage by drawing on its own endowment of mineral and energy resources to supply their needs. Soviet exports permitted the countries of Eastern Europe to follow the extensive pattern of using mineral and fuel resources lavishly and even wastefully.

There are many corollaries to these four features of the growth strategy, but supported by the structural features of the economic system, they constitute the backbone of the famous "extensive model" of economic development.

Growth Performance

For a long time this combination of centralized decisionmaking structure and extensive development strategy worked well. The USSR achieved an impressive rate of growth, particularly during its first quarter-century. In the light of what some other underdeveloped countries have accomplished in the years since the Second World War, the Soviet record seems less outstanding today, but at the time it was a distinctive success story in a world of market economies whose performance was characterized by depression and stagnation. Without trying to dig too deeply into the details of the Soviet growth record, we can review some major highlights that distinguish it from the general pattern of world experience.

First, all careful students of the matter reject the official Soviet data on the economic performance of the USSR. The picture presented by official statistics is highly exaggerated and distorted, for a number of reasons, and today even Soviet economists reject the official record. There are similar problems with official economic data for the East European countries, though on the whole the economic statistics of these countries are probably better than those of the USSR. A great deal of effort on the part of western sovietologists has therefore gone into trying to develop an independent picture of Soviet growth. The most careful western reconstruction of the Soviet national income accounts designed to satisfy more meaningful standards of measurement is that carried out by Professor Abram Bergson and his associates and followers. Those studies conclude that the Soviet economy grew at a rate of 6–7 percent per year over the first quarter-century. When we remember that the period we are talking about included the years of the Second World War, and that even in the nonwar years the USSR made a heavy allocation of resources to a military buildup, that rate of GNP growth is impressive.

Subsequently there was serious deceleration of overall Soviet growth. If in the fifties Soviet GNP was still growing at the rate of 6–7 percent per year, then in the sixties it fell to 5 percent per year, in the seventies to 3–4 percent per year, and by the end of the decade GNP grew at only about 2 percent per year. The average for 1981–85 was about 2.5 percent per year. The target originally set by the new Gorbachev regime for 1986–90 was a 4 percent growth rate, but that was a hopelessly overambitious goal, based on exaggerated hopes for rapid improvements from limited reforms. Actual growth during the second half of the eighties did not exceed about 1 percent per year, and by the end of the period a definite recession had begun.

Returning to the first phase of rapid growth (say 1928–55) and considering subaggregates within national income and output, there are some sharp differentials in growth rates for different end uses that are interesting for evaluating performance, for providing an insight into growth strategy, and for conveying an implicit scheme of priorities. Most important, household consumption grew very slowly in relation to investment and defense.

As shown in the following tabulation, it appears that per capita consumption fell in the early years of industrialization (and, not surprisingly, even further during World War II) and did not regain the 1928 level until about 1950.

GROWTH OF HOUSEHOLD CONSUMPTION		POPULATION GROWTH		
	Index		Millions	Index
1928	100	1928	147.0	100
1937	106	1937	165.0	112
1944	74	1944	175.0	119
1950	119	1950	178.5	121
1955	166	1955	194.4	132

One component of consumption, expenditures on health and education, did increase rapidly and indeed grew faster than GNP. Although we call them consumption, health and education services are also investments in human capital, important in raising the production potential of society. It is not surprising that a regime bent on growth would give them a high priority, even as it was neglecting more personal components of consumer welfare such as food, clothing, and shelter.

If consumption grew much more slowly than GNP as a whole, investment grew much faster, at 9.4 percent per year, compared to 6.7 percent per year for GNP. Defense grew even more rapidly—according to Bergson's calculations at 15.4 percent per year during the first quarter-century of growth under the mobilization model. This preferential priority for investment and defense expenditure over consumption has continued into the present, though in somewhat muted form in the most recent years. Whereas the rate of growth of investment had been triple the rate of growth of consumption in the first quarter-century of Soviet industrialization, it was only double it in the seventies and eighties.

These differentials imply very high shares for investment and for defense expenditures in total GNP. In the U.S., the share of investment in GNP has varied around 17–18 percent. In the USSR this share quickly rose to about 30 percent in the First Five-Year Plan, and has stayed high ever since (though it began to slack off in the eighties). There are difficulties in measuring the size of defense expenditure in the USSR that have led to sharp controversies over what share of GNP this end use takes, but the CIA calculates that in the seventies and early eighties, defense expenditures absorbed 12–14 percent of GNP, compared to 7 percent in the U.S. at the peak of the Reagan buildup, the roughly 3 percent characteristic of Western European countries, or Japan's 1 percent in the corresponding decades.

There are some interesting differentials by sector of origin. Industry grew at 6.9 percent per year in this first quarter-century. Also note in the table below the intraindustrial differences that reflect other aspects of the pattern. For example, the much higher rate of growth of civilian machinery over consumption goods is a reflection of the investment/consumption differential in the end-use allocation of GNP. These growth rates, too, show deceleration, and muting of the differentials in the more recent period.

AVERAGE ANNUAL RATES OF GROWTH
OF SOVIET INDUSTRIAL OUTPUT (*percent*)

	1928–40	*1928–58*	*1960–80*
all industrial output	8.3	6.9	5.2
civilian machinery	14.1	11.5	5.6
other producer goods	10.8	7.9	5.0
consumer goods	5.1	4.6	4.2

In contrast to the rapid growth of industry, agriculture grew virtually not at all during the first quarter-century of Soviet industrialization. A distinctive feature of the extensive strategy as it was implemented in the Soviet Union was a special advantage enjoyed in the form of an "output cushion" in agriculture. Russia had been a meat-eating country, and also relied primarily on animal draft power in agriculture. During the collectivization of agriculture, much of that stock of animals, both cattle and horses, was slaughtered as peasants decided to cash these assets in before they were collectivized. This freed large amounts of grain (or land for growing grain) to serve human instead of animal consumption. The conversion of grain to animal products, such as meat and milk, involves large calorie losses—it takes several calories in the form of grain to produce one calorie in the form of meat. As a result of the shift in the output of agriculture from converted products to grain, a caloric cushion was gained that enabled more people to be fed without the total amount of crop output having to be expanded. There was an important downside to this. It meant a decline in the quality of the diet, and some of the greatly increased industrial output that was mentioned above (in the form of tractors) merely replaced horses rather than constituting a net addition to total productive capacity.

The growth of output of the transport sector is easy to measure in physical terms, i.e., ton/km of freight work performed. In Soviet economic history, the amount of transport work performed grew faster than GNP, mainly for three reasons. First, the process of industrialization, with its heavy emphasis on investment and the production of bulky materials such as ores, steel, and energy products, meant that the share of products heavy in relation to their value grew in the total. Second, the process of regional specialization and exchange that accompanies modernization means that a larger share of the output is shipped interregionally rather than being used in the region of its production. In the great expanse of the Soviet Union, such regional interchanges generated huge additional amounts of freight work. Finally, the system and its decisionmakers did little to economize on transport. Transport is one of those sectors producing intermediate inputs that became so hypertrophied in the Soviet economy.[1] Within transport, there was a sharp differential between growth of passenger and of freight transport, an expression of the production-oriented, consumption-neglecting priorities of the system.

Services, generally speaking, grew slowly. Most of them—things such as housing, trade, personal services, public dining, travel, and entertainment—are elements of consumption, and their neglect reflects the low

---

1. As Soviet reformers today look back on and analyze the behavior of the traditional system, they conclude that the incentive system worked to stimulate the expansion of sectors producing intermediate inputs such as steel, coal, electricity, minerals, etc., while neglecting the task of getting more final goods—the consumer and investment goods and the exports—for a given input of intermediate inputs. The intermediate-input-producing sectors developed a kind of bureaucratic clout that enabled them to swallow up investment and other resources to continue output expansion. The argument is that if shifted to the final-good-producing sectors, those investments could have modernized the latter in a way that would permit output increases without requiring any growth of intermediate-product output. This is another illustration of the *zatratnyi mekhanizm* mentioned in chapter 10.

priority of consumption. One of the most neglected sectors in the services
area is housing, as can be seen from the following series on the amount
of housing space (measured in square meters) per capita in Soviet cities:

1923	6.45
1928	5.91
1937	4.17
1940	4.09
1950	4.60
1960	5.75
1970	6.32
1982	8.70
1988	~9.00

As urban populations grew, and the planners tried to sidestep the heavy
costs of investing in this capital-intensive sector, housing space per person
fell. To give some meaning to the 4.09 square meters per person in 1940,
this means 3.9 persons *per room*; the Soviet "sanitary norm" is 9 meters
per person, and in the U.S. in the sixties housing space per capita was a
little less than 20 square meters per person. As the table shows, housing
per person in urban areas in the USSR did not regain the preindustriali-
zation level until about 1960.

Productivity

It is also revealing to compare the growth in output with growth in inputs.
Two sources of growth can be distinguished in the process of economic
development. One is growth in the amount of resources devoted to production—labor, the services of capital, and natural-resource inputs. As
the amount of inputs devoted to production increases, more can be produced. A second source of growth is increases in *productivity*, which can
be thought of as more output per unit of inputs. This growth in productivity
takes many forms, such as more eggs laid each year per chicken, more
steel produced per steel worker and per physical piece of equipment in
steel mills, more passenger miles per passenger seat in the airplane fleet.

One feature of the extensive growth model is that it relies very heavily on the first source, relatively less on the second. This proposition can be illustrated by some calculations of productivity growth in the USSR made by Abram Bergson. The major inputs grew over the period 1928–58 at the average annual rates shown in the upper part of the tabulation below.

AVERAGE ANNUAL GROWTH OF INPUTS AND GNP	
Employment (workers)	2.0
Reproducible fixed capital	7.1
Farm land	1.5
Livestock herds	−0.2
Average	2.4 − 2.9%/yr.
Net national product	4.1%/yr*

*Late-year price weights to match the U.S. case.

Note the differentials here. The capital stock (and hence the flow of capital services) grew much faster than the labor supply, and indeed even faster than output. A growth of capital stock exceeding the growth in labor inputs is a general feature of economic development wherever it occurs, but for the capital stock to grow faster than output is unusual in world economic history.

Another interesting differential is the one between the growth of all inputs taken together and of output, i.e., a measure of productivity change. We can average the growth rates of the different inputs shown in the table by weighting their separate rates in proportion to estimated income shares. This is a far from perfect calculation. Although we cannot go into the details here, it is important to note that this set of inputs is incomplete. Specifically, the table does not contain any indicator for the growth in "human capital." The resources that went into the creation of steel mills and other productive facilities were outpaced by the investment that was made in educating people to design, create, and use them. Creating these human capabilities requires the same diversion of resources from production for current consumption as does investment in physical capital. This is the other side of the heavy emphasis on education noted above. Nor does this list of inputs include the growth in use of exhaustible natural resources.

The resulting rate of growth in general factor productivity for the Soviet economy was somewhere in the range of 1.2–1.7 percent. In the U.S. for a comparable period in our economic history, it was about 1.8 percent. This result is somewhat surprising. Many students of Soviet economic development thought Soviet productivity growth should have been faster, on the basis of the catching-up argument and the ease of technology borrowing, mentioned above as one of the advantages of backwardness.

The more recent period has seen a further slowdown in productivity growth. Calculations made by the Central Intelligence Agency, analogous in approach to those of Bergson, show productivity falling in the sixties to .82 percent/yr, and in the seventies to .70 percent/yr. By the late seventies, productivity growth actually turned negative; i.e., output was kept growing at all only by a more than proportionate growth in expenditure of inputs.

One of the most important reasons for this poor productivity record is poor performance on innovation. As explained in chapter 3, the USSR spends huge amounts of resources on "science," or in our terms R&D. It employs almost as many scientists and engineers in this activity as we do in the U.S. Also, this has been a fast-growing activity—increasing during most of Soviet history at rates exceeding the rate of growth of GNP. But this investment in R&D has not paid off very well, resulting in very little new technology, and little technical progress. The reasons are various, including, as explained more fully in chapter 4, defects in the organization and motivation of R&D organizations, and incentive defects at the level of the production enterprise discouraging the introduction of new ideas, processes, and products.

Conclusions on Soviet Growth

The important features of the Soviet development pattern can be empha-sized in the form of a few simple conclusions. The extensive model was dependent on continued growth of resource inputs. Rapid increases in a major input, capital, were one of the main instruments manipulated by the policymakers to accelerate growth. As expansion continued, it became more and more difficult to keep up the growth of inputs. The reasons include demography—population growth slower than economic growth and a drawdown of the reservoir of relatively underutilized labor in the rural sector—the need to replace obsolete capital, and the depletion of natural resources. Moreover, the system did a poor job of designing the new capital assets in which it was investing to adapt to "capital deepening," the fact that there was more capital per worker as the capital stock grew faster than did labor. To use a simple analogy, as the ratio of capital per worker increases, there is little to be gained from simply giving each worker additional shovels. More rubles' worth of capital per worker must, instead, take the form of modern earthmoving machinery. In machinery production, customized production lines must replace lathes and other kinds of universal machine tools. In the seventies some Soviet economists noted the futility of continuing to turn out millions of such machine tools in a situation in which there was no possible way to recruit people to use them, given the conditions of zero growth of the labor force. When all these decelerating factors had proceeded far enough, the old strategy was bankrupt.

Growth in Eastern Europe

After the Second World War, when China and the countries of Eastern Europe adopted the communist ideology and political system, they also adopted the Soviet development model as a way to industrialize and accelerate growth. Soviet-style central planning and the extensive growth strategy that went with it never did work as well in these cases as it had in the Soviet Union. We will first look at Eastern Europe, and more briefly at the Chinese experience in a subsequent section. There are, of course, other examples as well—Cuba, North Korea, North Vietnam, etc.—but they are less well studied and we will not try to deal with them.

Table 6-1 is an attempt to cover in summary form for Eastern Europe some of the same dimensions of growth performance covered earlier for the USSR. As in the Soviet case, western experts consider official national income statistics for Eastern Europe to be unreliable. The socialist concept of "net material product" (NMP), by omitting services, covers less than all economic activity, and the official series generally exaggerate growth. For some purposes, however, those data are useful, and the table includes data both from official sources—mostly from the statistical handbook published by the CMEA—and from independent western reconstructions of East European growth indicators using the Bergson approach.[2] Although the GDR no longer exists as a separate country, it is still shown in table 6-1 and discussed as one in what follows, reflecting the situation before the revolutionary changes of 1989–90.

First, a few words characterizing these countries in regard to their size and level of development. They form a three-tier system. The GDR and Czechoslovakia, as countries that had already undergone substantial modernization and industrialization before they became communist, rank highest in output per capita. Next come Hungary and Poland as semi-industrialized economies, followed by Bulgaria and Romania, the least developed and most agricultural of the group. The relative ranking by GNP reflects an interplay between physical size and level of development. The largest of these economies is Poland, whose large area and population give it a relatively large GNP despite its intermediate level of development. Next comes East Germany, which, though small in area and population, had a relatively large GNP in absolute terms because of high productivity (high GNP per capita) that went with its relatively advanced state of industrialization and modernity. Next is Czechoslovakia, a country inter-

---

2. A convenient source for a more detailed presentation of the western recalculations on which this table is based is the papers by Thad P. Alton in the series of reviews on East European economic developments published roughly every three years by the Joint Economic Committee of the U.S. Congress. The three most recent are Joint Economic Committee, *Pressures for Reform in the East European Economies*, 2 vols., Washington D.C.: USGPO, 1989; JEC, *East European Economies: Slow Growth in the 1980's*, 3 vols., Washington D.C.: USGPO, 1985; JEC, *East European Economic Assessment*, 2 vol., Washington D.C.: USGPO, 1981. Still more detailed data and explanations can be found in the series Research Project on National Income in East Central Europe, *Occasional Papers*, New York: International Financial Research, Inc., various years. The Russian version of the CMEA statistical yearbook is Sovet ekonomicheskoi vzaimopomoshchi, *Statisticheskii ezhegodnik stranchlenov Soveta ekonomicheskoi vzaimopomoshchi*, Moscow: Finansy i statistika, various years.

Table 6-1. East European Economic Growth Patterns

	GNP Bill $ (a)	MIDYR POP Mill	GNP $/Capita		GNP Growth, Western Estimates 1950-60	1960-75	1975-85	Official Growth 1960-75 NMP	CONS	ACCUM	1975-85 NMP
BULGARIA											
1975	19.0	8.7	2,180	INDEX	199.5	220.9	111.6	215.3	200.1	255.4	159.10
1985	57.8	9.0	6,450	AARG (%)	7.2	5.4	1.1	5.2	4.7	6.5	4.80
				/CAPITA			0.8				4.50
CZECHOSLOVAKIA											
1975	54.1	14.8	3,660	INDEX	160.8	156.9	119.7	201.5	173.3	332.4	120.00
1985	135.6	15.5	8,748	AARG (%)	4.9	3.0	1.8	4.8	3.7	8.3	1.80
				/CAPITA			1.3				1.40
GDR											
1975	61.5	16.8	3,650	INDEX	190.1	159.1	122.6	200.0	190.0	245.1	152.10
1985	174.4	16.6	10,474	AARG (%)	6.6	3.1	2.1	4.7	4.4	6.15	4.30
				/CAPITA			2.2				4.30
HUNGARY											
1975	25.2	10.5	2,390	INDEX	157.1	167.7	116.3	230.5	208.0	305.3	126.00
1985	80.1	10.6	7,521	AARG (%)	4.6	3.5	1.5	5.7	5.0	7.7	2.30
				/CAPITA			1.4				1.85
POLAND											
1975	82.9	34.0	2,440	INDEX	157.5	208.7	107.1	283.9	242.4	415.2	106.30
1985	240.6	37.2	6,467	AARG (%)	4.6	5.0	.7	7.2	6.1	10.0	.60
				/CAPITA			0.0				-.30
ROMANIA											
1975	46.7	21.2	2,200	INDEX	182.0	227.3	132.9	388.6	NA	NA	174.30
1985	123.7	22.7	5,455	AARG (%)	6.2	5.6	2.9	9.5			5.70
				/CAPITA			2.2				5.00
SUBTOTAL											
1975	289.4	106.2	2,726								
1985	812.2	111.6	7,275								
USSR											
1975	865.3	255.5	3,387								
1985	2062.8	277.6	7,432								

| | Sectoral Growth Indexes | | | | Share of Ag + For ~1975 In GNP Employ (percent) | | | Growth Indexes and Rates | | | |
	Ind 1960–75	Agric 1960–75	Ind/Ag 1960–75	Ind/Ag 1975–85	GNP	Employ		Employ CAP Stock (1960–75)		Population 1950–75	Population 1975–85
BULGARIA											
Western	297.1	141.8	2.10	1.70	25.1	28.1	INDEX	149.20	324.4	.740	.270
Official	455.9	161.1	2.83	1.60			AARG (%)	2.70	8.2		
CZECHOSLOVAKIA											
Western	170.3	109.7	1.55	1.10	17.5	15.1	INDEX	125.00	191.1	.714	.394
Official	201.5	140.7	1.43	1.20			AARG (%)	1.50	4.4		
GDR											
Western	249.1	129.5	1.92	1.00	13.5	11.0	INDEX	94.10	171.1	–.400	–.002
Official	170.2	125.5	1.36	1.30			AARG (%)	–.04	3.6		
HUNGARY											
Western	261.5	154.9	1.69	1.10	22.8	21.1	INDEX	108.70	206.2	.485	.100
Official	188.1	129.5	1.45	1.13			AARG (%)	.55	4.9		
POLAND											
Western	268.8	111.4	2.41	0.90	19.1	30.6	INDEX	138.60	195.6	1.268	.890
Official	364.4	150.0	2.43	1.27			AARG (%)	2.20	4.6		
ROMANIA											
Western	419.7	122.1	3.44	0.90	29.4	39.1	INDEX	111.60	329.2	1.065	.670
Official	613.3	169.1	3.63	1.34			AARG (%)	.70	8.3		

mediate on both counts. Romania is a fairly large country in terms of population, area, and natural resources, but got a late start on economic development and industrialization so that its low productivity gives it a low rank in terms of absolute size and output per capita. Hungary is a very small country, which offsets the relative modernity and productivity of its economy to push it down in the overall economic size ranking. Bulgaria is one of the smallest, and combined with relative underdevelopment this puts it at the bottom of the list in terms of total GNP. Not only did these countries embark on the socialist model from varied starting levels, but, as we will see, each has also been affected during its socialist development phase by individual circumstance.

The six countries in the table are individually small compared to the USSR, and even taken together their total GNP is less than half as large as that of the USSR (40 percent according to the estimates of the table). The group as a whole has a GNP per capita approximately the same as the USSR, but given the heterogeneity mentioned above, output per capita in Czechoslovakia and the area of the former GDR is appreciably above that in the USSR, while Romania and Bulgaria lag behind the USSR.

If we compare the first quarter-century of the East European growth experience under the Soviet model with the first quarter-century in the USSR itself (the 1928–55 period for the USSR and 1950–75 for the Eastern European countries), there are a number of interesting similarities and differences. First, the East European growth record is generally less impressive than that of the USSR during its initial phase. In the USSR, GNP grew at about 5.7 percent per year between 1928 and 1955. Romania and Bulgaria roughly matched this rate, but all the other East European countries were well below it. Czechoslovakia and Hungary grew at less than 4 percent per year, and although the GDR and Poland did a bit better, their rates were still below 5 percent per year. These are palpable differences, especially when we recall that the Soviet record included several years of all-out war. The Eastern European countries, despite some disruption through internal uprisings, experienced nothing during these years comparable to the cost and destruction of the Second World War.

These countries also recapitulated the Soviet experience of deceleration over time. Looking at the western estimates by period in the second panel of the table, we find that rates of growth fell sharply in 1960–75 compared to the first decade, and still further by 1975–85.

RATIO OF GNP GROWTH RATES BETWEEN SUCCESSIVE PERIODS

	1960–75/1950–60	*1975–85/1960–75*
Bulgaria	.75	.18
Czechoslovakia	.61	.60
GDR	.47	.67
Hungary	.76	.43
Poland	accelerated	.14
Romania	.90	.52

The first to cross over from growth to actual decline of output and stagnation was Poland, where output fell sharply after the debt debacle in the late 1970s. As table 6-1 shows in its third panel, the same kind of deceleration is evident in the official data on NMP growth.

These countries also exhibited the same consumption-investment-defense differentials we saw for the USSR. The western reconstructions do not provide calculations of GNP by end use of a kind that fit neatly into this table, but we can perhaps use as a substitute the relative rates of growth of consumption and accumulation in the official statistics, which show accumulation (which is fairly close in concept to investment) growing 1.5 to 2 times as fast as consumption. The data on the growth of defense expenditures in Eastern Europe are less complete than for the USSR, but unsystematic as the data are, they show that Eastern Europe did not choose, or was not encouraged by the USSR, to accelerate spending on defense to anything like the degree the USSR had in the comparable period.

As for sectoral differentials and structural change, the most important relationship is that between industry and agriculture. In all cases East European agriculture grew appreciably less rapidly than industry (see the fourth panel), and even less rapidly than GNP. The countries that started out most backward experienced the greatest imbalance in relative growth between these two sectors. The differential almost always appears lower in western recalculations than in the official statistics, which makes sense because the official statistics probably exaggerate industrial growth more than they overstate agricultural growth. This differential growth led to a transformation of the structure of these economies making them more industrialized and urbanized, but those that started out backward remain comparatively backward in terms of the relative importance of agriculture in their output and employment. Romania still has over a third of its labor force engaged in agriculture, and Bulgaria and Poland still have around 30 percent. These differences offer a potential for further transformation, and growth along with it.

Employment growth is an important determinant of the differing performance. Poland and Bulgaria had strong employment growth, and that helps explain good performance. East Germany had the special problem of people leaving, which hurt its growth badly. That is why the wall was built. Growth in employment was a big spur to Polish growth. The differentials in growth of employment are explained in part by differing population growth experiences. Bulgaria accomplished its labor-force growth without much help from population growth. Czechoslovakia obtained its employment growth largely by an increased participation rate, i.e., the share of people in the working ages who are in the labor force. The main variable here is participation by women, which is spurred by such conditions of Soviet-type economies as the push of low wages and a social policy of encouraging employment opportunities for women. Romania already had a high participation rate because it was so heavily agricultural, so if it had not had population growth, it would not have been able to increase employment. The potential for employment growth in East Germany and Hungary was hindered by adverse demographics, with a slow population growth.

The differentials between growth of employment, capital stock, and GNP are similar in character to those we saw for the USSR. The growth of the capital stock exceeds the growth in output, which in turn exceeds the growth in employment, so there has been a declining ratio of output to the capital stock. This is a characteristic feature of the extensive model.

These data seem to support an overall judgment that in general the imitators of the Soviet model in Eastern Europe have not done as well under it as the Soviet Union did. They never had as fast a growth rate, and the period of growth turned into a deceleration phase much sooner. The countries that were most developed to start with (the GDR and Czechoslovakia) had the least success. The most backward (Romania and Bulgaria) have done best.

Several factors are probably important in this difference. The East European allies were supposed to get "fraternal assistance" from the USSR, but probably did not, at least during the early period. In the first decade after the Second World War, capital transfer and technology transfer probably flowed in the reverse direction. The autarkic trade policy which they copied from the Soviet model probably hurt them as small countries more than it had hurt the much larger USSR. This comes through very clearly when we look in more detail at how trade influences the growth of individual countries. As noted above, Czechoslovakia and the GDR had the sharpest slowdowns. During the early period their growth was aided by the fact that they were in a position to expand their production and export of machinery to meet the rising rates of investment in the other less-developed socialist countries. They enjoyed a kind of export-led growth. But as the other countries repeated the Soviet import-substitution strategy, building their own machinery industries to achieve independence, the GDR and Czechoslovakia faced a falling export demand for their output.

A characteristic feature of the Soviet growth model is neglect of extractive and raw-material branches. The planners deliberately neglect agriculture, and always overestimate the potential for reducing material inputs per unit of output. Hence they tend to target output growth rates for primary sectors that are too low in relation to output growth targets for the processing branches that turn these inputs into final products. In execution, shortages of agricultural products, fuel, and minerals emerge. So in general the machinery that was scarce and hence the hard good of the early period (when all these countries were trying to raise the share of investment in GNP) became a soft good, replaced by agricultural and raw materials in later years. Fortune thus turned to favor the less-developed countries that still had capacities to export the new hard goods.

In general all the East European countries were less heavy-handed and less precipitate in their effort to collectivize agriculture. Whether this contributed to growth by avoiding some of the destruction and disincentives that resulted from collectivization in the USSR, or inhibited growth by reducing the diversion of GNP from consumption to investment is not clear.

The Chinese Variant

The experience of Communist China bears a somewhat ambiguous relationship to the Soviet development model. There were profound differences in the conditions for economic development, and long periods of political turmoil meant that the Chinese leaders operated a Soviet-style program only intermittently and inconsistently. Once the Communists gained control of the mainland and had completed a period of reconstruction, they set out very deliberately to follow the Soviet model. The institutions, policies, and mechanisms of their First Five-Year Plan (1953–57) aped the Soviet model very closely and were based on Soviet assistance in the form of loans and technical assistance in building some key industrial facilities. Performance under the First Five-Year Plan was a success in many ways, as evidenced by a rate of GNP growth of around 6 percent per year. But whether emboldened by that success or frustrated by the prospect that even that kind of change would do little to solve the underlying problem of transforming the society from its rural and agricultural condition into a modern urban industrial system in any reasonable period, the Chinese leaders set in motion for the next phase a much more ambitious effort in the form of the Great Leap Forward. The economic rationale of the Great Leap Forward was to better exploit the resource China had in abundance—surplus labor in the countryside—to build up the society's capital stock and to enhance *industrial* growth. The countryside was organizationally strengthened by creation of the communes, and an effort was made to mobilize more rural resources for industrial development, symbolized by the campaign to build backyard steel furnaces. The Soviet leaders did not approve of what they saw as adventurist departures from the Soviet model, and together with other frictions this led to the Sino-Soviet split, a break in relations that included cessation of Soviet aid and the withdrawal of Soviet technicians in 1959 and 1960.

The Great Leap Forward turned out to be a disaster, with a fall in agricultural output that led to famine, and waste of resources in ill-advised projects. The years 1961–65 were a period of adjustment and recovery from that debacle, in which a more traditional Soviet-style strategy was followed, but this was then interrupted by the Great Proletarian Cultural Revolution, which seriously disrupted production and diverted attention from economic policy to ideological goals. The Cultural Revolution was followed by another period of relative stability in politics and consistency in economic policy in 1970–73, but political conflict again disrupted economic efforts during the period of control by the "gang of four" in 1974–76. In 1975 Chou En-lai had outlined a sensible program of economic growth, which was embodied in a ten-year economic plan covering 1976–85. The period started off with political instability following the death of both Mao and Chou in 1976, but by 1977 Deng Hsiao-ping was in control and the political situation remained stable. The ensuing period saw a consistent focus on economic development, but with numerous departures from the Soviet institutional structure and development strategy. This was a period of creeping reform in which the leaders shifted the system significantly away from the Soviet model.

Given the turmoil and setbacks beginning with the Great Leap Forward, overall growth in 1958–75 had averaged somewhere between 3 and 4 percent. But with a consistent economic line after 1976, the Chinese outperformed what the USSR had done in 1928–40, although in conditions where they had departed significantly from the Soviet model. GNP grew rapidly and steadily, at something like 9 percent per year. The process of reform continued during the eighties, as did growth, until at the beginning of the nineties the standard difficulties experienced by half-reformed economies—especially inflation and problems with income distribution—became serious. This period ended, of course, with the political turmoil and reaction associated with the Tienanmen Square demonstrations and repression.

In this history there are enough perturbing forces, distinctive policies, and unusual conditions that we are hardly justified in treating the Chinese experience as another case of the Soviet development model. China faced a situation much less suitable for the Soviet model than had the USSR and Eastern Europe. The pressure of people on the land was much more serious at the outset. Communist China had rapid population growth during its first years (before the government dropped its ideological line that Malthusian concern about population growth was a capitalist canard and adopted a one-family, one-child policy). The Chinese leaders could not ignore the need to feed a growing population, and were forced to seek a better balance between industrial and agricultural growth. They started out with something the USSR did not have—aid from a socialist ally— but when that failed, they adopted a policy regarding international economic relations that was even more autarkic than characteristic of the Stalinist model. This autarkic policy was, however, again sharply reversed in the seventies. Also, very important, the Chinese initiated significant reforms fairly early, especially in agriculture, where the introduction of the family responsibility system substituted family decisionmaking for bureaucratic management, and price incentives were used to guide agricultural producers. The stimulus of this reform was basic to good overall performance in 1975–89. So despite its origin in the Soviet model, the Chinese case was really a different animal. But it does have some special relevance to thinking about reform and the half-reformed economy. First it showed that a diminution of the central command model might indeed elicit a response. China's gain in this respect was mostly in agriculture, and part of the lesson of Chinese reform seems to be that agricultural reform ought to come early. The Chinese experience also shows the seriousness of the macroproblem of a half-reformed economy that has not instituted the institutions of a hard budget constraint. It shows the benefits that come from an open economy, and the role that decentralization, perhaps regional or through special economic zones, can play in using open-economy policies as a spur to growth.

To sum up, we have found quite a few similarities in these patterns— there is a distinctive Soviet growth strategy that depended on the centralization of power to achieve a high rate of investment, and that mobilized labor by increasing participation rates and shifting it en masse into higher-productivity occupations in the industrial sector. But once we get below the general level and look at the growth experience of individual countries in detail, the explanation for the differences becomes very complicated, and we get lost in a morass of particular development situations that have very little to do with the fact that they were socialist planned economies, or that they were following a Soviet-type growth strategy. Examples are the difference in demographic variables, the perturbations caused by trade variables, and the differences in resource base.

A corollary of this is that although all these countries started out with a very close imitation of the Soviet model and strategy (mobilization, autarky, collectivization, structural transformation), they realized fairly early that it did not fit their conditions, and rather in advance of the Soviet leaders concluded that it was necessary to shift to an "intensive" strategy. This implied a need to change the system as well, and several East European countries experimented with reform of the economic system in the sixties.

The failure to sustain growth at the high rates they experienced in the beginning has been a major force in all the centrally planned economies in stimulating reform. Poor performance in growth is what finally pushed them to question the validity of the strategy. And as suggested earlier, since the system and the strategy were created as a unified package, it is not possible to change to an intensive growth strategy without changing the economic system as well. Reform began in the sixties in Eastern Europe, and then spread to the USSR. It appeared in a distinctive form in China in the seventies. Reform has been proceeding for a fairly long time in some countries—Hungary, for example, and even longer in Yugoslavia—but in others serious efforts at reform have been long delayed. We now have a long enough experience with the most common elements in reform measures and their effects to make some generalizations. The length of previous experimentation, the current degree of commitment to a radical shift toward private property and marketization, and the constellation of political forces that will affect the process vary greatly across the countries of the socialist world. But the conclusion drawn in this chapter—that this system and the growth strategy that rested on it lost in the seventies its capacity to expand the material base for national power— means that today economic reform is inescapably inscribed on the agenda. As Gorbachev likes to say to those who are reluctant to face change, there is no other way, there is no place to which the USSR can retreat, *perestroika* must go forward.

7.
The Semi-reformed Economy and Its Characteristic Problems

The Semi-reformed Economy

In response to the inefficiencies described in earlier chapters, and especially in response to the growth deceleration discussed in chapter 6, the leaders of the socialist countries have been trying for years to reform their economic systems. Especially as these societies began to open up to the outside world somewhat in the seventies, they became painfully aware that their systems were sluggish at innovation, had an outmoded production structure, and were far behind those of western countries in meeting the desires of the population for variety and quality. We might distinguish two elements in the reform process. The first is revisionism in theory and economic doctrine, the second is institutional change.

As the managers of the system wrestled with specific problems, they became more sophisticated about issues of value, pricing, and allocation. Novozhilov's invention of the concept of opportunity cost in the form of the *zatraty obratnoi sviazi* is a good example. The biggest of these doctrinal breakthroughs was Kantorovich's invention of linear programming, which, when it was finally accepted in the Khrushchev era, provided a more sophisticated way to think about value and allocation than the Marxian economic doctrine with which the USSR had formerly been saddled. The new insights from linear programming were used in numerous ways—in development of more sophisticated foreign-trade planning procedures, in generating shadow prices that would be better than the arbitrary prices established by administrative fiat, in applications for improving allocation in individual sectors and branches. For example, the electric power industry began to use linear programming to better allocate the fuel supplies available to it among generating stations. This growth in economic sophistication could not really begin until Stalin had died, but it did increase significantly during the Khrushchev period. It was to provide the ideological underpinnings for understanding how an economy might operate in a decentralized way on the basis of prices, but it takes a long time for improved theory to be translated into new policies or institutions. So although this is a fascinating history in itself, we will largely pass over it to concentrate on institutional change.

The simplest version of institutional change is what is sometimes called "institutional tinkering," a process that has gone on for a long time. The administrative-command economy can be administered more or less well. It may be possible to do a more effective job of managing without going outside the basic administrative paradigm. One could change the form of the commands (measuring output in value rather than in physical terms, or measuring it in value added rather than in gross value), redraw the organizational chart to reallocate responsibilities, create more ministries to reduce the span of control, or consolidate small enterprises into larger ones to put an important interaction under one boss. To take the USSR as an example, Khrushchev made a great many such changes—shifting from branch principle to territorial principle when he abolished most ministries and introduced the regional economic councils, changing the prices the SPE paid agriculture, abolishing the machine-tractor stations, changing the R&D planning process, etc.

In the sixties a general wave of reform affected most of the centrally planned economies. The pace of reform has always been limited by what the Soviet big brother would allow. When one country moved much ahead of what the USSR was doing, as the Czechs did in 1968, the Soviets checked the pace of progress. The Czechs, in fact, did not recover from that shock for twenty years. The Hungarians have always been a bit cautious in their experimentation, looking back over their shoulders to see how the USSR was reacting to the changes. Much of what the Hungarians would have liked to do along the way, for example, decentralizing to a point that would permit a new kind of foreign-trade system within the CMEA, was impossible because it was inconsistent with what the other members of CMEA were doing. Yugoslavia, the country which early embarked on the most radical economic experiments in decentralizing decisions and turning control over to the workers, was able to do so only because it left the bloc and escaped effective Soviet control. Nevertheless, there was a great deal of experimentation in the sixties. In Hungary the "new economic mechanism" (NEM) was adopted in 1968. The Poles worked out one fairly comprehensive reform scheme as early as 1956 and another in 1972, though neither was actually adopted. The Czechs did an analysis of their system, and concluded that in place of the bureaucratic economy they would decentralize decisionmaking to give socialism a human face. In the USSR in 1965 a program for decentralization was adopted by the government, the intent of which was to considerably loosen central control. Enterprises were to get much greater freedom to make their own choices about investment and output and input mixes. It was even intended that at a later stage, the traditional central allocation of materials would be replaced by a system of wholesale trade. In the end much of this reform program was blocked by the recalcitrance of the ministries and other central authorities. Despite that setback, reforms have continued in the USSR, with another fairly extensive package being introduced in 1979. But rather than going into all the associated backing and filling, intentions and results, and intercountry differences, we can sum up this period in the words of Gertrude Schroeder, as one in which the Soviet economy (and to a large extent Eastern Europe) trudged along on a "treadmill of reforms" that in fact took it nowhere.

A more advanced form of administrative tinkering could be characterized as administrative *decentralization*, in which decisions are moved down the administrative hierarchy to, or closer to, the enterprise. This usually means that planning targets and success indicators passed down from above are made more aggregative and are reduced in number. For example, targets may be set only for total output in value terms, rather than specifying in detail the assortment. An enterprise may be permitted to retain its own funds for investment to spend as it sees fit without having to apply to the central authority for approval. Such decentralization is usually accompanied by a price reform, in the hope that better prices will channel the greater freedom into directions consistent with planners' goals.

In its fully mature form administrative decentralization relies primarily on general "economic levers." The essence of such a "regulator reform," as it is sometimes called, comes down to something like the following.

The economic authorities abandon to a considerable degree the direct commands or allocations in physical terms characteristic of the traditional administrative approach, and allow enterprises to make the related decisions (about output level and mix, input mix, investment, degree of participation in foreign trade, size of labor force, introduction of new products, and many others) on their own. The center tries to "steer" enterprises using new kinds of policy instruments. These are largely financial levers—tax rates on general income, taxes on enterprise wage bills, subsidies, an exchange rate in place of the former direct orders to export and import, an interest rate, bank credit instead of the traditional government grants to finance investment.

In addition, at this stage of reform, the reformers may allow a considerable increase in private activity through easier creation of cooperatives and joint ventures with foreigners. These new enterprise forms operate outside the framework of state plans and allocations altogether, usually even have the right to set their own prices, have full ownership rights in the assets they accumulate, and so on. Another form of semi-privatization is to lease state-owned facilities to those who work in them, with the leased firm subject only to the conditions of the lease contract rather than to day-to-day administrative direction by the superior organ. In Hungary, groups of workers were permitted to contract for use of the equipment of the state factory in which they worked to produce in off hours products and services they could sell on their own. The reforms generally allow firms to retain and spend on their own initiative some of the foreign currency they earn, and may even go so far as to let individuals own foreign currency. Another feature of this stage is that administrative price fixing is likely to be somewhat relaxed. Typically the reformers let some prices go free of all control, set ranges or ceilings on other prices, and retain traditional administered pricing for only a fraction of the items traded in the economy. Another thing that may happen at this stage is removal of some administrative interference from what markets already exist.

As all this was going on in the late sixties and seventies, a great deal of attention was invested by western observers in analyzing these reforms, assessing what difference they might make, and applauding the improved understanding they seemed to reflect. But in retrospect, it is clear that we overestimated their importance. By and large they left the administrative principle untouched. The ministerial bureaucracy was still in place, and still tried to direct the behavior of individual enterprises, though it was using new instruments to do so. There is a long and fascinating history here dealing with what the reformers thought they were doing, how their intent was frustrated by the entrenched bureaucratic structures, how the new measures often turned out to be ineffective because they were incoherent. But by now it *is* history, and the point of this chapter is not to recapitulate the vagaries of that odyssey but to look at the terminal stage of those efforts, the stage from which radical reform began at the end of the eighties. The premise of this chapter is that as these economies sought reform, they all tended to introduce similar kinds of measures, despite the variety of national circumstances. They converged ultimately into something we can think of as a kind of generic "semi-reformed economy," by which I mean the kind of administratively decentralized, regulator-controlled system with some elements of privatization and marketization described above. This semi-reformed economy differs in detail from country to country, and different countries arrived at this point at different times. In particular, the Soviet Union lagged behind Eastern Europe, but today it has joined the forward march to reform. At the end of 1990 it seemed finally to be committing itself to the kind of radical reform measures Poland and Hungary had already embarked on at the end of the eighties.

Just as all the reforming economies have some common features in the reform measures adopted, the generic semi-reformed economy has some standard problems. For large areas of decisionmaking the reforms may amount essentially to "administrative decentralization" rather than marketization, and so may not much ameliorate the defects of interference from above and self-protective behavior on the part of the controlled firm described earlier for the administered economy. The semi-reformed model retains a fairly high degree of central control over enterprise activity in "addressed" terms, i.e., in a specific interaction between the central authorities and individual enterprises or sectoral groupings. The addressed commands may concern different matters and be less detailed than previously, but the practice of sending signals from above tailored to the individual plant or sector remains pervasive in the semi-reformed model.

The system of guidance by means of economic regulators is in many ways incoherent, and may induce enterprises to act in perverse ways and contrary to the authorities' aims. This problem will be analyzed more fully below. The reforms thus fail to achieve the improvements in performance that the reformers expect. Also, the first stage of reform generally fails to deal with the problem of ownership and property rights. To the authorities socialism *is* state ownership of property, and they overlook the need for properly motivated "stewards" of social property—agents with a direct stake in the efficient use of society's wealth, enough control to effect it, and an equity stake that gives them property rights in capital gains. Too little is done to overcome the lack of financial discipline, or, as it is often described, a "hard budget constraint," a concept to be explained further below. In particular, the semi-reformed economy inherits a banking system that has not in the past played the role of regulating the money supply, and that does not know how to play that role. As an administered economy begins to decentralize in a situation in which macroeconomics is not understood, and in which too little attention is given to creating fiscal and monetary institutions and policies appropriate to a more decentralized system, it begins to experience serious problems of macroimbalance. The result is inflationary pressure and, if direct price control is abandoned, open inflation. This macroimbalance is also likely to spill over to the external account, exacerbating balance-of-payment problems. The new economic regulators give enterprise managers more latitude in determining wage payments, and to the extent market pricing is allowed, enterprise incomes begin to be determined by market forces rather than by government policy. The result may be an income distribution among workers in different firms or different regions inconsistent with the official ideology or popular norms. This looser kind of system thus requires a more sophisticated fiscal system that can serve the goals of micro-regulation, macrocontrol, and equity in income distribution.

Another weakness of most of the reforms in the early stages is that most marketization and decentralization applies only to production and allocation of current output. It does not extend to investment, which is still largely centrally controlled. In Poland and in Hungary, even after they had gone some way in marketizing the allocation of current input, three-quarters of all investment resources were still allocated by central organs rather than on the basis of decisions made by enterprises themselves.

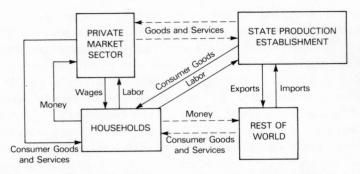

Figure 7-1. New Sectors and Markets in the Semi-reformed Economy

Addition of New Sectors and Markets

To reflect the new features of the system as it undergoes reform, we need to modify the scheme introduced in chapter 2. There are now more sectors and more markets to be distinguished. The main modification is to add a private/cooperative sector. If that is defined to include private-plot agricultural production, we no longer need to distinguish urban and rural households. In a way the new sector represents an enlargement of the private-plot principle, which in the original model was limited to private plots for collective-farm households. The kind of freedom that goes with the private plot is extended to a number of *nonagricultural* production activities, and to other households outside the agricultural sector. These new activities are predominantly service activities such as repair, restaurants, catering, and so on, but this private/cooperative sector *could* embrace a much wider range of activities, including industrial production, transport, and construction. The scope of activity in agriculture may also be widened beyond the private plot, by permitting leasing of collective-farm land to individuals, or by transferring effective control to brigades or families, as in the Chinese family responsibility system. The relations between the state production establishment and households, and between it and the rest of the world, remain as before.

Along with the creation of a private sector goes the legalization of some new kinds of exchange, and some new markets. The private sector can engage in exchanges with households, drawing on their labor and selling goods to them—agricultural goods from the private plot as before, and also now various kinds of services. One variable in the design is whether the private/cooperative activity remains organized around the household (or a few households) or is on a larger scale requiring the hiring of labor services from households via a labor contract. Another variable is whether the private/coop sector is given significant access to the foreign sector with the right to engage in buying imports and selling output abroad. Another difference turns on whether or not the private/cooperative sector engages in exchanges with the SPE. The intention of the reformers is usually to allow the private/cooperative sector to operate only in areas where it does not depend on the socialized economy for inputs of intermediate goods, or on the state budget for capital, or on the state-controlled bank for loans and hard currency to finance imports. In figure 7-1, these ambiguities are indicated by the use of dashed rather than solid lines for transactions between the private sector and the SPE. But even if the private sector does not conduct much trade with the SPE, it is not really independent of it since the latter, in its role as the government, has fiscal powers over the private sector. It can levy taxes on the incomes of participants in the private/cooperative sector, and on its outputs.

Another variable in the reform design is whether there is a possibility of exchange between the household sector and the outside world. If this is permitted, households can have access to foreign goods with little intervention by the SPE, and can hold foreign currency. Households can *acquire* foreign currency through remittances from abroad (Poland is a famous case), or the authorities may permit nationals to earn some foreign currency. For instance, the Soviet system has traditionally allowed specialists who have worked abroad in various capacities to keep part of their foreign-currency earnings, to be spent (after conversion to a special scrip) for foreign goods in special stores. The supply of foreign goods to these consumer-goods markets may be regulated to some degree by the SPE, but for the moment, let us assume that these stores are free to buy goods abroad, in quantities sufficient to meet demand. This assumption gives us two new markets, one in which households buy foreign goods, and one in which foreign currency (or the goods which can be bought with it) can be exchanged for the domestic currency. In this latter market relationship there will emerge an unofficial exchange rate, which may not be the same as the official one.

The reforms may go far enough to create embryonic market relationships *within* the old SPE. Market relationships here means a situation where q's and/or p's are no longer set by the plan but are determined by the free interaction of state enterprises acting as buyers and sellers. We might think about this in terms of whole sectors moving out of the old SPE into the market sector, or in terms in which individual enterprises may have one foot in the SPE, the other in the market sector. At one stage in the Chinese reform, enterprises were assigned output plans that covered part of their output which had to be disposed of in accordance with centrally determined plans, and at state-fixed prices. They were allowed to sell any output they produced beyond the plan to whatever customers they could find, and at prices they negotiated with those customers. The Soviet version of this mechanism is the idea of "state orders" (*goszakazy*) in which part of an enterprise's output is determined by the plan (this is the state order) and is supported with an allocation of inputs from the center. But the extent, composition, and allocation of the rest of its output, together with the acquisition of inputs to support that output, are determined by the enterprise itself. One important distinction here is whether the enterprise must adhere to centrally set prices in the transactions that are outside the plan or is allowed to negotiate a price with the partner to the transaction. If the state sets the prices this is not yet quite marketization.

There is also an important distinction to be made between a state enterprise controlled by the market and truly "private" market activity, where the enterprise is not owned by the state. That is, an enterprise may have the freedom to engage in activity according to the rule of maximizing profits, and interact with all its partners via markets, in which prices are set by supply and demand, but still be owned by the state and directed by a bureaucrat working for the state. How this may affect the behavior and incentives of enterprise management is an aspect of the issue of privatization to which we will return in a later chapter.

Despite all these distinctions not captured in figure 7-1, the idea of the diagram is that there is now a much larger area of production activity where the mechanism that drives production is based on market links involving interaction between buyers and sellers about prices and quantities, with profit as the motivator. Its motivating significance may depend on the fact that the firm is directed by its private owners, or that the success indicator and bonus system for a state-subordinated manager are based on profit as the bottom line.

As this market-type sector expands, its links with whatever remains of the SPE must ultimately expand. There are only a few activities that really satisfy the criterion of weak interaction with the SPE mentioned earlier, with autonomous firms selling their output (and purchasing their inputs) to (from) each other or to (from) households. As the market-based sector expands, the links indicated by dashed lines in figure 7-1 become ever more substantial. Private activity becomes more and more dependent on the state sector as a source of inputs, and as an outlet for its products. The implication is that these links become subject to the kind of pricing considerations described earlier for relations with households or with the world market. To the extent the state still fixes prices for the goods and services it exchanges with the private sector, those prices must satisfy the conditions for macroequilibrium, microbalance, and efficiency explained in chapter 4. One of the most interesting questions is the distribution of market power between the marketized firms and the state sector. In most of these cases it is found that as enterprises get freed from SPE controls in various respects they sometimes acquire a degree of monopoly power that reverses the former relationship between them and the rest of society. In the USSR, for example, R&D organizations were the first SPE firms to acquire the privileges of a nonplanned firm, specifically the right to negotiate prices for their services with customers they chose themselves, and to allocate the incomes received to uses they decided on themselves. Given the high degree of specialization among them they became able to charge very high prices, and in many cases to give their employees very high incomes. The Ministry of Finance found that prices charged for R&D services rose in one year alone (1988) by 35 percent, and wages, including premium payments out of profits, in many cases doubled in the course of a couple of years.[1]

Furthermore, all these markets begin to be connected. The area in which

---

1. *Ekonomicheskaia Gazeta*, 1989:25, p. 24.

the market rather than the SPE sets prices, or the volume of SPE-related transactions in which the SPE needs to satisfy market rules of pricing, is now enlarged. That fact limits the ability of the managers of the SPE to steer behavior and allocation by price setting in the markets it *does* control—the state labor market and the consumer-goods market—and in whatever transactions it carries on with the private/cooperative sector. If it wants to affect allocation, or income distribution within the household sector, or within the private-production sector, public finance becomes much more important as a policy tool.

Difficulties of Coherent Decentralization through Regulators

It turns out to be very difficult to design a system of "economic regulators" (i.e., indirect policy instruments) that is coherent and able to reach the actors in their new environment to guide their behavior in directions that will satisfy planners' goals for the economy.

First, the authorities are often trying to achieve multiple objectives through this mix of some central control and some reliance on markets. For example, they may want to achieve full employment without inflation, to maintain external balance, to stimulate regional development, and, until CMEA is totally disbanded, to satisfy CMEA obligations. They may also want to change the sectoral structure of output, employment, or investment. It may be that there is no way all these things can be achieved in the desired degree at the same time. In the traditional system the planners managed to maintain full employment with minimal inflation, even when they set targets well above potential output, by a well-tested system. They controlled prices from the center, and reconciled excess demand with supply by a well-understood system of microcontrols in the form of informal priorities and buffer sectors, applied hands-on in the process of plan execution. In the new situation the package of levers to reconcile excess demand with real potential may be incomplete, or the planners may have too little experience in handling it to make it work.

This point about incoherence can be illustrated with a couple of examples. One goal of reform in Eastern Europe has been to stimulate exports to balance the external account. Under the reform, enterprises began to operate in an environment in which they were interested in profit. But the reforms have generally failed to fully shift the attention of enterprise management from the wishes of central organs to market signals. Decisions by an enterprise continue to be much influenced by the pressure and the signals it gets from the center (its own ministry, the Ministry of Finance, the State Materials and Price Office [in Hungary], the Planning Office, etc.) as well as price signals that affect profit. It might face complicated tax penalties on wage increases. It might be allowed to spend hard currency earned from its exports, but the temptation to earn foreign currency may be diluted if the enterprise has to run a bureaucratic licensing gauntlet to import anything with it. The enterprise may be eligible for subsidies of various kinds. Most important, its management knows that its fate still depends on retaining goodwill and clout at headquarters, i.e., at the center. The central authorities' task is to manipulate these various elements in the enterprise's environment to get it to export more. It is going to be very difficult to predict the enterprise's export response to the manipulation of these variables. And if the authorities want to steer enterprises not only to expand hard-currency exports, but also to meet continuing export obligations to CMEA countries, to shift employment and investment from old to more modern product lines, they may find their manipulations drive the economy into the ditch, rather than straight down the road.

The steering mechanism may have internal inconsistencies. As an example, Hungary used devaluation of the forint to encourage exports. But it also introduced a domestic price system that set internal prices on the basis of external prices. So devaluation, along with the extra profitability for exporting that it promised, also raised the *domestic* price of the goods in question and undercut any motivation to shift sales from the domestic to the export market.

In both Hungary and Poland, since the authorities could no longer control prices directly, they tried to control the *price level* by influencing the *wage level*. That is, they operated an "incomes policy." The instrument was a tax on any increase in an enterprise's wage expenditure. In practice it turned out to be impossible to make these policies stick. Units incurring losses lost laborers, and in their interaction with central authorities, they managed to win exemption from the tax so that they would be able to raise wages to retain them. The USSR attempted a similar policy beginning in 1989, and had a similar difficulty in making it stick, because it conflicted with numerous other goals, such as shifting the composition of national output and avoiding unemployment. For example, enterprises besieged the Ministry of Finance with the argument that they should not be subjected to this policy since it made it financially ruinous for them to increase wage expenditures to expand consumer-goods output, which they were being urged to do.

A final example of the unintended effects of reform through regulation involves investment. New projects are financed by loans, and when a project does not get finished, or it is liquidated, there is pressure to excuse the investors from repayment. So the Ministry of Finance budget is in deficit, and the only way it sees to cover the deficit is to tax profits more heavily. So the growing, exporting, cost-cutting, productivity-improving enterprises that have responded to the indicators as hoped are punished for their success by the remnants of the old ratchet effect.

Monetary Institutions and Policy

The designers of the semi-reformed economy have typically not found a way to impose a "hard budget constraint," and as decentralization begins to give money real command over resources, one of the biggest problems is to control the money supply, aggregate demand, and inflationary pressure.

The dichotomy of the soft/hard budget constraint, first introduced by Janos Kornai, has acquired a wide variety of meanings. Basically it refers to the fact that the Soviet-type economies, even in the semi-reformed version, lack institutions that force financial responsibility on the state and its creatures, such as the Ministry of Finance, banks, and enterprises. The crucial sanction that is missing is bankruptcy and enterprise liquidation, which the authorities have always been reluctant to accept.

The softness of the budget constraint has micro- and macroeffects. On the micro level, it reduces the pressure to correct past errors in investment, economic structure, and allocation. The economy abounds with enterprises that produce the wrong things, do not try to control cost, systematically overexpend resources, and often fail to cover their costs out of revenues.

Soviet critics of the old system have captured this behavior neatly in their description of the administrative-command system as an "expenditure machine" (*zatratnyi mekhanizm*) that eats up resources without generating output. But these inefficient enterprises can continue to operate because the bank extends credit to cover their overexpenditure period after period, and not infrequently forgives the loan. When the bank faces the alternatives of extending credit beyond the amount planned or holding the enterprise to that limit and thus forcing a shutdown of production, the rules of the system have generally called for the bank to provide liquidity for continued operation. In the USSR at the beginning of the nineties it was acknowledged that nearly 100 billion rubles of the total indebtedness of enterprises to the State Bank (about 400 billion rubles) represented extension of credit purely to cover losses against no real collateral at all. In the semi-reformed systems, central authorities also often extend special treatment to weak enterprises in other ways—special exchange-rate coefficients giving them an advantage compared to the general rate of exchange, relief from taxes, special dispensation with respect to wage payments, and direct subsidies. So uneconomic production—activity that eats up more resources than its product is worth—continues, and resources are not shifted to more desirable activities.

On the macro level, either of these processes (direct extension of unrepayable credit by the bank, or extension of budget-based or budget-wrecking favors) creates excess aggregate demand. The first leads directly to an expansion of the money supply. In the second variant, budget deficits are covered by the monobank's extending credit to the state rather than to enterprises. Whatever the mechanism, this excess liquidity generally ends up as cash held by the population. This excess cash leads to loss of incentives, black markets and corruption, price increases for those consumer goods and services that are not price-controlled, or "price creep" for those that are price-controlled, through such devices as quality deterioration. The monopoly bank does not worry about the growth of outstanding liabilities in the form of its notes which are backed on the asset side of its balance sheet only with worthless IOUs. As an agency of the state, it will never have to redeem those notes.

A hard budget constraint could perhaps be imposed at the micro level by "commercial banks" operating under a "solvency or bankruptcy" rule.

In such a situation the bank system would be forced to operate in its dealings with the enterprise sector on truly commercial principles, extending credit only to credit-worthy borrowers for economically justified purposes. But we know from the experience of market economies that even hard-headed and hard-hearted capitalist bankers may extend so much credit to firms that in the aggregate there is excess demand. So there must also be a liquidity constraint imposed by a central bank. Specifically what is needed is a reform of the banking system embodying a separation of functions between a central bank and a network of commercial banks in a two-level system. In such a system, the top level is a central bank like the U.S. Federal Reserve Bank that does not itself make loans to the economy, or to the government. Instead, its main task is to control the supply of "reserves" to the lower-level banks. The second component is a network of lower-level banks that actually extend credit (make loans) and by doing so determine the supply of money. Their ability to do so depends on the amount of their reserves, usually in a fractional reserves system, and the supply of reserves to the system can be raised or lowered by the central bank to control the money supply.

An illustration of how this works, using the following schematic accounts, may help. Such a system consists of a central bank and 100 commercial banks, typically with balance sheets like the two shown. The commercial banks are required to hold "reserves" in the form of deposits in the central bank equal to, say, one-fifth of whatever their deposits amount to. The deposits of firms and individuals in commercial banks, against which they can write checks, are the major component of the economy's money supply. A commercial bank's business is to earn income by lending money at interest to borrowers, i.e., by taking the borrower's IOU and giving in return an addition to his/her deposit, a process which creates money. The bank's ability to make loans this way is limited by the "reserve ratio" which says the bank must not have more than $5 of deposits for each $1 in its account with the central bank. In the situation shown, if a customer were to propose borrowing $10 million from the 1st National Bank by giving the bank an IOU and getting a corresponding increase in its bank balance, the bank would have to say no, as that would make its deposits more than five times its reserves.

The ability of the central bank to control the money supply lies in its

I. CENTRAL BANK BALANCE SHEET

Assets		Liabilities	
Gold	$10B	Deposits of commercial banks	$100B
Government securities	$90B	First NB	$1B
		. . .	
		Last NB	$1B
Total	$100B	Total	$100B

II. BALANCE SHEETS OF COMMERCIAL BANKS
   (100 such banks of similar size)

1st Natl Bank				other banks	Last Natl Bank			
Assets		Liabilities		A. L.	Assets		Liabilities	
Dep in CB	$1B	Customer checking accts	$5B		Dep in CB	$1B	Customer checking accts	$5B
IOUs	$4B	Gen Manuf	$10M		IOUs	$4B	Schmidt	
Acme Mach	$11M	Jones	$2M				Brown	
Gen Manuf	$20M	Smith	$1M				Ajax	
etc.		etc.					etc.	
TOTAL	$5B	Total	$5B		TOTAL	$5B	Total	$5B

ability to force increases or decreases in commercial banks reserves, either enabling the latter to expand loans (hence deposits and hence the money supply) or forcing it to contract them. If the central bank sells $1 million worth of the government securities it owns by going to the securities market (the "open market" in government securities) and selling them to Jones, say, Jones pays with a check drawn against his account at the 1st National, i.e., a note which tells 1st National to pay $1 million to the Federal Reserve Bank. The central bank collects in effect by adjusting *downward* its own debt to 1st National, i.e., the deposit 1st National has with the central bank. The 1st National Bank now has only $999 million of reserves, and so must reduce its deposits to stay within the required 1 to 5 reserve ratio. When General Manufacturing comes in to pay off its 90-day loan of $10 million by drawing down its account, that reduces total deposits of the system by $10 million. And because it is short on reserves the bank is *not* in a position to renew that loan or extend new loans to anyone else. The reduction in the money supply will continue until total deposits have fallen by $5 million. If the central bank *buys* securities in the open market, the process works in reverse, *adding* to commercial bank reserves, and so permitting an expansion of the money supply.

This kind of banking system does not yet exist in the USSR or most of the other reforming CPEs, and the reformers either have not understood the need for one or have been reluctant to move toward it. Moreover, some important prerequisites are missing. In the U.S., as indicated in the above example, the central bank increases and decreases the amount of reserves held by commercial banks (and hence their ability to expand credit) by buying or selling government securities in the open market. This is a common model in market economies. In fact, it is not possible to have sophisticated monetary policy without the existence of government securities and markets for them. This permits monetary policy to be separate from fiscal policy, and to be exercised by a bank which is independent of the treasury, and independent of the actions of the commercial banks. It also gives the central bank a second variable it can use to influence aggregate demand: the interest rate. When the central bank sells securities in the open market, it increases their supply and depresses their price. This causes a rise in interest rates for new issues and ultimately in interest rates generally. The decline in money supply and the rise in interest rates reinforce each other in depressing aggregate demand.

The Hungarians have gone furthest in trying to create such a system and now have something close to the kind of system described. This is one area where the USSR ought to be able to telescope the reform process a bit, but the bank reorganization effort undertaken in the early stages of Gorbachev's economic-reform program did not touch the essential features of the monobank system in which there is no real restraint on the issue of money. The first Soviet effort split the bank system into the Gosbank and five specialized banks (Prombank, Agroprombank, Vneshekonombank, Zhilsotsbank, and Sberegatel'nyi Bank) with which enterprises now have their accounts and from which they get loans. This was supposed to leave the Gosbank to "implement a unified policy in the field of monetary circulation, lending, financing, settlements, cash and foreign exchange operations," as N. V. Gostev, chairman of the board of the Gosbank, described it. But the specialized banks are still not commercial banks, and the Gosbank is not a central bank in the sense explained above. The decentralized banks are essentially subcontractors for performing the loan and settlement operations that the Gosbank used to perform directly.

Failure to plug this hole for money creation is one of the central flaws of the semi-reformed system. There are considerable variations in this process from country to country. In the first five years of *perestroika* in the USSR the government ran a cumulative budget deficit of about 360 billion rubles financed by extension of bank credit, when the annual GNP was only 875 billion rubles. The resulting excess monetary holdings— the "monetary overhang"—and their potential for causing inflation under a market regime had at the beginning of the 1990s paralyzed the reform leadership. In China the inflationary fiscal and monetary mechanisms were exacerbated by strong regional authorities who expanded the money supply with little control from the center. The Czechs claim that, on the basis of a long fiscal-responsibility tradition and a relatively independent position for the monobank, they have been able to keep better control of the money supply and intend to maintain tight fiscal and monetary policies as reform accelerates. But to some degree the soft-budget constraint and its consequences for the monetary supply are inherent features of all the semi-reformed economies.

The consequences of failure to control the money supply are obvious in the form of inflationary pressure when prices are freed. Partial marketization in a situation where the bank system is incapable of imposing a liquidity constraint leads inevitably to inflation. The Yugoslavs in the late eighties were experiencing an inflation rate of over 20 percent per month! The Poles were suffering 200 percent per year just before the shock therapy administered by the new noncommunist government. Ultimately, the reformers realize that they have to either give up on reform (which they now see as impossible) or move forward, allowing even more marketization. As creeping or galloping marketization restores money to its full authority, they have to control the money supply, or it will destroy them.

As suggested, one of the conditions for an effective central bank is that it be insulated from coercion by the treasury. One of the goals of having monetary policy is that it be able to operate in opposition to fiscal policy.

But if the government has sufficient power to force the central bank to finance its deficit, say by having the bank buy the government's issues of new securities and thus monetizing the debt, it is no improvement over the present situation. The question of independence of the central bank extends far beyond the socialist countries, of course—central banks often are not independent. In many less-developed countries they are forced to cover the deficit in demand for government bonds, and so are turned into an instrument for monetizing the budget deficit—no different from the present Soviet situation.

Fiscal Instruments and Fiscal Policy

The other gaping hole in the policy toolbox of the semi-reformed economy is the absence of a proper fiscal system. The classic administered economy operated with a very primitive system of manipulating government revenues and expenditures to regulate the economy, and the reformers have been slow to understand the need for a fiscal system consistent with the greater importance of market forces in the semi-reformed economy.

As was explained in chapter 5, the fiscal system in the administered economy is not an independent agent of policy. Its function is to serve as a channel for collection and redistribution of funds among various accounts of USSR, Inc. Its flows are the financial expression of allocation and pricing decisions carried out by more direct means. The economists and planners of socialist countries have little experience in thinking about or understanding the fiscal system as an independent tool of policy.

It may be useful here to take a detour through some fundamental ideas about the function of fiscal policy, starting with an explicit definition of the term. Fiscal policy is the government's actions regarding government revenues and expenditures, including its decisions about taxation, government expenditure either for goods and services or in the form of transfer payments, and government borrowing. (Transfer payments are government expenditures for which no goods or services are received in return, such as subsidies or welfare payments.) It may be useful to recall here that there are three main rationales for a government sector in the market economy, and for the taxes and government expenditures that go with it. These are the provision of "public goods" or "collective goods," redistribution of income, and regulation of aggregate demand.[2]

"*Collective goods*" are those that will not be adequately supplied by the market system because of a "free rider" problem. National defense is the prototypical collective good, which serves all citizens of the nation whether or not they have made any contribution to paying for it. For this class of goods there is a "free rider" problem, providing a rationale for the state to use its coercive power to collect taxes in order to make sure that an appropriate amount of resources are made available to provide for national defense. This is a process in which the distribution of the cost is made according to some collectively derived social judgment as to who ought to bear the burden, rather than according to willingness to pay. The issue of what is and what is not a collective good gets very complicated, but let us leave it at that.

The *redistributive use of the fiscal system* flows from some social consensus about fairness that is unwilling to accept the income distribution generated by the market. The market distributes income in proportion to the productive contribution of the factors provided. It awards large incomes to some people (especially if the institutions of property and inheritance exist) and doles out very little to others whose productivity and contribution to the society's production are low, even if this low productivity is no fault of their own (a result of mental and physical handicaps or lack of education, say). This market-based distribution may violate some fairly widely held notion of what every citizen may rightly claim from society.

In an economy with decentralized decisionmaking, like the market economy, or the decentralized socialist economy, the savings decisions made by households and enterprises at full employment may not be consistent with the amount of investment the government and enterprises decide to make. For example, the *stabilizing function* of fiscal policy in this case is to reduce the total flow of demand by collecting more from the income stream in taxes than it adds to it in the form of expenditures.

---

2. Another important function, less closely related to the financial activities that concern us here, is the government's role in defining the rules of the market game and monitoring adherence to them.

Alternatively, when total demand is too small, the government may need to inject additional spending into the income stream by running a deficit, i.e., spending more than it collects in taxes.

The general prescription for combining these aims is as follows. First, assume that the full potential output possible from full employment of society's resources will be produced. Then by some process of political decisionmaking a choice should be made as to how much of that output should be available for current private consumption, how much set aside for investment, and how much for the provision of public goods. The function of the tax system, including the "negative taxes" we call transfer payments, is to influence the allocation of income between saving and investment, and distribute the associated tax burden in a way that seems equitable. So equity is achieved by differentiating taxes, transfers, and the provision of government services among various groups. Redistribution takes place both on the taxation side and on the expenditure side.[3]

In settling the final element of the fiscal equation, the total size of tax collections, the principle is to adjust them to whatever amount is needed to adjust aggregate demand to aggregate supply. If the result is a budget deficit, government should borrow the necessary amount not from the central bank, using its power to command, but from the general public, by selling government bonds. This permits the separation of fiscal and monetary policy.

Macrostabilization in the Socialist Economy. Socialist economies have not generally depended on borrowing by issuing securities when they need to finance a budget deficit. They are reluctant to create instruments giving private individuals significant financial claims against the state. So the socialist state borrows mostly from the State Bank, which produces the money via the printing press, or by tapping people's savings-bank deposits, paying no interest in either case. It has sometimes borrowed by issuing

---

3. It should be added that in a market economy there is *shifting* of taxes, and this complicates knowing what the final *incidence* of the tax is on *personal* incomes. To achieve the redistributive goal of a fiscal policy, it is probably best to tax closer to personal income, not tax enterprises. It may be worth noting here that there is a kind of symbiosis between taxes and prices. In perfect administration neither prices nor taxes were the policy instrument. But as prices come to be set in the market, and taxes are used as an active policy tool, taxes begin to have an independent impact on prices. What the impact is depends on how they get shifted. And here the answer is in terms of how markets work—how free they are.

state bonds. But domestic borrowing by socialist states has always offered rather limited rights to the lender. Low interest rates are paid on government bonds, bond maturities have frequently been rescheduled, and bonds are generally not transferable.

Taxes and Income Distribution. In the traditional SPE, taxes were collected mostly via pricing of consumer goods, and in that arena there is a big gain from following the rules of correct pricing described earlier in chapter 4. But these rules are all "efficiency rules" that are not concerned with distributive effects. One reason the old system departed from efficiency rules (as in setting rents far below the equilibrium level, for example) was that it was trying to use the price system to ensure that access to goods (in this case to housing) did not depend on income. In the semi-reformed economies as income distribution begins increasingly to reflect market forces, it becomes important to retreat from distributing income by *price* manipulation, and to find other tools for income redistribution. Earlier we noted the absence of a government control instrument for affecting the distribution of income between the urban households and the rural households that face each other in the collective-farm market. If underfulfillment of the food component of the consumer-goods plan leaves urban households with unspent money, they can spend it for food in the collective-farm market, thus redistributing income toward peasant households. With the emergence of a private sector, there is another channel through which the consumption total allocated in the national plan is redistributed between urban households, rural households, and private-sector producers. The spread of markets creates new areas for application of the income-redistributive function of the fiscal system.

So far the reformers are groping to adapt the fiscal system to these new needs. But I suspect that in most cases they try to deal with it by introducing some kind of tax on producers, taxing away income before it can be distributed to individuals. In the USSR the Ministry of Finance proposed in 1989 to limit the large earnings of those who worked in cooperatives by a tax on cooperative profits (and at one point on gross revenue) with a rate of 90 percent. A more effective approach toward equalizing incomes would be to tax personal incomes. Some of those who work in co-ops may have second incomes from the state sector, and the profits of a cooperative may be distributed very unevenly among its different participants. Taxing co-op profits *before* distribution is a clumsy way to try to equalize incomes between those different individuals.

The Problem of Monopoly Power

As central control over prices and output decisions is relinquished, the issue of industrial concentration becomes important because of the potential for turning enterprise autonomy into exploitative market power. These economies are highly concentrated. The administrative passion for specialization, elimination of duplication, gigantomania in projectmaking, etc., has created many situations where the overwhelming majority of some product is produced by a few plants or firms, and in some cases all of it by a single one. Ironically some of the earliest reforms (such as the creation of "large economic organizations" in Poland) strengthened this concentration by bringing together all the firms in a given industry under the umbrella of a single organization, which could become a kind of cartel when marketization began. If enterprises are now turned loose to maximize profits, they will have the market power to raise prices to obtain those profits and will distort allocation in the process. Also it is likely that such freedom will add to inflationary processes by creating a cost-push pressure in addition to the demand pull of the monetary overhang. One objection of the anti-reformers is the high prices and profits earned by firms not under central control. But in this case as in many others a defect of the semi-reformed economy is best combated not by retreating to the old system but by moving forward to still more radical reform. In this case the need is to combat monopoly by making entry easier.

For examples of how to do this, the experience of the East European pioneers is useful. The Poles broke up industrial concentrations. But a trust-busting approach that delays the introduction of market pricing until the old monopolies have been reorganized into smaller units may not be the best approach. It may be easier to let prices go and focus on creating the conditions for the entry of new competitors that will be powerfully attracted by the resulting high prices for the corresponding products. Another tactic is to control market power through opening the domestic economy to foreign competitive pressure. Marketization of foreign-trade decisions is important not just for better allocation, but also as a support for creating a climate of competition. It is important to ease conditions for the formation of new enterprises, to which there are many approaches. Some self-organizing initiative can come from cooperatives and joint ventures. Leasing is another backdoor to creating new entrants. It is important to remove artificial constraints on production profiles of enterprises that exist *de jure*, or because of administrative pressure from above. It is also important to ease the transfer of assets between enterprises, preferably by purchase and sale. An illustrative case that occurred early in the Soviet reform was that of an insolvent enterprise in the Ministry of Machine Tools and Instrumentmaking taken over by the Ministry of Automotive and Agricultural Machinebuilding. The Automobile Ministry assumed the enterprise's debts, and provided investment to reequip it and change its production profile. It thus created a supplier for itself at a much lower cost than building a new plant from scratch. The case reported leads to vertical integration, which we know may pose dangers to competition, but on the whole such acquisitions are beneficial. Purchase and sale of enterprises and facilities encourages potential entrants to scout out underutilized assets to be used more effectively. In addition to facilitating better use of the abundance of underutilized assets that is a major feature of the centrally planned economy, it is also a method of encouraging entry to counter market power.

Even if these steps are not sufficient to control the market power of large enterprises, with its disruptive effects on allocation, it may be possible to overcome some of the effect of such power on income distribution by an appropriate system of taxation.

What Remains to Be Done

To summarize, the experience of socialist economic reform gives rise to the concept of the "semi-reformed economy," a kind of "halfway house" represented in variant forms in Yugoslavia, Poland, China, Hungary. It is clear that the semi-reformed economy is still burdened with much of the allocative ineffectiveness and incentive defects of the old system, along with some special problems all its own. These problems can be solved only by moving farther in the direction of reform.

The Poles took such a step in the most resolute and rapid shift to market principles in the socialist world. The Hungarians followed, but at a somewhat slower pace. The issue was solved for East Germany in a more radical way. With all the old planning and supervisory structures being simply abolished, enterprises were thrown directly into the much larger West German market environment. The economically most weighty of the countries of the old socialist camp is the USSR, as we saw in chapter 6, and its reform travail is of special interest. On a reform thermometer calibrated by the experience of the other socialist countries, economic *perestroika* in the USSR by the end of the eighties had brought the system barely above the freezing point. It is not yet to the halfway house. It is sometimes thought that the USSR could learn from the experience of the smaller socialist countries and telescope the two stages, going much more directly to a fully reformed, marketized economy. What is needed to complete the reform has already been suggested along the way, but it may be useful to restate it a bit more systematically here.

I take it as axiomatic that real reform must involve marketization. If the reformers want significant improvement in performance, the reform must cross the threshold between the "regulator approach" of the semi-reformed model to full marketization. East European experience suggests that effective administration of the economy is no more attainable via financial levers wielded by the policymakers than by production commands. This is mainly because of the gamelike character of the relationship between the managers and the managed, between the central authorities and the enterprise-level executors of commands. An asymmetric distribution of power between top and bottom of the administrative hierarchy (with formal authority concentrated at the top, and information, which confers a less explicit but effective form of power, in the hands of the managers) results in a defective bargaining structure in which both sides lose. The three pillars on which the administered economy rests are the setting of output targets and allocations, administered pricing, and a cyclically repetitive control process. The main difference in the semi-reformed economy is the substitution of economic regulators for the output/allocation pillar. As long as those pillars remain, the attention of management will be focused on pleasing (perhaps by deceiving) their superiors, not on catering to customers or bargaining with suppliers. The only way to get rid of the three pillars is to destroy the apparatus whose job it is to perform those functions.

The Soviet reformers had at the beginning of the nineties adopted a schizophrenic stance toward undermining those three pillars. At first they talked about "combining plan and market." They tried to institute a hybrid system where some production activity was market-directed while the remaining production was to be guided by the old principles under the guise of the *goszakazy*. They legislated freedom for the enterprise in the new law on the enterprise, but left in place the old bureaucratic apparatus to interfere with the exercise of that freedom. As of the early nineties they had done virtually nothing to move away from administered prices. As time passes and experience accumulates, they are coming to realize they must go farther toward real marketization. In general, policy and actions have moved in the direction of radicalizing the reform. The reformers have come to realize they cannot really change the behavior of the bureaucratic apparatus, but must simply abolish it.[4] They are held back in this task more by the political problem than by any expectation that they can reform the bureaucrats. The tactics are to chip away at the administrative apparatus, to free individual sectors, to marketize certain categories of prices, and so on. Under such a piecemeal approach, there will be inconsistencies, like those familiar in the earlier experience of Eastern European countries. The important thing is to keep moving in the right direction. I am reminded of Albert Hirschman's view on economic development. Critics of development programs always decry their inconsistencies and disproportions. Hirschman's idea is that this is an unhelpful point of view. The important thing is to do *something*. It is not possible to deal with all aspects of a program in a fully coordinated way, so imbalances and bottlenecks will inevitably emerge. But that is no excuse for not starting—imbalances and bottlenecks will define very clearly what direction the next steps must take. Similarly in reform, the idea is to *act*— to start somewhere.

---

4. This line of thought is systematically developed in a very interesting little book, A. G. Khudokormov, *Ekonomicheskie korni biurokratizma*, Moscow: Ekonomika, 1988.

It is not possible to marketize without reforming the price mechanism. Marketization, properly understood, is a process in which markets not only allocate resources but generate the information needed for the economic decisionmaking underlying allocation. In shifting from vertical communication between bosses and executors to lateral negotiation between producers and users, the goal is not only to settle decisions about q's, but also to get a reading from all interested parties on how much inputs and outputs are worth. What has to be reformed is not prices per se but the price *mechanism*. If economic reform is to improve economic performance, price reform must go beyond having a state price-setting agency such as the USSR's Goskomtsen introduce "reformed prices" to removing the process from the hands of a central price-setting agency altogether. This is one of the cases where it may be necessary to take one step first, and then a second, but in this case such a transition is like the policy of tariff protection for "infant" industry.[5] As long as Goskomtsen is there to reform prices, it is itself the biggest obstacle to reforming the price mechanism. The big argument here is one of sequence. The Soviet line is that markets must first be brought into equilibrium before prices can be freed. There are too many shortages, and freeing prices would lead to disaster in the form of inflation and redistribution of income. I favor the counter view that unless prices are freed from the beginning, to operate as powerful signals of what is worth doing and what is not, the adjustments that have to be made to improve efficiency and output structure will be put off indefinitely. The problem of sequencing is a separate topic that requires a more systematic discussion, and we will return to it in the final chapter.

The above prescription for marketization is meaningless without development of fiscal and monetary tools. The monetary/financial/fiscal systems must be created, almost from the ground up, and the planners have to develop a policy process to use them correctly.

Just how to create a central bank is not clear, but one feature of the

---

5. Tariff protection for industries just being established as part of a country's development strategy is often proposed on the grounds that in its early stages the "infant" industry cannot survive competition from more mature and experienced producers in the rest of the world. The burden this tariff puts on consumers of that product in the form of higher prices is to be repaid by vigorous development of the industry once established. The difficulty is that, spared the rigors of competition, such an infant may never become efficient, and may require tariff protection indefinitely.

semi-reformed stage is the emergence of real commercial banks alongside the official state banks. In the USSR, there quickly sprang up cooperative banks, and joint-stock banks, owned by various kinds of state production units. The Avtobank is an example, formed by capital contributed basically by enterprises and ministries in the automobile industry or with a client relationship to it. Such banks feel a hard budget constraint inherently— they are outside the Gosbank system and without the patronage of the Ministry of Finance and must fail if their borrowers default on loans. If they were the main source of credit creation, that would solve the problem. At the moment, however, they are small in relation to the main banks, and in the language of western banking they are "financial intermediaries" rather than commercial banks. They simply transfer excess funds from one unit to another that needs them, and do not have the power to create and destroy money and thus affect the money supply. Conceivably they could grow in importance, and eventually be a force for creation of a two-level banking system, but at the moment they have a hard time even surviving in the face of the hostile power of the regular state bank system. Some Gosbank offices have tried to undercut the new banks by threatening to withhold Gosbank's banking services from any enterprise which does business with them.

The managers of the socialist economies are now handicapped by the fact that there is no distinction between fiscal and monetary policy—the two always work in the same direction. A budget deficit always leads to an increase in the supply of money, and a reduction in the money supply is possible only by running a budget surplus. Issuing government securities could potentially keep these two tracks separate. The creation of a government securities market would incidentally provide a means by which a more sophisticated central bank could regulate the supply of liquidity in the system. By creating a more complex system of financial instruments that can serve as forms of property (commercial paper, enterprise stocks and bonds, government bonds), the reformers could solve other problems as well. The creation of a government bond market would create a new influence on the rate of interest to encourage saving and control investment.

This sounds like a recommendation that the socialist reformers create carbon copies of the market economies, and it may be objected that it is unrealistic to expect them to do so. My answer is that although tremendous variation is possible in the forms fiscal and monetary policy take, they are the most important economic policy tools appropriate to a marketized economy. It does not make much sense to marketize the economy without attending to the creation of this macrocontrol instrumentarium as well. When finance, money, fiscal policy, etc., become important it is indispensable to develop more complex financial instruments and markets.

A more subtle fiscal system to deal with the issue of income distribution is necessary not only for the finally reformed economy but to permit the reform process to proceed. As control of prices is relinquished to the market, the leaders lose control over the distribution of real income— some people earn high incomes, others are stuck with stagnant incomes or even lose their jobs. This rouses opposition to the reform idea, and offends whatever ideas about distributive justice are held by either the leaders or the population at large. These phenomena (which appeared especially strongly in China) are appearing today in the USSR. Popular revulsion at the high prices and high incomes the co-ops are exacting has been well publicized, and there was an attempt by the Ministry of Finance (later aborted) to tax co-ops out of existence. There is also a need to build a safety net for those who lose out under market pricing through some combination of disadvantage on the income and cost-of-living sides. In East Germany's transformation that problem was mostly taken care of by the fact that there was already a safety net in place in the West German economy into which it was absorbed. But the others must build such institutions *ab ovo*. Here is where political reform and economic reform are clearly tied. The tax system will be able to deal with the equity issues which marketization raises only in the context of a political process that will involve and win the support of the public for economic change.

There is a great deal of analytical groundwork that will have to be mastered by the reformers in this sphere. As the economy becomes marketized, incidence and shifting become important. In the old system, which depended heavily on the turnover tax, it was clear who paid the tax— households. The only issue was interpersonal welfare incidence (the tax burden was heavier on those who liked vodka than on those who bought children's shoes). Even when Soviet tax policy deemphasized the turnover tax to collect more taxes from enterprises in the form of profit deductions, there was little shifting, since prices were administered and input menus determined administratively. But in a reformed system in which price and cost interact with allocation, the shifting and final personal incidence of taxes is likely to be an important issue but much more difficult to sense. Most Soviet economists seem not even to know that this issue exists. The ideas of shifting and incidence are central enough to any notion of fiscal policy that they are introduced in the first sophomore economics course in the West, but I have never seen them even mentioned in a Soviet discussion. Hungary's discussion of this issue has been more sophisticated, and in reforming their tax system to rely mostly on VAT and a personal income tax, the Hungarians understood and were trying to deal with the incidence problem.

In the author's view this agenda and end point are obvious and eventually inescapable. But the understanding and acceptance and the will to get on with the task vary considerably across the old socialist camp. The Soviet Union, in particular, as of the summer of 1990 was still in the throes of a debate over how to proceed. One government reform program had been turned down in the spring, and Gorbachev had instructed his reform commission to come up with a new one. In doing so the USSR government had additionally created a separate commission to canvass alternatives, and in the meantime the RSFSR government had produced its own "500 days" program. Still another group was appointed to meld the RSFSR and USSR versions, amid assertions by some that the two conceptions were so different they could no more be mixed than oil and water. This drama occurred in a situation of increasing impatience at the level of republic and local governments with the foot dragging and irresolution of the USSR government and a determination to proceed on their own. It seems likely that when reform actually happens in the USSR, it will be because the power of the center is broken by regional forces, with the emergence of a much more fragmented structure for the USSR, if, indeed, it holds together at all. We will return to these momentous themes in the final chapter.

8.

The Foreign Sector in the
Semi-reformed Economy

There is a great deal of talk on the part of the socialist reformers about making their national currencies convertible, engaging in a broader range of international economic relations, and becoming normal members of the international economic community. As indicated in chapter 4, the international economic relations of the socialist countries were not normal in that they were conducted under conditions of a state monopoly of foreign trade, as part of the highly centralized economic decisionmaking apparatus. Moreover, the socialist countries directed much of their trade to each other through their involvement in a preferential trade bloc, the CMEA or Council for Mutual Economic Assistance.[1] As part of the breakdown of the USSR's "external empire" at the beginning of the nineties, and radical domestic economic reform in several of the East European members, CMEA was left with no clear role, and the regime of preferential trade began to collapse. Interest in associating with the institutions of the international economic order (the World Bank, the International Monetary Fund [IMF], and the General Agreement on Trade and Tariffs [GATT]) began to grow. Romania had joined the IMF and World Bank in 1972, Hungary in 1982, and Poland in 1986. But by the end of the eighties those who were not members were applying to be, and the USSR, too, had indicated its interest in applying for membership in all three. In 1990 the USSR gained observer status in GATT.

Foreign-trade links not only offer opportunities for improving the func-

---

1. The CMEA did not include *all* the Soviet-type economies—a notable omission being China. The original members were the USSR and the six East European nations, joined later by Cuba and Vietnam. Yugoslavia has had observer status for a number of years.

tioning of the economy, but also pose obstacles for reform. In their current relationship with the world market, many of the socialist countries are burdened with a foreign debt so large as to cause burdensome balance-of-payments problems, and constrain the degree to which they can loosen central control over international economic relations. What can be expected to happen to foreign trade and other international economic links as these economies proceed with their transition to a more marketized economy?

Let us begin with a reminder about foreign trade in the two polar cases of the classic administered economy and a normal market economy. In the fully centralized economy, the size, composition, and direction of exports and imports, like all the other quantities in the resource allocation pattern, are determined via the centralized balancing process described in chapter 3. Imports and exports are components in the material balances for any good. The foreign currency earned from exports to the capitalist world market is banked abroad, and used to pay for the goods imported. The domestic currency is inconvertible, both in the sense that it cannot be bought and sold freely against other currencies, and in the more important sense that it is not routinely convertible into goods. Under these conditions the exchange rate plays no equilibrating or guiding role in decisions about what to export and what to import, and it can be completely arbitrary. Trade with other socialist countries works in essentially the same way, except that earnings from exports to another administered economy are not convertible in the way hard currency earned by exporting to a market economy is, ultimately because of the absence of goods convertibility. The rubles the Czechs earn by exporting machinery to the USSR cannot be exchanged for Soviet oil unless the Soviet planmakers specifically allocate oil for that purpose. This inflexibility has led to "bilateral balancing" in CMEA trade. Each country strives to make the value of its exports equal those of its imports *separately* for each of its socialist trading partners. One special twist is that the socialist countries have been unable to develop a system to generate an indigenous price system for goods being traded within the socialist market. The established practice has been to use the prices of the capitalist world market in these transactions, though over time a great deal of informal bargaining has opened up a considerable gap between the CMEA and world-market price structures.

At the other extreme lies the familiar pattern of trade among market-economy countries, in which any firm can decide what to import or export, these decisions being guided by prices and a meaningful exchange rate. There is convertibility at an exchange rate set in a foreign-exchange market. Since any currency can be changed into any other in these markets, trade between any given pair of countries need not balance—as long as a country's total earnings of foreign currency are enough to pay for its import needs, it need not be in balance with *individual* trade-partner countries. There are also international capital flows, transactions in which actors in one country buy the other country's currency not to pay for commodities but to buy assets, i.e., to invest. Such a system can exist only among countries with more or less completely market-directed economies. In such a system, macro policy levers may be used to influence the exchange rate— directly, or indirectly as a part of the general macroeffort at stabilization— and there may exist controls on certain kinds of international transactions, such as capital transfers. But the level, composition, and direction of foreign-trade flows are generally not controlled by any central body. In a reforming economy, the question is how fast and how far to shift from the centralized pole to the open-economy, market-directed pole of this spectrum.

Tasks of the Transition

A country might consider going all the way at once, simply declaring its currency convertible. This would mean letting it be bought and sold through the central bank, say, in unlimited amounts at the official rate, or letting it be bought and sold freely in a general market, accepting whatever rate emerges from supply and demand.[2] Such a decision implies

---

2. Market economies can operate under alternative exchange-rate regimes. One is a fixed-exchange-rate regime. In this regime, short-term fluctuations in exports and imports are not equilibrated by exchange-rate fluctuations, but by macrofluctuations and capital flows. Exchange rates are changed only when they become clearly inconsistent with longer-term equilibria. The alternative is for the authorities not to intervene in the foreign-exchange market, so that the value of the dollar in relation to the D-mark, say, will rise and fall in accordance with demand and supply. The reformers in socialist countries prefer the fixed-rate regime, and in what follows, the discussion will generally assume that the government tries to maintain something near a fixed rate.

a corollary: that purchasers of foreign currency could spend it without hindrance to buy foreign goods, and that the foreigner's right to buy the domestic currency would be coupled with the right to spend it on whatever goods he/she desired. But this is unlikely to happen.

First, such an approach would be extremely disruptive and destabilizing. The most fundamental obstacle to a quick transition to market rules in foreign trade is that the reforming economy has inherited a profoundly deformed production structure and price structure. In terms of the discussion of comparative advantage in chapter 4, it is producing a great deal of output in which it does not have a comparative advantage, with high domestic costs and prices. If the economy were opened to the world market, many enterprises would fail, and the people employed in them would lose their jobs. For other goods, low relative prices by world-market standards would make them attractive as exports, and (unless the exchange rate for the domestic currency is kept artificially high) these commodities would be drained away and hence become unavailable to domestic consumers. Ultimately the domestic structure of production would shift, and the resources thrown out of production in some industries would be absorbed in the industries stimulated by export demand. But these adjustments take time, and the heritage of inflexibility in the newly reforming economy would make them especially problematic. The reformers want to avoid these disruptions and effect the transition to a rational production and price structure over a time period long enough to permit firms and people to adjust.

As a second difficulty, making trade fully market-directed would be inconsistent with the other features of a half-reformed economy in which elements of central administration still coexist with market rules. Until marketization proceeds much further than in the usual halfway-house reform, the phenomena of independence for economic actors, profit motivation, and flexible market-equilibrating prices will not be pervasive and reliable enough to permit them to guide decisions about foreign trade. As for convertibility and a market-determined exchange rate, currency convertibility in the usual sense is not fully feasible. Currency convertibility rests on "goods convertibility," which does not yet exist throughout the economy, since the economy is still incompletely monetized.

In the semi-reformed economy, the usual first step in the foreign-trade area is to give some freedom to enterprises to choose between exporting their output or serving the domestic market, and in choosing whether to import inputs or buy them domestically. Usually, some of the foreign currency which enterprises earn by taking advantage of the freedom to export is left at their disposal. The spirit of the reform is to let enterprises make their own decisions about spending whatever hard-currency income they earn, as with any income. But some hard-currency income will continue to be channeled into the hands of the state, and will be distributed among possible imports and importers in the traditional centralized way. Hard-currency revenues and expenditures by enterprises freed to make their own decisions will certainly not match within each firm or even each industry. So the nation's supply of hard currency will be allocated among demanders in part via some central mechanism and in part via a market. Hard-currency earnings turned in to the State Bank at the official exchange rate would be allocated in some administrative way without regard to exchange rates, profit calculations, or any other market rules. If any is to be distributed via a market, the usual approach is to permit a free market in which those with more hard currency than they need can sell it to those who want to import. This market often takes the form of a hard-currency auction, supervised by the state. The auction generates a market exchange rate reflecting a calculation by many actors as to how many rubles a dollar (or other hard-currency unit) is worth for their purposes, given what can be purchased with a dollar compared to what could be purchased domestically with the rubles that must be exchanged to obtain a dollar. This rate is likely to depart sharply from the official exchange rate. In a semi-reformed economy such a free market process typically generates a value for the domestic currency much below current official rates. This market exchange rate will then influence some enterprises' choices between domestic and foreign sales and purchases.

Another inconsistency between full market-driven foreign-trade-cum-convertibility and the half-reformed institutions flows from the continued existence of CMEA trade. Even when an individual socialist country goes a long way toward marketization, as Hungary did, for example, in the early eighties, it is still likely to conduct a considerable share of its total trade with other socialist countries because of its membership in CMEA. The amount and composition of exports and imports to and from CMEA countries are determined as before in a bargaining process conducted by the center, and some central planning machinery must be used to see that CMEA export obligations are met, and that CMEA imports are absorbed domestically. This set of decisions will have to remain in a planned core or enclave within the economy. When CMEA as a system for binding the socialist countries to one another disappears, as it is scheduled to do by 1991, so will the problem. But it is an acute problem for the transition period.

The general problem of how to regulate the relationship between these two parts of the semi-reformed economy—one free and responding to market forces, the other still run by the administrative-command system—thus appears in the area of foreign-exchange relations as well.

Finally, a significant problem in marketizing foreign trade, opening up decisions about exports and imports to the influence of prices and the exchange rate, is that it is likely to expose the country to balance-of-payments problems. Typically, administered economies are tempted to set exchange rates that severely overvalue their currencies. In this situation, when the official exchange rate is used to translate the world-market price of a good into rubles, say, many foreign goods look cheap, and few seem to have world-market prices high enough to cover their high ruble costs if they were to be exported. In this situation export and import decisions based on profit calculations using the official exchange rate would lead to a large volume of imports and too few exports to pay for them. This is connected to the failure of the semi-reformed economy to solve the problem of establishing a hard-budget constraint in the early stages of reform. The excess aggregate demand that results from the soft-budget phenomenon spills over into the foreign balance, in the form of greater demand for imports than can be paid for by exports. (The U.S. is a good example of how this happens in a market economy experiencing excess aggregate demand.) A reforming administered economy thus typically faces the prospect that it will incur foreign indebtedness if it tries to maintain an overvalued currency, or that it will experience a serious depreciation of its currency if it lets it float. A foreign-trade deficit might be covered by loans from outside, but there may be serious disadvantages to letting the country go deeper and deeper into debt. Letting the exchange rate depreciate is an unwelcome course since that would make it more and more expensive to service whatever foreign debt the country has already accumulated. At a value for the ruble compared to the D-mark (2 rubles = 1 D-mark, say) it takes more rubles to pay 6 percent on a million D-marks of debt than if the rate of exchange were 1 ruble = 1 D-mark.

The upshot of the phenomena described is that foreign trade is likely to be one of the last aspects of a reforming economy to be fully marketized. Currency convertibility, the reforms intended to attract foreign capital and entrepreneurship that depend on it, a real exchange rate, and so on work with limited effect until the economy as a whole is marketized. The interesting and controversial problem is what form "semi-free trade," "semi-convertibility," and other beginnings of market-driven international economic relations can take in a semi-reformed economy. If full market-controlled international economic activity is not possible until the economy is fully reformed, what are the possibilities for "halfway" versions of such features in a half-reformed economy?

Compromises and Halfway Houses in Foreign Trade

CMEA Obligations

As indicated earlier, one of the halfway problems is that even if some trade flows are determined by decisionmakers at the enterprise level in response to the exchange rate, prices, and the profit criterion, trade flows with CMEA partners will be determined by the traditional central planning machinery. The first step is likely to be to treat the CMEA obligations by analogy with the *goszakaz* principle described in chapter 7, under which the central planners still set output and allocation targets for some goods. Export obligations will remain part of the *goszakaz*, and on the other side of the equation enterprises which receive their inputs by allocation from the center will find that part of those allocations consist of CMEA imports. This will work all right if all the usual export goods come from state-planned enterprises, and if this group can absorb all the imports. As the nonadministered sector expands and the centrally planned sector shrinks, this cannot remain the case, and the Foreign Trade Ministry will have to scrounge for export goods via the market and peddle the goods it imports from CMEA for what it can get. In the process it is likely to find that the ruble cost of its exports exceeds the ruble value of its imports, requiring a subsidy. This is how general excess demand spills over into the external balance.

The interesting result here is that if the marketized part of the domestic economy has come into a reasonable equilibrium with the world-market prices, then the country's foreign-trade responsibility toward the other CMEA countries need have nothing to do with the domestic economy. The foreign-trade agency could as well meet its CMEA export commitments by buying on the world market as on the domestic market, and similarly dispose of its imports from CMEA countries. In this case, the Hungarian foreign-trade agency, to make the case concrete, would become an agent of its CMEA partners, with no necessary connection to its own marketizing country.

Convertibility, the Exchange Rate, and the Dual Economy

In trying to make the transition to a real exchange rate and convertibility, the reformers always start out very gingerly. As they move toward local enterprise decisionmaking as regards exports and imports, the first action on the exchange rate is usually to differentiate it in application to different commodities and industries so as to cushion the impact of exposure to the world market. Enterprises that shift to a profit-guided regime will find that some goods they exported in the past are not profitable, because they are too expensive domestically. Very high-cost producers would find that they could not compete with imported goods and so would suffer losses and have to close down. Producers of goods that are underpriced domestically will see big profits from shifting their activity from supplying domestic customers to exporting. So as the first step the reformers are likely to introduce special coefficients that modify the impact of the official exchange rate as it applies to different firms, sectors, and products.[3] The goal is to differentiate the rates so that the profit-motivated choices about trade will not be much different from the planner-directed choices of the

---

3. These coefficients are used to correct the official exchange rate as it is applied to different exports and imports, so we can think of the coefficient system as a system of differentiated exchange rates.

past. Succeeding steps move gradually toward unifying the exchange rate, or reducing the spread of the coefficients. The move toward a unified exchange rate is usually accompanied by some devaluation of the original arbitrary official rate to a more realistic value. At the same time the reformers revise somewhat the domestic price system, setting prices on some goods to reflect world-market prices (domestic price = world price converted at the exchange rate) or establishing a formula that tells the enterprise that in exercising whatever price-setting freedom it may have acquired, it can set the price it charges domestically at something like the world-market price converted at the official exchange rate. They may also put a twist on this formula to enhance the profitability of exporting, or to enhance the attractiveness of buying inputs domestically rather than importing them.

The variables and issues in this approach can be illustrated by what the Hungarians did. Their goal was to accept the external prices as real and let them rule the internal price system. Since the Hungarian economy is very small in the world as a whole, it is always a pricetaker. The external world-market prices *do* represent real tradeoff possibilities available to domestic decisionmakers, and those prices will not change as Hungarian sellers and buyers make their internal decisions.[4]

Under this system, a manufacturer could export goods and receive in forints the world-market price times the exchange rate. If he wanted to sell the same output on the domestic market, he could sell it at a forint price covering the domestic cost plus an average profit markup equal to that earned on exports. That made him indifferent between the two. This rule applied only to firms that exported at least 5 percent of their output to hard-currency markets, and other producers of those products had their prices tied to the prices of exporters. Raw materials (in Hungary these were for the most part imported) were priced domestically at the world-market price times the exchange rate. For other imports the general rule was to use the foreign price converted at the official rate plus tariff and transport. Domestic producers of these goods selling them internally could charge up to the price of the imported good. They set an exchange rate

---

4. This whole system was intended to apply mostly to tradeable goods, and affected prices of nontraded goods only indirectly.

fixed more or less on the grounds of purchasing-power parity for tradeables, and adjusted from time to time in relation to a basket of hard currencies as external prices changed. The general impact of this system was to confront Hungarian buyers and sellers with a domestic price system that was close to world-market prices and, as a corollary, to make them indifferent between selling or buying on the world market or the domestic market. That is, it was a way to let the tradeoff possibilities embodied in world-market prices drive Hungarian producers into levels of production compatible with the principle of comparative advantage.

But this system was not fully applied. Because the planners did not want to accept the unemployment and the output shifts that would take place as these conditions made some enterprises unprofitable, they used subsidies to existing exporters who could not survive under these rules. Or in case a devaluation raised the prices of imports, and so made some import-using line of production unprofitable, the government might subsidize it. So the price guidance and disciplinary effect and the potentials of gains from the right choice of exports and imports were somewhat attenuated in favor of preventing dislocation. On the other side the price formula meant that a devaluation did not increase the attraction from export, since the *domestic* price could be raised to the same level, which circumscribed the usefulness of exchange-rate manipulation to achieve balance in the external account.

The Hungarians' situation was complicated by the fact that about half of their trade has been with other socialist countries, settled in transferable rubles. As explained above, that trade is fairly heavily directed from the top, in regard to both which firms are to supply the goods and which are supposed to absorb the imports. Given arbitrariness in choosing these exports and imports and the peculiarity of CMEA pricing, the profitability of these goods to the user or producer turns out to be highly variable. That means that in terms of profit, participation in some exports is desirable, in others undesirable, and the situation is similar for absorbing imports.

Without going into all the details, it is obvious from this description that an enterprise's choice as to whether to export a good to the capitalist market, sell it domestically, or sell it for rubles, and whether to buy an input domestically, from ruble sources, or from hard-currency sources, is a complex mix of the relative profitabilities, the possible existence of subsidies, and the likelihood of getting a license, or of getting a specific assignment with respect to ruble trade. So the outcome is a good illustration of our earlier point that control via economic levers may be unpredictable in its impact on outcomes, and internally contradictory. It is difficult to design a set of equipment for a pool game in which the loading of balls, warping of cues, and waviness of the table will neatly counteract a player's astigmatism to enable him to get the balls into the pockets as easily as in the normal game.

The Hungarian case is also a good illustration of the interaction of the system reform with the external environment and with economic policy. The compromise system created by Hungarian policymakers in the first half of the eighties intended to permit them to maintain half their trade with CMEA, with corresponding implications for the domestic output structure, and to let the trade with the West be guided by a market-mimicking set of economic levers. They were hurt by the terms of trade for the structure of trade that policy created as the prices on the goods Hungary exported fell relative to prices on the goods it imported. This can be thought of as a reduction in real income, and the policymakers' response was to accept a deficit in the hard-currency balance of payments. The policy response to this adverse shift in terms of trade was not to shift structure much, redirect trade between the two halves, or seek equilibrium via exchange-rate changes. The application of all the administrative instruments—quotas, investment incentives, exchange-rate devaluations, subsidies, suasion, etc.—kept them from really letting price and comparative advantage enhance earnings from trade. The continual crisis led to the reimposition of more and more direct centralized policy instruments that distorted structure, composition, and volume of trade and allocation of resources away from a market-dictated pattern.

What the Soviet Union did in the first stages of its foreign-trade reform can provide another concrete case of temporizing reform. Beginning January 1, 1987, a select set of enterprises received the right to export on their own, and were allowed to keep part of their hard-currency earnings, to be spent at their own discretion. These enterprises were allowed, in effect, to make their own decisions about amounts to export and import. As of April 1, 1989, this right was extended in principle to all enterprises. Unfortunately, that was essentially a hollow right, because of a requirement to get licenses to import, because of prohibitions on exporting and importing certain goods, or because getting hard currency to *finance* the imports one has the formal right to buy is still an administered process. There was still no foreign-exchange market in which a would-be Soviet importer could exchange rubles for hard currency. In the beginning the reformers kept the old official exchange rate (about $1.60 per ruble) but introduced highly differentiated coefficients (nearly three thousand of them, ranging from .3 to 6) to produce in effect a highly differentiated exchange rate. Thus while one producer might be able to earn a ruble by exporting goods salable on the world market for 48 cents, another would have to sell goods worth $9.60 to earn a ruble. It was intended that in 1990 the differentiation would be reduced to three rates, applicable to different kinds of transactions, but with essentially a unified rate for all decisions about goods trade. The new unified rate was to involve a significant devaluation, roughly halving the old official rate for the ruble. The timetable for this change originally envisaged the new system being in place by 1990, but it has been significantly postponed. One of the new exchange rates *was* introduced in 1989, namely, a very low value of the ruble for household transactions. A Soviet citizen who wanted to get hard currency to travel abroad no longer got $1.60 for the ruble but only 16 cents, and vice versa for foreign tourists. But this exchange rate was limited in its application since the prices most foreign visitors had to pay such as hotel bills continued to be quoted in dollars at prices that did not pass on the gain from the devaluation.

At about the same time a currency auction was introduced, which generated a free-market rate for the ruble. We can use this case to illustrate the function of a currency auction. For the first auction in 1989, firms were invited to offer hard currency for sale, indicating the amounts they wanted to sell and the exchange rates they would accept, and analogous bids were invited from those who wanted to buy hard currency. How such an auction would work is shown in figure 8-1, which should be read as follows. Starting up the dollar offer curve, we see that someone has placed an offer to trade $1M for 1 MR. That is, at the exchange rate of 1 R/$1 he is willing to sell $1M. Proceeding up the staircase, there are two offers, each of which says the seller of dollars will accept 1.5 MR for $1M, three offers each to accept 2 MR in exchange for $1M, and so on. After sorting

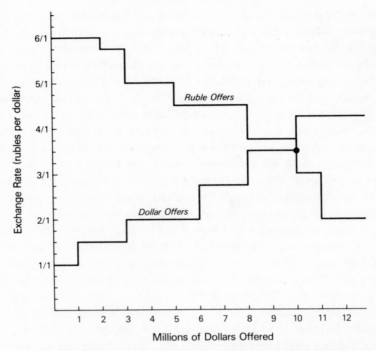

Figure 8-1. Supply and Demand in a Currency Auction

the offers to *buy* dollars, we see that some buyers are so desperate to obtain dollars that they are willing to give up 6 rubles for each dollar they get. The next-best offer on this side of the market is from a dollar demander willing to pay as much as 5.75 MR to obtain $1M, and so on.

Figure 8-1 is a kind of supply/demand diagram. We find that the bids to take dollars at an exchange rate of 3.50 R/$1 or more total $10M, and the offers from enterprises willing to sell dollars at any price up to 3.50 R/$1 total $10M. So all the people to the *left* of the $10M mark on the horizontal scale can be satisfied. Everyone to the right of that mark has to go home without having been able to make a trade. Those who did not succeed in changing their rubles into dollars are content to take their rubles home, because the dollars they could have gotten from some would-be seller cannot do as much for them in terms of meeting their goals (imagine that for the actors in this semi-reformed system the goal is profits) as the rubles they kept. The argument is the same for those who did not sell their dollars.

In this diagram there is a *clearing exchange rate* (3.50 R per $1), and a trade volume of $10M. One way to run this auction would be to fill all the orders at that clearing rate. In that case some people would get a bargain—the person who was so eager to get dollars that he was willing to pay 6 R/$1 would get them at 3.50 R/$1. In line with the argument above, this trader would get a windfall. Next time around the price might change a bit. Some people who did not consider that it might have been to their advantage to participate might come in as sellers once they see what the going price is, and the same is true on the buying side. As time goes on a rate will emerge which people will use in their calculations. We can imagine an enterprise purchasing official saying, "Well, if I can buy hard currency at a rate of 3.50 rubles per dollar, and I can buy tires, polyethylene [or whatever inputs he needs for production] abroad at such and such a hard-currency price, that will be better than buying them domestically."[5]

The exchange rate that emerges from such an auction might be far

---

5. An interesting footnote here is that the Soviets decided to organize this auction in what seems an economically illiterate way. The rule for their auction is to fill bids not at the clearing price but at the offer price. That is, the party who offered 6 MR for $1M will pay that amount, and the one who was willing to sell $1M at 1 R/$1 will get 1 MR for them. On this transaction the auction committee as broker will net 5 MR. We can figure that for all the matches it can make, the auction committee will collect from the buyers 48.75 MR, and will have to pay the sellers of dollars only 22.5 MR, keeping the other 26.25 MR for itself. This is interesting as an example of the state as monopolist, which we have seen in other contexts, as well as a long-standing proclivity in the administered economy. The planners' mentality is to extract all surpluses for the state.

From the economists' point of view, that is thoroughly misguided—the goal of this auction is not to enrich the state but to generate information, i.e., a price that tells all the decision-makers out there what the value of a dollar's worth of imports is in replacing domestic goods for the last use in which it is worthwhile. Then anyone can see if he/she is making the right choices about using domestic vs. foreign inputs, or selling her/his product domestically or abroad. But the auction committee did not even announce the clearing price, which is the whole purpose of this exercise.

Moreover, it is a very shortsighted kind of approach, as we can see if we think of the auction as an ongoing institution. Next time around the offers would likely be a lot flatter—if someone who paid 6 R/$1 hears that someone else got dollars at 3.50 R/$1, he will figure that in the next round he can still get dollars even if he offers less than last time. So the auction committee is unlikely to be able to make this monopoly profit a permanent thing.

different from the official exchange rate—suppose it is a lower value for the ruble than the official rate. Then in the *other* channel for distributing dollars earned from exports, i.e., where the state collects and allocates foreign currency at the official rate, some people may get dollars at a bargain, others may be required to turn them in when they have a better use than the last enterprise that got some. That is the nature of arbitrary allocation from the center.

One feasible halfway measure between the old system and full convertibility might be to make the domestic currency convertible for limited classes of transactions. One important example would be to let foreign firms or foreign investors in joint ventures operate under something close to market rules. Among other things, they would be allowed to freely exchange currency either way for any kind of transaction, including export of output, purchase of equipment and materials abroad, repatriation of profits, and so on. A narrower option would be to permit them this free convertibility only to repatriate profits. Any such actor would thus have a firm operating with two kinds of currencies—domestic rubles for purchase of labor, sales on the domestic market, etc., and foreign currency for exports, imports, etc. To figure what the firm's profit is, the joint-venture entrepreneur has to have an exchange rate, and the state would have to set it so that it was advantageous to operate. There is no reason to believe that an exchange rate that would do that is the same rate that makes demand for dollars equal to the offering of dollars for rubles in a thin auction in which very few firms participate, and the state might have to intervene in this free market with dollars earned by enterprises in the state-planned sector.

Given the impossibility of going to full convertibility immediately, another compromise is the idea of a parallel currency, a "hard" ruble that would be real money internally (i.e., it would fit the definition of money as anything generally spendable for goods, services, and obligations, and so satisfy the goods convertibility criterion) and that would be convertible to foreign currency at a rate fixed by the state. In effect it would be the currency of the market-based part of the half-reformed economy. Its exchange rate would have to be set at an equilibrating level, and its supply would grow as the reform spread.

The problem is in defining the new economy within which this hard ruble would be used as the transactions medium—what firms would use this kind of money, how it would be introduced, and in what kind of transactions it would be used. The basic idea is that the state would offer it in exchange for the old ruble to any comer at a high premium; it would cost lots of old rubles to get one of the new. It would circulate internally at a rate at least that high. Persons with the right to sell under market rules, i.e., anyone outside the state-planned sector, who could choose their own customers and negotiate for as high a price as they could get, could ask for payment in the hard ruble, and those operating in a setting where they received hard rubles would have an advantage in acquiring goods. This currency would meet the needs of foreigners. Any product from a joint venture which they sold abroad, any hard-currency contributions they made to a joint venture, could be translated into the hard ruble, and they could repatriate soft-ruble profits by buying the hard ruble at the going soft/hard rate, and into their own currency at the fixed foreign-exchange rate for the hard ruble. Since the hard ruble would be convertible, the demand for it would be like the demand for dollars in the auction described above. Eventually the government might ask that taxes be paid in hard rubles, and might itself use them to pay for certain government purchases, including *goszakaz* purchases. As the share of the two economies changed, the demand for the old ruble would fall and its value would decline, a process the authorities could hurry along by issuing more of the soft rubles while controlling the output of the hard ruble. Citizens might be permitted to own hard rubles, and there could be certain kinds of transactions in which they would be paid in them. I have in mind something like the current system of offering collective farmers hard currency in exchange for obligatory deliveries of agricultural products above past levels of deliveries. Households could own this currency, as an option to holding the soft currency. As marketization proceeds, eventually they could use it to buy foreign goods.

Something just like this happened in the Polish economy, except that the Poles simply used the dollar to serve this purpose instead of introducing an "ersatz dollar" in the form of a "hard zloty." Polish citizens have for some time been allowed to own dollars and other hard currency, buy dollars at a special rate from the savings bank, and spend them for foreign goods in special stores, i.e., the PEWEX stores in which goods were sold only for hard currency. After the introduction of radical reforms in 1990, this interchangeability of hard currency and the zloty became even simpler, and in the Polish economy today in its significantly marketized form, foreign currency circulates about as freely as zlotys.

The problem with the parallel currency idea is that it just moves the convertibility frontier back within the domestic economy. In terms of the original sectoring diagram in chapter 7, a portion of the old SPE becomes an enclave within the economy or is shifted to the "private or market" sector and is allowed to function as if it were a bit of the world market, but within the borders of the socialist country. This enclave may be defined in terms of particular kinds of property (e.g., all forms except land) or some kinds of transactions (e.g., transactions on current account only, meaning that one could buy dollars for any purpose except to export one's savings), or perhaps on a territorial basis (e.g., *any* activity on the territory of the three Baltic nations). The convertibility problem that formerly applied to the whole SPE as it faced the rest of the world is shifted back to the interface between the enclave and the remaining unreformed portions of the economy. The planners who still ran the latter would have to figure out what exchange rate they wanted to set between the two currencies, but it would be artificial. They would determine what "imports" they would acquire from it for use in the SPE, what outputs of the SPE state-administered economy would be sold to pay for those imports, and so on.

But this would be a transitional form that would work, and as time passed more and more enterprises, more and more transactions, could be transferred to the rules that operate in the reformed part of the economy. The reformed part could still not be allowed to have access to outputs, or sell goods to enterprises in the nonreformed process. The process would operate exactly as in the original SPE, but now not over the Soviet border, but over the frontier between the old economy and the new economy.

The Chinese adopted this approach in the form of free economic zones, which became in some respects as open to the international economy as to the mainland Chinese economy. The USSR began in 1990 a timid experiment with the establishment of three "special economic zones" in Nakhodka (on the Pacific rim), Vyborg (on the Finnish border), and Novgorod.

This "enclave" way of thinking about the process is helpful in understanding what may become an important part of the economic reform in the USSR as time passes. If some of the national regions in the USSR really manage to obtain economic independence, including the right to issue their own currency, they would be a good example of the kind of enclave described above. This might happen in the Baltic states or other regions in the USSR. Elsewhere in the socialist world it could happen with Slovenia in Yugoslavia, though it might be simpler for the Slovenes just to drop the dinar altogether and use some foreign currency, such as the Austrian schilling or the D-mark, for all transactions.

There has been a confused argument about whether the Baltic region or other small units within the USSR could survive as separate economies. A full analysis of the issues involved is probably inappropriate here. A country such as Lithuania obviously could not survive as an autarkic unit, and any such small unit is vulnerable to economic sanctions like those the USSR did indeed impose on Lithuania. There is a problem here analogous to that of disentangling Hungary from CMEA. But the above discussion suggests that Lithuania's economic relations with the rest of the USSR could be like those of any independent country, or like those of a reformed enclave nominally within the old USSR. We know from the discussion of foreign trade in the administered economy in chapter 4 that when one of the partners is an administered economy, its clumsiness and "trade aversion" inhibit close relations and an optimal level of trade. The calculations and negotiations involve extensive transactions cost. Since this kind of trade fails to generate as much trade as is optimal, the Soviet side would still fail to get all the benefits from trade with Lithuania that foreign trade would normally offer. But if economically independent from the USSR, Lithuania (or other separatist enclaves) could seek its trading partners in many other places in the world, and if its economy had been reformed to become really flexible and market-directed, it could thrive as many small nations do. This is even more the case for the three Baltic nations taken together. They have a population of about eight million people, which is larger than that of Belgium, Finland, Austria, or many other small nations which manage quite successfully. The transition might be rough, but the end result could be an improvement in terms of economic productivity and welfare.

Household Behavior and the Foreign Sector

Another step in marketizing is to allow individual households as well as enterprises to own foreign currency (or the hard version of the domestic currency), to bid for it in some kind of market, and to spend it as they want. This would mean, in terms of figure 7-1, drawing in full market links between households and the rest of the world. This is likely to be one of the last steps in marketizing international economic relations. But as foreign trade becomes marketized (say by the enclave approach), it is desirable to let households have some access to the new currency (as pay for working in the new sector, for example), and to let them spend it for goods from this sector. Since the market sector is open to the world economy, this implies giving households access to the foreign balance. This adds a new dimension to the consumer-sovereignty aspect of the earlier discussion of the rules for pricing in the household-SPE relationship. Giving households access to the world market is economically rational. If the designers of the reform do not let households have the choice of allocating their income between domestic and foreign goods and services as well as among various kinds of domestic goods, one of the household-expenditure rules is violated. Remember that the rule was that relative prices were to equal relative costs, and if households have access to world markets, relative prices on tradeables should come into equilibrium with world-market prices. Failure to honor this rationale in an open economy has the same consequences for diminishing efficiency as in the closed economy. This would be another example where the planners lose control over an aspect of allocation. They could no longer control the composition of imports as between consumer goods, intermediate producer goods, and investment goods, and we can expect that they would object that their ability to use the country's hard-currency earnings in the way that best meets society's needs was being infringed. But of course that is just another version of the conceit that central planners know the best allocations without having to make them pass the test of market forces.

The conflict of planners' notions of what is best for the country and individuals' notions of what is best for them arises in many contexts, of course. One of the most confusing cases, which falls under the heading of international economic relations, is the current agonizing in many socialist countries over the threat of a brain drain. As soon as political reform began to make it possible, many of the best scientists in these countries sought to emigrate. An individual can take advantage of some of the tradeoffs that are announced in the form of world-market prices only by moving physically across national borders. A talented Soviet mathematician can sell his skills to an institution of the SPE for rubles at a certain rate. If the economy is marketized in its international trade activities, he could decide that the rubles will give him more satisfaction converted to yen and spent on a Japanese VCR than on domestic caviar. But this is still not the best outcome. If he is allowed to sell his skills to an American university, the dollars he earns (and the D-marks or yen into which they can be converted) buy him a lot more western consumer goods than the previous bargain would. This is true even if the SPE follows the rule of paying him as many rubles as he is worth. The reason is that the SPE is unable to fully utilize his potential. There is a temptation to think that the USSR loses something by letting the mathematician take advantage of this opportunity to increase the payoff to his abilities. But this involves a deep-seated fallacy incompatible with the ideas of universal humanist values and a global perspective that is part of the "new thinking" that underlies *perestroika* and economic reform. If the mathematician is allowed to take advantage of that opportunity, the total output and welfare of the world as a whole are increased, probably by more than the increase in the welfare of the mathematician alone. If the state can see itself as responsible for the welfare of all the people who happen to be born within its borders, the movement of the mathematician has helped, not hindered, it in realizing this goal.

Another interesting problem at the intersection of convertibility and households' relation to the external market is letting citizens of one socialist country cross the borders of another as tourists. Such tourists have generally been allowed to convert some money. Suppose Czechs can visit Poland and buy zlotys, and vice versa for the Poles. Since the price structures differ, some Polish goods look cheap to the Czech tourists, and some Czech goods look cheap to the Polish tourists. So there is a mutual stripping of shelves, and anguished cries to stop this thievery by the foreigners. In response to a similar phenomenon in which Soviet stores along the border with Eastern Europe were stripped of goods for sale across the border in those marketizing economies, the Soviet government made it illegal to export consumer goods. If the stores in *each* country operated in a market-driven sector, the prices would move in a way to eliminate this problem.

A final aspect of giving households access to the foreign sector via convertibility that might be mentioned is that it complicates the demand-for-money issue. If households can exchange the domestic currency for the hard currency, they will have a choice about how to hold their assets. In the usual situation, when currency emission is not controlled and people have more money than they feel comfortable holding, convertibility gives them another choice—holding their cash in the form of foreign currency. This will be another influence on the exchange rate, and will transmit excess demand domestically into pressure on the balance of payments.

Our analysis of the foreign-trade aspect of reform has covered this complex topic only in part. But in addition to specific issues, it also illustrates well a fundamental dilemma of the transition. There are many kinds of markets—foreign-exchange markets, financial-asset markets, producer-goods markets, labor markets, etc. All are interconnected, and reform in the form of marketization should ultimately embrace them all. When the economy is only half-reformed, if marketization has not been comprehensive, the result is an "interface problem," which involves some loss of efficiency or welfare. The essence of economics is that everything is connected to everything else. As markets are added, the market/nonmarket interface shifts. In this case, for example, opening an enclave to the world market shifts the issue of convertibility from the national border to the enclave/SPE border. But *wherever* there is a market/nonmarket interface, the inefficiencies in the nonmarket sector have to be preserved by blocking signals from the market sector, and by ensuring isolation of the two with some kind of administrative interference. If one tries to isolate the markets in this way (if households can spend their incomes on whatever they want, except for foreign goods because they cannot get hard currency as in the above discussion), then the result is some violation of an efficiency or welfare condition. The economy that is only half-converted to market principles is only halfway to efficiency.

9.
Property, Ownership, Privatization

The socialist system has primitive arrangements for stewardship of "property," or what a Marxist would call "the means of production." In a socialist society, the means of production are owned by the state on behalf of and in the name of the working class. Unfortunately, the state and its agents have proved to be feckless stewards in managing that property.

The priests of socialist thought have an ideological hangup about this issue, having always treated "public ownership of the means of production" as the *sine qua non* of the socialist order. But many reformers both in Eastern Europe and in the USSR have come to see that ritual assertion of the primacy of state ownership as a hallmark of socialism ignores the question of effective use of that wealth for the good of the working class.

A more pragmatic approach to ownership and property has become an important element in reform programs throughout the socialist world. Many new departures have been suggested and debated. One route is to retain *public* ownership but decentralize it to lower-level governments. Another is to lease state-owned assets to individuals or collectives to operate them. The idea of complete privatization has also gained many supporters. This may mean letting individuals form private enterprises, and own and operate them like any private capitalist in the market economy. It would also include selling off existing enterprises and other assets to private individuals. The activities of co-ops, a form which might be thought of as a kind of small-group private ownership, have been expanded. These alternative forms of ownership imply the creation of various kinds of financial instruments and contracts to permit the shifting of some of the functions associated with ownership to private individuals and institutions.

One example is the creation of joint-stock companies either as completely new entities or by conversion of existing state enterprises to corporations issuing stocks that individuals might own. Stock ownership would give the owners certain rights with respect to control of the enterprise and claims against any profit it earned. Ultimately, the rights embodied in these various kinds of contracts such as leases, stock ownership, tenure rights for use of land, etc., ought to be transferable, i.e., salable to other parties. Thus, marketization of property rights is another dimension in a general shift toward the market principle.

How to understand ownership and devise some alternatives to state ownership is an important part of the debate on reform in the socialist countries. It did not arise in the first stages of the discussion, but toward the end of the eighties it became a hotly debated topic. Many elements of privatization have begun to be introduced in these countries, and Hungary and Poland, in particular, embarked on far-reaching privatization programs in the early nineties. In the Soviet Union privatization was introduced into the reform debate at a fairly early stage in its elaboration, and timid experiments with the new forms were undertaken from the first stages of the reform. "Privatization" and "private property" are uncomfortable words for the socialists, and they employ all kinds of euphemisms for these concepts. To avoid saying "private property," the Soviets introduced the term "citizens' property" (*sobstvennost' grazhdan*), and before the term *privatizatsiia* was accepted, they created and used the euphemism "de-etatization" (*razgosudarstvlenie*) of ownership. Better understanding of the functions of ownership will probably eventually result in extensive institutional and policy reforms in this area in all the reforming socialist societies.

I want to talk in this chapter about "ownership," "property," "claims," "equities," and other concepts associated with managing the "means of production," in two stages. The first lays some theoretical and conceptual foundations regarding the functions of property, ownership claims, equity, and so on. The second stage takes up the issue of what the socialist economies are doing to institutionalize a shift from state and collective property in the means of production to more flexible approaches to ownership.

Theoretical Considerations

The concept of ownership is a slippery one, as indicated by the many different terms we use to deal with it. In addition to ownership and property (what is the difference between those two ideas anyway?) we also talk about assets, equity versus other forms of claims against the income of a firm, property in the form of physical assets, such as land or a factory, and property in the form of financial instruments, such as stocks and bonds. Russian, by the way, has an equally complex set of terms connected with property and ownership.

Property as a Bundle of Rights

The key to understanding what is involved here lies in recognizing that ownership is a "bundle of rights," or a complex of functions with respect to property. Some of the important rights in this bundle might be listed as follows:

1. the right to appropriate the income generated by property;
2. the right to control or manage productive assets;
3. the right to transfer and dispose of assets—by sale, lease, bequeathal, etc.;
4. the right to trade in—buy and sell—these rights;
5. the right to acquire or assemble assets and devote them to organized productive activity, including the formation of new firms.

In addition, it is sometimes useful to think of property rights that exist outside ownership of or claims against specific productive assets, such as worker or citizen *entitlements*, or the perks associated with bureaucratic position. For example, the bureaucrat's or professor's assurance of tenure is a kind of property right.

An "unbundling" of ownership rights can be accomplished by means of contracts, such as leasing, or the more complicated forms of claims on assets characteristic of capitalist economies. This unbundling permits specialization among parties in the various functions and responsibilities of ownership. We can separate ownership in the sense of title to assets from the function of controlling and managing them, and can separate control over use of assets from rights to receive income from them. The owner of land may give up control over its use to someone else, retaining only the right to claim the income from it, through a lease or other tenure and income-dividing arrangements such as sharecropping. The stockholder-owners of a corporation may borrow from other sources of finance (such as bankers or bondholders) under a contract that does not give the lenders any say in the management of the property, but does give them an unconditional claim against the income from the property in the form of interest payments. There are voting and nonvoting forms of stock. The economist Henry George proposed a single tax—a tax on land—under which land would still be private property, with the owner retaining most of the rights of any property owner, except that any capital appreciation, as "unearned" income, would be appropriated by the state on behalf of society as a whole. This specialization among agents in exercising the various functions of ownership is very important for efficient production. Moreover, it is possible to stipulate that the rights laid out in the contracts may be transferred to others, which means that some of the rights associated with ownership can be marketized. For example, the bonds that represent a claim on an enterprise's income can be bought and sold just as onions are bought and sold.

The important distinction we have learned to make among the various members of the coalition with a stake in the economic activity of a productive entity (the customers for its output, the suppliers of produced inputs, those who contribute land, the workers, the various classes of owners) is between those who have their claims determined in a market and a "residual claimant," i.e., the party whose income consists of whatever is left after all those claims are settled. That party is sometimes also described as the equity holder, a rent-seeker, or a net-worth maximizer. The income of the firm and some of the claims on that income are settled in markets. The gross revenue of the firm is determined by the prices it can charge. That revenue gets distributed to some of those who contribute to the firm's activity on the basis of market valuations—such as market prices for purchased inputs, interest on capital to banks or bondholders at the going interest rate, compensation to routine management at the going rate for those skills. With most of the interactions with the rest of the economy settled at market prices, the income of the "owner" of the firm is the residual—positive or negative. This residual income is associated with an exceptionally important function, namely, ownership interpreted as the risk-bearing and entrepreneurial function. Property income, or "economic profit" as it is often called, is the return to those functions. As the residual claimant, the owner is the party with the greatest interest in the effective use of the property, and the rationale for property income is to link income with the right to have the final say in strategic decisions about the activity of the firm, the disposition of its property, the right to contract out some other functions.

Some Soviet economists understand this way of thinking about ownership clearly enough. The person chosen at one point to design and implement economic reform in the USSR, Leonid Abalkin, distinguishes clearly in one of his statements between the right to appropriate the surplus value created by capital, and the right or function of "control," i.e., managing the use of property.[1] Abalkin goes so far as to say that the difference between managerial income (one of the routine, market-valued payments) and entrepreneurial income familiar in the analysis of market economies can have an analog in socialist economies.

Socialist Attitudes toward Property and Ownership

In the history of socialist thought, socialists never had much use for the ideas of entrepreneurship or riskbearing, and have always scoffed at explanations of profit and property income that depend on them. They equate property and ownership almost exclusively with the mere *appropriation* of income, not based on any real *functional* justification. This attitude was unequivocally summed up in Proudhon's famous slogan "Property is theft." Even the more enlightened and more economically sophisticated

---

1. *Kommunist*, 1989:10. Beginning in 1989 nearly every issue of any economic journal had at least one article on issues of property, and proponents of a private-property approach have their say frequently in articles in the central press. A big conference to try to work out a position on ownership was held in spring 1989. The reform-minded sociologist Tatiana Zaslavskaia says we have to have many forms of property. Oleg Bogomolov, an important figure in the radical reform camp, asks what is wrong with the desire of an individual to have a bit of land on which to build a house. But again one of the most direct and clearly stated sets of ideas by the reformers is what Abalkin and Petrakov said in their conference with the Czechs in an article in *Kommunist*, 1989:11.

socialists such as Oskar Lange and others who tried to develop an "economics of market socialism" in the thirties had little appreciation of the role of ownership. In the theory of market socialism developed by Lange, management of the socialist enterprise was just a specialized form of labor, and the other ownership functions discussed above were handled by the state or the planners at the center. Central planning *eliminated* riskbearing, it was thought, and hence the need for a return to entrepreneurial responsibility. The founding of new enterprises and indeed *all* investment decisions were in the hands of the Planning Board. The center would collect all non–labor factor incomes and use them on behalf of society. Ludwig von Mises, one of Oskar Lange's opponents in the famous debate over the feasibility of socialism, likened the notion of socialist managers acting as real entrepreneurs to boys playing with trains as an imitation of the real thing. Without the spur of real ownership they would be a pale imitation of real capitalist owners. Lenin was similarly naive about the role of ownership—he had the notion that once socialism was established, and the working class had rid itself of the capitalists, the management of productive assets would be a simple routine job. He asserted in a famous passage in his work *State and Revolution* that the administration of socialist firms would be no more complicated than running the post office.

Stewardship of Property in the Soviet-type Economy

Decades of experience have demonstrated that the socialist state and the bureaucracy through which it administers the economy are *not* capable of this stewardship function that socialist theory assigned them. The center is inept and clumsy in performing the role of entrepreneur. It is slow to see opportunities to start new firms and new lines of production, and is wary in exercising another function of the entrepreneur—what Schumpeter called "creative destruction." It is reluctant to discard or abandon property, or to license activities that will undercut the routinized use of existing property. The central organs of the administered economy have too little information to really manage the use of productive assets in detail, and they hand this function over to the bureaucrat/managers, who might be considered stewards of the state in this task. The problem is that these stewards are *not* motivated to ensure that property is used in the most

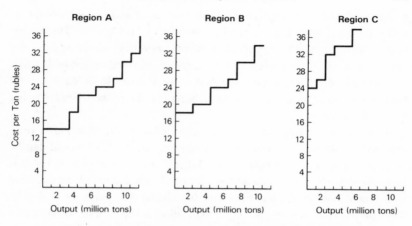

Figure 9-1. Marginal Cost Pricing and Differential Rent

productive way. Their reward system does not motivate them to take the long view or to seek to maximize net worth or capital appreciation.

The socialist state, which claimed the prerogative of exercising ownership rights over natural resources as one element of the means of production, never understood how to appropriate the income from the use of those resources. More fundamentally, it more or less denied that there was an income there to be appropriated. This point is worth a short excursus. Natural resources (such as agricultural land, or deposits of coal underground) are productive, and have value as a consequence of their ability to increase society's output. The income associated with these forms of property is called rent. There are different ways to understand rent, but let us consider the case of "differential rent" in the oil industry, or in agriculture. Pieces of land or deposits of mineral resources situated differently have differential capability to add to society's output. This superior capacity of some natural resources may lie in fertility, richness, location, or ease of utilization. In figure 9-1, there are several oil-producing regions from which the demand for oil (or the socialist production plan) could be met. The steplike lines are marginal cost curves showing the cost to produce various amounts of oil. In region A, if it were decided to produce at a rate of only 3 million tons per year, the cost per ton would be 14 rubles. But if the region is to produce at a higher rate, producers will have to resort to expensive measures that will make the cost of an additional million tons a year (making total output 4 million tons/year) 18 rubles/ton. This higher cost for additional output (a phenomenon economists call rising marginal cost) may result from having to use expensive stimulation methods (such as injection of gas or surfactants) that make it possible to leave less oil behind, or from having to tap deeper horizons. There is a similar rising cost curve in each region.

If it is necessary to produce a total output of only 3 million tons a year, obviously it should all come from region A, where this amount can be produced at a cost of 14 rubles/ton. But if 6 million tons/year is needed, it would be a mistake to get it all from region A, since some of the marginal tons would cost more than oil from the alternative source in region B. The approach, obviously, as the planners allocate the total production plan among regions should be to distribute output so as to make the cost at the margin equal—that will assure that the total is produced at the lowest cost. If the total production plan were 18 million tons, it should be assigned as 9 million tons from region A, 7 million tons from region B, and 2 million tons from the very high-cost fields in region C. The marginal cost, i.e., the cost/ton of the last million tons from each region in this case, would be 26 rubles. To depart from this pattern, reducing output from any region and compensating by increasing output in another, would raise the total outlay required to produce the 18 million tons.

A second implication of this situation is that *the price for oil should be set at this marginal cost*. Such a price would convey a message to anyone considering doing something that takes some extra oil (as in one of the projectmaking calculations we considered in chapter 3) that any decision requiring the production of another ton of oil will cost society 26 rubles' worth of resources. Similarly, if anyone has some idea for saving oil, and wants to know whether it is worth the cost of doing so, 26 rubles is the measure of how much such a saving would be worth. (Incidentally, 26 rubles is the price that would emerge from a linear-programming optimized plan for the economy.)

Pricing oil at its marginal cost generates *rent*. If the price of oil is set at 26 rubles per ton, the producers operating in the cheaper regions will receive income in excess of their outlays. In region A their revenue for 9 million tons of oil at a price of 26 rubles/ton is 234 million rubles, but their outlays are much less—3 million tons at 14 rubles each plus 1 million tons at 18 rubles each, and so on, for a total of 178 million rubles for the whole 9 million tons. The difference of 56 million rubles is "rent." The most important thing about this income is that it is attributable to the fact that favorable conditions in this region make it possible to produce most of the output at less than the price of 26 rubles/ton, rather than to any superior efforts or wisdom on the part of the managers in region A.

Operating with their Marxian average-cost-based idea of value, the Soviet planners traditionally calculated as follows: "Outlays for producing the 18 million tons of oil summed over all regions totaled 378 million rubles for an average of 21 rubles per ton, and so we should set the price at 21 rubles per ton to cover the 'socially necessary expenditures of labor.' " The requirements of *khozraschet* would be met by having the low-cost producers subsidize the losses of the high-cost producers out of their extra profits.[2] But this method of pricing is a bad solution in that it sends the wrong signal to users of oil. The real drain of an additional ton of oil on the society's production potential is *not* 21 rubles but 26 rubles, and it would be worth spending 26 rubles to save a ton of oil, though it would apparently save the user contemplating such an action only the 21 rubles paid for a ton of oil.

Eventually in the USSR it was recognized that an average-cost price was not a good signal. The idea has gradually won acceptance that price should be set at something like marginal cost, and that the state should collect as "rent" the large profits accruing to the advantageously situated cheaper producer. Unfortunately, it was not understood that this rent should be collected in the form of a lump sum, i.e., a per-year charge to each set of managers for the right to use the resources over which they are given stewardship. Such a lump-sum rent payment would force the enterprise to produce at the optimum level if it is to earn the rent it must pay to the owner. When the USSR finally introduced a rent charge for oil, it was formulated as a per-ton payment. Dividing the total rent of 56 million rubles possible in region A by 9 (= 6⅔), the producer in that region was

---

2. At 21 rubles/ton, the producers in region A would still have a net revenue, after covering costs, of 11 million rubles. The producers in region B would have a loss of 3 million rubles, and those in region C would have a loss of 8 million rubles.

told that it would get the marginal cost price of 26 rubles per ton less the rent of 6⅔ rubles per ton, or 19⅓ rubles per ton. This enterprise thus finds that some of its output (everything beyond 4 million tons) incurs a loss. To the extent that its success is measured by a bonus function that gives some role to profit (remember the bonus function?), it is tempted to underfulfill the plan. This example might be described in various contexts as a pricing problem, or as a problem in correct establishment of a bonus function. But the point being illustrated here is that by not distinguishing the income attributable to a particular form of property, and by failing to perform the ownership function of acting as a "rent-seeker," the state as owner is failing in its responsibility to see that property is exploited in the most productive fashion. Although we are dealing with the issue of rent here in a very simple and schematic way, this general conclusion about the consequences of the state's failure to exact rent for the resources over which it exercises ownership rights holds for all kinds of natural resources.[3]

Property income is sometimes interpreted in bourgeois economics as a motivation for saving—people save and invest in property in order to receive a long-run return exceeding the original investment. The Soviet-type economy in its control over the physical division of GNP into consumption and investment created a powerful alternative mechanism to ensure saving. The rate of saving can be thought of as a choice between income now and income later, which has as one dimension the inter-generational allocation of the society's income. A high rate of saving means a sacrifice of consumption today in favor of more capital formation generating larger consumption possibilities for the next generation. A state-imposed high rate of saving is one of the hallmarks of the classic Soviet-type model. This mechanism substitutes the preferences of the leadership for a consensus on the part of the population regarding the right rate of growth and the claims of the current generation versus those of later generations. So privatization, the extension of property rights to indi-

---

3. Although I will not go into it here, the student of Econ 1 may recognize that the argument can be extended beyond natural resources. Much of the man-made capital already in existence is in fixed supply just like natural resources, and the income from those resources is a "quasi-rent." The problem of how to assess and collect that quasi-rent depends on correct pricing as in the oil example.

viduals, is at the same time a way of transferring the decision about intergenerational equity from the state to the most interested party, i.e., the currently active generation.

Creation of New Property Institutions in the Reforms

The question of what to introduce in the way of new laws and approaches concerning property is one of the most controversial aspects of reform programs, and the response has varied among countries and over time.

Eastern Europe

The reformers moved earlier and more boldly on privatization in Eastern Europe than in the USSR. Those economies have generally allowed the emergence of larger private sectors than the USSR. Considering all types of legal private economic activity, including co-ops (private-plot agriculture, construction services, and so on), the private sector in the early eighties accounted for almost 15 percent of all output in Hungary and Poland, almost 10 percent in Bulgaria, and about 3 percent in Czechoslovakia, East Germany, and Romania. This latter figure also holds for the USSR.[4] Beginning in 1989, with a new noncommunist government in Poland and a new reform agenda being worked out in Hungary, these two countries began to sell off considerable blocs of assets either to domestic citizens or to foreigners. An example of the latter was the sale of a controlling interest in the Tungsram enterprise (which manufactures light-bulbs) to the General Electric Company. Poland has begun extensive efforts in this direction under the new noncommunist government, and presumably the other East European economies, especially Czechoslovakia, will be doing the same. Since these countries have gone further or thought it out more, we can usefully look at them more carefully to see what some of the problems are. Privatization turns out to raise a host of difficult problems.

One requirement is to set a valuation on the enterprise and its assets, i.e., to figure out the "net worth," or the equity potential, of an enterprise.

---

4. *Planecon Report*, vol. V, no. 38–39.

Table 9-1. Balance Sheet of a Socialist Firm (in thousands of rubles)

Liabilities		Assets	
Charter capital	1,700	Plant, at original cost	2,000
Accumulated profit	200		
Indebtedness to state		Settlement account in	
bank	300	bank	100
		Receivables from other	
Payable to other firms	150	firms	200
Pay due workers	50		
Depreciation reserve	500	Inventories	600
TOTAL	2,900	TOTAL	2,900

The balance sheet of the traditional socialist firm looks something like table 9-1. Starting with such a balance sheet for a firm, we can define its net worth as assets minus liabilities, which in this case consist of indebtedness to the State Bank, amounts payable to other firms, and accrued wages due workers. We should probably also subtract the depreciation reserve, as a correction to the original-cost value at which the assets are shown on the balance sheet. So for this firm the net worth would be figured as 1,900.

But that calculation has taken the balance-sheet figures at face value, which may be highly misleading. It may be that there is little prospect of this firm's ever repaying what is due the bank, and as part of a reform package the government may simply wipe out that indebtedness. Or it may be that the prospect of collecting what is due from other firms is very slight. In the calculation in table 9-1, we corrected the value of the plant for an estimate of the *physical* wear it has undergone, but it may be that in the face of a reform of the whole economy, the plant has lost value in other ways as well. In many cases these plants are equipped with old technology, are located in the wrong places, or are suited to producing only old-fashioned product lines. In the new situation, with market pricing and the prospect of competition from newer domestic firms or from the world market, the plant is worth much less than the cost at which it was acquired and at which its equipment is shown on the balance sheet.

However the net worth is valued, the task is either to sell that equity as a complete package, or to divide it up into a number of shares, to be sold or perhaps given away. Alternatives include (a) handing over the plant, or the shares indicating ownership of it, to the workers who happen to work in that plant; (b) distributing the shares gratis to the populace at large, in randomly chosen combinations, or against vouchers previously issued to the population; (c) handing some of the shares over to the government; (d) selling shares to foreigners, other firms, banks, or individuals. These various transfers of shares might be unrequited, or payment might be required in the form of (a) full payment in cash; (b) a down payment, with the buyer to pay in the remaining value in regular payments or by pledging future earnings; (c) credit extended to buyers by the state so that they can pay the full cost of shares but have a debt to the bank. These many alternatives can be combined in numerous ways.

Now we can begin to see what some of the problems are. If the equity is to be distributed gratis, a distribution formula must be chosen—should everyone get the same number of vouchers, or should the number be differentiated by years of previous employment? If the workers in each plant are made the owners, some will inherit old, loss-making plants worth essentially nothing, while others who have sacrificed no more under socialism than the former will inherit more modern plants perhaps equipped with modern American machinery. If the ownership is turned over to the workers, how are they to organize to exercise their rights to control how the firm is managed? If these shares are made easily transferable, the new worker-owners might choose to sell them massively to foreigners, exchange the hard-currency proceeds for consumer goods, and thus exacerbate the problem of the external balance. If a large overhang of cash exists, selling shares for cash would be a way to pull in a lot of the excess cash, but that raises issues of economic justice. The cash may be very unequally distributed, and we would likely be transferring shares of the national patrimony to those who have managed to enrich themselves in some illegal way under the old system. There is a danger that manager/ bureaucrats currently in charge of enterprises, who will organize the sale, will engage in self-dealing. That is, they may sell the equity in the new firm to themselves at a price well below its real value, or to foreigners at bargain-basement prices, against an assurance that they will be left undisturbed in their control of the firm or given a "golden parachute."

So privatizing existing property is not an isolated component of reform.

Rather, it must be part of an integrated package of reforms that offers some solution to such problems as the treatment of the foreign sector, reform of the banking and fiscal system, and establishing rules for company formation and governance, and is based on some appropriate macroeconomic arithmetic.

Privatizing land and urban real estate present distinctive problems. Most land in socialist societies is being used by enterprises or other organizations under some rather ill-defined use rights. State enterprises usually have what amount to long-term use rights to the land they occupy or the natural resource they exploit. Agricultural cooperatives are often said to have "rights of use in perpetuity" of the land assigned to them, but in fact the state has been arbitrary in taking land away from one collective farm and transferring it to another, or to state uses. Urban land and the structures (commercial premises and housing) on it likewise have a confused status. For industrial enterprises we might just convert those use rights over land into outright ownership. Most of the proposals regarding agricultural land involve keeping it in state ownership or in the hands of the cooperatives, and leasing it on a very long-term basis to the members of the co-op who work it. The special difficulties here come from the fact that land has been so poorly utilized that its return and hence its value are currently low, but are likely to appreciate rapidly if reform is successful. So there will be a big windfall to whoever is granted ownership rights over land, which raises serious equity questions. For urban land and urban infrastructure such as commercial buildings and housing, title might be transferred to the local governmental units, which would then manage the property, collecting rent, or maybe selling it to occupants and lessors after market forces have begun to signal realistic values for land.

We might summarize by characterizing the problem as one of access and equity. Once ownership is transferred to private hands, we can assume that the owner will exercise her/his ownership rights more effectively than the state did. The owner will be the residual claimant, will have rights to make decisions about its use, and will make these decisions with an eye to maximizing his/her income, the capital gains, the market value of the property. But the scheme we use for getting this equity into the hands of some owner raises big issues of fairness. One of the most vexed problems is how to value the firm. In the USSR there was a proposal made in 1989 to sell off most loss-making firms to the workers, but obviously the workers would be a bit wary about what they pay for a firm that incurs losses and has accumulated debts. Similarly, many firms in Eastern Europe come not only with assets but with huge liabilities in the form of the prospect that in a more environmentally conscious regime they will be called on to do an expensive cleanup of past pollution. Privatization also raises important issues of macroeconomics. If existing equity is *sold*, then the funds needed to buy equity may crowd out other kinds of investment. The reformers see a second channel of privatization in the formation of new firms (co-ops, private firms, joint ventures with foreigners, etc.), and these firms, too, will be trying to raise funds by selling stocks. If privatization involves selling off too much of the ownership rights to formerly state-owned property to the public, there is a danger of crowding out sources of investment for these new, more entrepreneurial firms.

There is also a problem of creating a stock market. Whether as a source of finance or as a method of social control over management, there needs to be both a primary market (in which new issues are sold) and a secondary market (in which existing stocks are traded among owners). Such a secondary market is necessary to give an owner a way to get rid of a stock when he or she loses confidence in the management of the firm. This process both enhances the willingness to buy stock in the first place, since it is not an irrevocable commitment, and motivates managers to be attentive to the rights and interests of the owners. It will be necessary to create a whole apparatus of brokers, agents, and rules of the game. The special problem here, familiar in other societies as well, is the danger of fraud, use of insider information, and efforts to avoid competition.

The USSR

The reformers in the Soviet Union have gone through a long period of sharp debate and some experimentation on the issue of ownership and property. By the beginning of the nineties they had made modest beginnings on a few aspects of this complicated problem. In the first round of reform in 1986, two important changes were a law that permitted expanded scope for cooperatives and individual labor activity, and the law on the state enterprise. The law on cooperatives was intended to open wider the door to private economic activity, including ownership. The rules for co-ops were defined in a way such that the cooperatives' assets constituted private property. The earnings of a co-op after meeting tax obligations, and any productive assets purchased with this income, belonged to the members of the co-op. Its members could make their own decisions about setting up a business, exercising full managerial control, transferring or liquidating the co-op, and disposing of its property if they saw fit. But this form catered to the socialist notion that ownership income must accrue to the workers, rather than to someone who had only put in capital. The co-op members were owner-workers enjoying the product of their labor and assets with no one exploiting them. The legislation also set size limitations on these co-ops. Unsurprisingly, inventive entrepreneurs soon found ways around these limitations, and many co-ops became in effect private companies in which managerial and income rights were concentrated in the hands of a very small group.

One new idea for improving performance was to establish joint ventures with foreigners. The Soviet-type economies have always drawn the line at simply letting foreign firms and foreign capital operate in their economies, but the idea of joint ventures was that foreigners could establish new firms in partnership with domestic socialist enterprises, and that the foreign partners would be co-owners of the new venture along with some domestic firm. The foreigner would put in part of the investment, participate in running the venture, receive a share of the profit, and, if the joint enterprise was liquidated, retain a share in ownership of whatever was realized on liquidation. This means the rights of the foreigners in the important areas of control and rights to appropriate the income must be defined. Soviet rules started off with rather restrictive controls on the rights of foreign partners, but were later relaxed to give them more and more rights. In the beginning foreigners did not have the right of control, being limited to an ownership share of less than 50 percent, but this was later changed. They did have a right to appropriate their share of the income. But how meaningful this right is depends on the ability of the foreigner, in a situation where the domestic currency is not convertible, to repatriate these earnings or the capital itself in case of liquidation.[5]

---

5. The East European reform legislation dealing with joint ventures has usually treated foreign capitalists much more leniently.

The Soviet "law on the state enterprise," introduced in 1986, offered the idea that the means of production assigned to state enterprises were "property of the people as a whole" but that the labor collective of the enterprise was to think of itself as boss, using this property on behalf of society. That seems rather an internally contradictory idea, but it was an attempt to give the workers a sense of one of the ownership functions, *management* of property. That law also permitted the leasing of enterprises or parts of enterprises to the workers, in which case the enterprise was no longer subject to direct day-to-day control by its nominal superior. Its responsibilities to the state as owner were spelled out in a lease contract rather than in the form of a cyclical planning and evaluation process. Leasing overlapped with the creation of cooperatives, since the workers to whom a plant would be leased were usually organized as a cooperative.

When the Soviet reformers took the first steps in developing a serious reform program in 1989, the program was said to rest on "five whales." (This is a variation on the three whales which in some Russian cosmologies hold up the world.) One of these whales is the law on property. This law and the activities under it go partway toward establishing a basis for private property, but the Soviet effort as a whole has been much more equivocal than the East European programs. The more serious reformers have expressed an intention to shift a large part of all state industry (the majority of it, in fact) away from state property to other forms. Unfortunately, the original law on property is not an adequate base for that goal. It allows the formation of joint-stock companies, but only vaguely. What is needed is an unequivocal acceptance of private property, the clarification of how equity in an existing enterprise should be distributed when it is transformed to private ownership, etc. Also important is a more complete company law that tells how to organize companies, authorizes the creation of new firms on a routine and nondiscriminatory basis by anyone, and settles issues concerning the apportionment, monitoring, and disposition of worker equity in worker-owned firms. In the USSR, more elaborate legislative enactments on the subject of company law, issuance of stocks and bonds, encouragement of small business, and others have since been passed, laying the basis for a private business sector. Nevertheless, there is a still a great deal of ideological and popular opposition to moving ahead strongly with privatization.

One pioneer Soviet enterprise undertook to sell shares to its workers, and in a number of cases enterprises were given the right to sell shares to other enterprises and institutions. Some banks were formed on the basis of selling shares to institutions. But as of the beginning of the nineties, these experiments were generally primitive and tentative, advanced in a climate that provided no clear signal that they were considered normal, and where there was no clear law as to what was possible. In all these experiments shares were sold only to an enterprise's own workers or to other enterprises, not to the general public, and there was no provision for trading in these shares. Moreover, most of them did not really settle how the stockholder/owner's equity in the enterprise was to be translated into control over management, or make clear how the stockholder's claim against the income of the enterprise was to be settled.

Under the guise of the law on the state enterprise, some schemes were advanced for turning state enterprises into entities jointly owned by the state and the workers' collective. One of the first was an experiment at the Saratov aircraft plant, which was to become the model for similar transformation in many plants in the aerospace branch. Workers would either buy out part of the state's share, or over time finance expansion through their own contributions, evidenced by ownership of shares. The income after other obligations had been met would be divided in proportion to ownership, and control of the enterprise would be in the hands of a council representing both classes of owners. This experiment had a hard time obtaining approval, and has not gone very far. Another big step in this direction was a law on leasing and an announced intention to get many loss-making enterprises out of the state sector and off the state budget in 1990 by leasing them to their workers. The law also offered the possibility of letting workers ultimately buy the enterprises. It was planned to thus dispose of some 8,000 of them. But absolutely nothing was done in 1990 to carry out this plan.

All of these nonstate forms that transfer some rights to the workers in an enterprise lead to a problem of how to distinguish and handle income and equity claims of individual workers. As an enterprise continues to carry on production, its income (to which the workers have a claim) will be partly shared out, partly invested. The growth of assets if they are used correctly will mean a growth in income, and perhaps a need to add new workers. Inevitably the workforce will undergo some turnover, with some workers moving or retiring and some new workers being recruited. The question is how to share out the portion of the income attributable to income invested in the past, how to let a retiring member of the collective recover his equity, how to treat a new worker who has not previously contributed to the capital and hence to the current earning power of the enterprise. There is a similar set of issues about the *management* rights that go along with ownership. All these issues take on another dimension if the workers and the state are co-owners of the enterprise.

This problem of how to juggle equities and management rights was first faced in the Yugoslav case in which cooperatives were taken as the true embodiment of worker ownership of the means of production. There has been a great deal of debate among analysts of the Yugoslav model about whether worker/owners would have interests that would induce them to make decisions that were nonoptimal for the economy. As an example, if the new workers were to have equal rights with existing workers in sharing the income of the enterprise, workers in a profitable enterprise might be reluctant to expand output by adding new workers. In the usual case, the productivity of the marginal workers would be below the average, and giving them equal incomes with the workers already in the co-op would lower the income/person of the latter. The worker-owners of the co-op would thus be motivated to keep output too low, in effect acting like monopolists. The existence of profits is a signal that the firm's output *should* be expanded. Without reviewing all the theoretical considerations and actual experience with this problem, I will say only that there is a solution to this and other such difficulties with cooperative ownership, namely, properly distinguishing and accounting for incomes accruing to workers as workers from those due them as owners. There are ways to do this, as can be demonstrated both theoretically and by the practice of cooperatives in many countries. But this part of the problem is still very poorly understood in the socialist countries, and is yet to be worked out. Many of the co-ops formed in the USSR in the first year or two operated with very short-term horizons, and have not been in existence long enough to come up against these issues.

A third important step was to allow peasants to lease land for long periods of time. But all these were very small, tentative steps, much less complete than a full-scale program. And in the early stages there was no coherent understanding of how the response of agricultural producers was related to security of tenure and the environment in which private agriculture would function. There are discussions of the need to charge rent for urban land, and even to let some agent of the state auction the right to use it.[6]

To sum up the Soviet experience as of 1990, it seemed clear that ideology, public attitudes, and bureaucratic resistance constituted an evil alliance that made it impossible for the USSR to proceed as rapidly with privatization as did some East European economies. But sooner or later the Soviet reformers will have to follow the East European precedent in this area. All the more radical reform programs, such as the RSFSR 500 days program or Lithuanian plans, embodied extensive privatization schemes.

The conclusion I want to draw is that "state ownership of the means of production," the last bulwark of the administrative-command system, is coming to be seen in a new light by socialist economists, and arrangements are being proposed that will permit the privatization and marketization of some property rights along with the marketization of other economic valuables. The semi-reformed economy that marketizes everything except property rights will find that one of the crucial tools for effective production—rent-seeking by an active residual claimant—is still missing. "Privatization," understood in this way, appears to be one of the necessary conditions for effective reform.

---

6. "Tsena zemli Moskovskoi," *Ekonomicheskaia Gazeta*, 1989:12, p. 18, and other articles in earlier issues, 1988:33 and 49.

10.

The Problem of Transition and the Future of Reform

The goal of this final chapter is to cover three main questions: (a) What kind of system might we imagine as the end point of reform—how far will the process have to go before the system becomes stable and effective? (b) How fast should the transition be attempted, and with what sequences and priorities? and (c) Is a full transformation of the centrally administered economy into a market-type economy in fact possible?

There is a standard process at work in socialist economic reform that has come to be understood and generalized in a large literature that has accumulated over the years.[1] The experience of reform has consistently been that it creates new problems even as it generates some improvements in the functioning of the economy. Various components of the reform package are inconsistent and work at cross-purposes. Since reform upsets established ways of doing things, it results in confusion and economic disruption. The introduction of reforms is hindered by those whose private interests they contravene. As the defects inherent in partial reforms are revealed, the enemies of reform are emboldened to renew their attack on it. At this point the leaders face a choice between going forward or retreating. If the choice is to go forward toward loosening central control still further in favor of market principles, the intensified reform measures may well lead to new undesirable side effects, such as the inflation and income-distribution issues discussed in earlier chapters. This cycle may continue through several iterations.

This dynamic pattern has occurred over and over again in Eastern Eu-

---

1. A number of relevant works are included in the Suggestions for Further Reading at the end of the book.

rope, in China, and especially noticeably in the first several years of *perestroika* in the USSR. In Eastern Europe, reform began in the sixties in Hungary, whose leaders moved it forward slowly and cautiously over a quarter of a century. At about the same time reform programs were mooted in Czechoslovakia and Poland. In the first case, however, they were aborted by the Soviet invasion, and in the second the leadership used reform promises as a stratagem to allay public dissatisfaction with economic failure, but never moved consistently to implement reform proposals until the eighties. A real acceleration of reform and an extension to other East European countries that were still run essentially along classic lines came at the end of the eighties. In China reform started slowly in the seventies, then became more radical, but always with important limits—the major effort did not extend much beyond agriculture. In any case, as the inconsistencies appeared in the Chinese reform program in the eighties and motivated some to demand further reform and political change, the process was reversed after the Tienanmen Square demonstration and repression.

In the USSR, important decision points have emerged several times since reform measures were first promoted by Khrushchev, but until Gorbachev, the decision was usually to shrink back from radicalizing the original efforts. Even Gorbachev's energetic push for reform has exhibited the "two steps forward, one step backward" syndrome, but forward progress continued all during the 1985–90 period. As he has encountered obstacles, in the form of either political opposition or failure to improve performance because of inconsistency and incompleteness of the reforms, he has usually found a way to confound the enemies of reform, widen the scope of reform to include politics, and push economic reform to the next stage. The reformers appear to believe that if they do enough, fast enough, the process will become irreversible, and the option of stopping or going back will disappear. The Gorbachev administration seemed to have come to a decisive stage in reform at the end of 1989 and the beginning of 1990. Gorbachev had altered the political system to give himself the authority to reform, and the reformers had developed several general schemes and concrete legislation that would represent a real move toward marketization. But the decisive move had not yet been made by the end of 1990, and it was not certain that the USSR would follow the Hungarian and Polish paths.

Issues of the End Point

As reform moves forward, where will it end up? How far will these societies go toward full marketization? Throughout the history of reform in the socialist world, there has always been a line of criticism that accepts the need for some reform but is opposed to the idea of completely abandoning socialism and planning. As reformers conclude that halfway-house reforms are not going to solve the basic problem, and move on toward more extensive marketization and privatization, the opponents begin to ask, "If we do all these things, have we not ceded victory to capitalism, our mortal enemy?" The reformers have to come up with some response to the question, "What is *socialist* about the new system that you are creating?"

For some, whether the end result is socialism or not is not especially important. As time has passed, more and more people have come to believe it is necessary to reject all the old slogans and all the fundamental institutions of the communist order—the monopoly of power of the Communist party and the bureaucratic state, state ownership of the means of production, the whole economic mechanism of the administered economy. One strand of radical reform thought considers it necessary to go beyond just reforming the economy and create a "law-based society" or a "civic society." In general this means copying such features of a western society as a constitutional order, the rule of law, political accountability to the people, the legitimacy of political opposition, as well as a market economy. It was relatively easy for this line of thought to emerge and dominate in some of the Eastern European countries, where the whole Soviet-type system had long been resented by many as an alien imposition from outside. In rejecting Soviet dominance and the Soviet model, the people in Hungary, Poland, Czechoslovakia, and East Germany were regaining both their national sovereignty and their older, originally western, traditions. As part of that return to older traditions, many among the population were willing to give up some of the security of the old system and accept the hazards of an economy based on private property and the market, in the hope that such an economy would permit them the kind of life they saw in the West.

Other societies, and some groups in all of them, greet this prospect with much less enthusiasm. Bulgaria and Romania seem unlikely to shed the communist ways so easily—they do not really have a democratic western tradition to go back to. The leaders of some socialist societies have been able to fend off reformist ideas long after the strategic choice was clearly settled in favor of the market in Eastern Europe. North Korea and Cuba are obvious examples. In many of these societies, notably China and the USSR, a great deal of power has remained in the hands of the bureaucratic and political elites, who naturally have a material interest in preserving the privileges and rewards that system has provided them. But beyond these self-interested forms of opposition to marketization, there is an ideological residue in the minds of many ordinary citizens of socialist countries from the notion drilled into them for decades that socialism is good and capitalism is bad. There is also a broad current of popular feeling disturbed by the abandonment of what some see as positive values and features of socialism. In the USSR, for example, many citizens dislike the prospect of sharp inequalities in income. Wealth-creating activities and entrepreneurial push are not really accepted or valued by many. Probably most important is a preference for the security of a known system, versus the unpredictable consequences of change. These attitudes are probably more prevalent and powerful in the USSR than in Eastern Europe. The system has operated so long in the USSR that many people have adjusted their expectations and behavior to it, and have little appreciation of how they could possibly benefit under what they see as the harsh institutions of the market.

The first taste of reform confirms all these fears. Even halfhearted efforts at reform result in incipient inflation, growing losses for some enterprises, and threats to job security. In the USSR as the old system began to disintegrate, shortages of consumer essentials sprang up all over the map. Once the bolder reform pioneers take really significant steps to marketize and privatize, as in Poland, the feared results are glaringly clear for all to see—unemployment, price adjustments that threaten particular groups with destitution while others become rich through taking advantage of the profit opportunities that grow out of the distortions of the old system. Unemployment went in East Germany from virtually nothing to a figure in the millions; agricultural producers in Poland have been caught in an impoverishing price squeeze; some of those in cooperatives in the USSR and in private firms in China have managed to attain incomes exceeding those of state workers tenfold and more.

In all those societies the response of the reformers in the early stages to the question of where they aim to end up has typically been that they do not intend to abandon "socialism." The reformers usually resolve this issue by saying that the system they aim to build as an alternative to the administrative-command system will be different from capitalism. It will have markets and other forms of property besides state ownership, but this will be a market system with a difference—market discipline and private interests will be controlled or modified to ensure that "social justice" is achieved. During the first five years of *perestroika* as the Soviet leaders inched toward accepting the idea of the market, they usually said that they wanted to "combine plan and market" even in the final system. Those who appreciate and advocate privatization are still likely to say that they expect state ownership of the means of production to be maintained in the "commanding heights" of the system—transportation, communications, the banking system, the production of mineral resources. The farther the reformers move forward toward the fundamental measures required to solve the problem, however, the harder put they are to say what is distinctively socialist about the system which they are creating. Soviet reformers moved in 1989 and 1990 from the slogan of the "socialist market" (they were at a loss to explain how the socialist market differs from a market in general) to the slogan of the "regulated market." In trying to define an end point, many of the reformers refer to the combination of market and plan that they think they see in Sweden. As reforms move forward, the conflict between security and change, between stagnation under the old system and possible revival by market institutions, becomes ever sharper, and the conflict between those who do not want change and those who do will be exacerbated.

Issues in the Transition

Whatever the end point, it is still a long way ahead. In Poland and Hungary the transition to a market economy operating reasonably effectively may be basically completed by the mid-nineties, but for others the process may not be finished for a couple of decades. In the meantime there are urgent shorter-term issues to be settled on which there is little agreement.

One of the main controversies concerns the speed of transition. Should reforms be introduced gradually, giving institutions and individuals time to adjust, or is it better to abandon the old system "cold turkey"? The transitions will involve extensive turmoil and adjustments. Many enterprises will fail, many workers will lose their jobs and face the need to retrain and relocate. Firms that fail to innovate, modernize their production lines, and get rid of unproductive workers will lose income and market viability. If the economy is opened to the rest of the world, foreign competition will undercut the position of many producers and even whole sectors. The argument for going slowly is that it would be too painful to absorb all these adjustments at once. Moreover, for a government to try to *force* such a painful transition is not a politically sustainable course. The argument from the other side is that failing to reform rapidly merely prolongs the agony. A slow pace gives opponents the chance to drag their feet, and to entrench themselves in various ways to frustrate the reform. In this view it is better to move fast, get the pain over in a hurry, sweep away the obstacles all at once, creating conditions in which the situation can then get better quickly. In early 1990 Gorbachev formulated the question as whether the USSR was prepared for the Polish-type "shock therapy," and answered "no."

By the end of the year impatience with rapidly deteriorating performance under the old system had created support for a bolder approach, and such a reform plan was developed in the form of the "500 days program," also known as the Shatalin program. Unfortunately by the end of 1990, the USSR was caught in the turmoil of a constitutional crisis over the division of power between the all-union government and the republics. With this constitutional issue unresolved, without some consensus regarding such important economic issues as the division between the two of ownership rights to state property, taxing power, control of the money supply, responsibility for national defense or for a social safety net, it seemed impossible to design a program for reforming the economy that was acceptable to both sides.

Whatever pace is chosen, a related issue of phasing arises. Given the interrelated nature of economic institutions and behaviors, it can be argued that all the individual reforms (creating banks and introducing a hard budget constraint, accepting market judgments about prices and output mixes, privatizing and accepting private profit as the bottom line in economic decisions, etc.) have to be introduced simultaneously or *pari passu* with one another as the reform intensifies. This argument is the more compelling the more one believes it is crucial to carry out the reform in one big readjustment. But even in a crash program, and all the more so if the reformers envisage a transition period stretching out over several years, it seems reasonable to hold that there is some logical sequencing of measures in which one change sets the stage for another. To turn the argument around, it will do no good to introduce a particular change until the prerequisites for its proper functioning are in place through a previous reform step. For example, it is often said that until the monetary overhang is reduced or eliminated, it will be disastrous to introduce free markets for consumer goods, since the inevitable result would be rapid inflation and redistribution of incomes. It is also sometimes argued that getting rid of surplus labor in some of the most egregiously overstaffed enterprises must come before they are privatized, since private owners will face political constraints on their freedom to fire thousands of workers in high-visibility firms, causing mass unemployment in the socialist economy. Even if transferred to private hands, therefore, those firms would continue to incur huge losses, and gradually have to be renationalized to bail them out. Similar is the argument that privatization will not work unless some of the larger entities are broken up to forestall the exercise of monopoly power.

The structure of these economies is indeed highly concentrated. Most sectors are dominated by a few huge firms, with small and medium-sized firms conspicuously absent. Any given product is likely to be produced by one or a very small number of producers, and if enterprises are given freedom, and if administered pricing is abandoned in favor of the market, these firms will use their market power to push prices up. This will aggravate inflation by unleashing cost-push pressures, reinforcing the demand pull caused by the monetary overhang. To the extent that market power is unevenly distributed, the result will be to shift incomes from one group to another, one region to another, one industry to another. So it is argued that it is necessary first to break up the big enterprises, encourage entry for smaller ones, and open the economy to foreign competition before turning prices loose to be set by market forces.

Unfortunately, as this list of sequences gets elaborated, it begins to resemble the problem of the chicken and the egg. It may well turn out that measure A, which is a prerequisite for carrying out change B, turns out to be impossible until B is accomplished. There is thus a strong case for the simultaneity argument, and on that ground a quick transition. Since all these changes have to be made at the same time anyway, they should all be made quickly to shorten the period of disruption and turmoil during which there will be inflation, shifts in the price structure, balance-of-payments problems, enterprise bankruptcies, and a surge in unemployment.

One approach to the sequencing issue is to prioritize firms, sectors, and products for marketization and privatization. The general consideration that would seem relevant is differences in their expected ability to respond to the new conditions. Since it is impossible to do everything literally at once anyway, priority in marketizing ought to be given to those firms and sectors that promise a quick response to the new freedoms. The general determinants of this flexibility are size, length of the production cycle, and how much a firm depends on inputs from other firms. For instance, services are often chosen as one of the first activities to be opened to co-ops, joint ventures, and private entities on the grounds that their main input is labor, so that they can respond to market demand without depending on materials supplied by the still-unchanged old system. In privatizing, smaller firms are probably better bets. Focusing on the giants first would be a mistake because they have market power, they are wasteful, and they are likely to have managements that will not respond quickly. And they are likely to be tied in to the rest of the economy with extensive forward and backward linkages. Firms that have export possibilities are likely to appeal to foreign investors and attract outside capital, and on that ground might deserve special priority.

But analyses of where to start based on economic logic can take us only so far, and it is important to keep in mind important political considerations. It is a fundamental desideratum that there be some successes early, to maintain public support for the reform process. It is especially crucial to improve the living conditions of the population, and the reform program ought to give special priority to reform in those parts of the economy supplying consumer goods and services.

Another dilemma is the design of a "safety net." There seems to be general agreement that the government must provide some protection and compensation to people threatened by losses from the twin forces of unemployment and inflation. Unfortunately there is an inescapable conflict here—all the devices for providing a safety net are likely to slow the adjustments that reform is intended to force. Subsidies or tax relief that would cushion enterprises against losses and enable them to avoid major layoffs of employees prevents precisely what *must* happen to make the economy more competitive. Indexing wages of certain categories of workers, or indexing pension payments so that inflation will not inflict hardship on pensioners, or promising compensation to particular groups who will suffer from a jump in consumer-goods prices requires either inflationary budget deficits and money creation, or tax increases which will exacerbate the costs of adjustment felt by others.

If this list of hard choices persuades one that reform and transformation must be carried out cold turkey, then the question is whether the leadership can muster the political will and muscle to follow that course. It may be overly optimistic to expect that a government can get away with a rapid, all-encompassing reform with all the disruption it will bring. We have to keep in mind that reform is taking place in a situation where normal political institutions have begun to emerge, and with electorates who are demanding accountability from the government. But those political institutions are still weak, and the experience of democratic responsibility and compromise is still unfamiliar to many of the players. In the USSR, 1989 and 1990 saw the emergence of consciousness of power on the part of workers in coal, transportation, and the oil industry, the exercise of which could scuttle any reform program. There is a danger that popular discontent will topple governments through less-orderly processes than elections.

It would be foolish to pretend that there is some clear-cut answer to how to handle this political task. Nevertheless, it seems obvious that if reform measures are to be sold in the conditions described, it is important that the program be grounded in realism, that it address the fundamental issues, and that it be reasonably consistent and comprehensive. Moreover, it must be carried out in a political style of honest explanation by the government. The costs have to be acknowledged, and a clear explanation must be offered as to what results are expected. The longer reform drags out, the more the leadership temporizes and tries to soften it, the less likely it is that radical-enough changes will be made to actually improve economic performance.

Is Transformation Possible?

A textbook is obviously not the proper forum in which to offer short-term prophecies about the outcome of the reform process that has begun in the socialist world. Events are moving faster than the production cycle for writing and publishing textbooks. Ultimately, the issue is whether there *exists* a passable road from the old system to something much like the modern market economy, whether it is possible "to get from here to there." Without taking a dogmatic position on this question, it may still be useful to think over some possibilities.

An optimistic scenario for finding a way through these difficulties would go as follows. With skillful political maneuvering by reform-minded forces, with some material help and advice on economic policy management from outside, after some political turmoil and economic disruption, the economies of the old socialist world will turn the corner and take off on a course of economic renewal. What is required is a clear understanding on the part of the reformers of where they are heading and how they expect to get there, enlightened and resolute leadership, and enough political reform to establish the government's legitimacy in the eyes of the population. Using the example of the USSR, we can illustrate some possible ways through the economic pitfalls.[2]

As for the biggest obstacle, the monetary overhang, consumer-goods prices can be permitted to rise significantly, which means that the amount of money in existence becomes needed because of a rising transactions

---

2. Clearly we have to differentiate among the various cases. For East Germany, reunification offers a self-evident, straightforward path through these dilemmas. Reform there represents a simple takeover and absorption by an ongoing, vital system so large compared to East Germany that it can be absorbed with barely a ripple.

demand.[3] Some of the overhang can be channeled through banks to co-operatives and to private firms, so that it appears not as consumer-goods demand but as demand for real estate and existing assets. Some fiscal blunders can be reversed, as the Soviet government reversed itself when it backed off from its anti-alcohol campaign and thus restored some of the huge tax revenue from alcohol. It is possible to whittle away at cash hoards by selling government bonds and offering higher interest rates on savings deposits. The real supply of consumption goods can be increased by some borrowing abroad to finance imports, from conversion of the defense industry, and from a reduction in investment. The reformers can find plenty of expensive and unproductive capital investments that it will be no great loss to abandon. A complex of measures of this kind can get the consumer-goods market functioning again so that people can find goods to buy when they go to the store, and so that inflation can be held to tolerable levels. The Polish experience in 1989–90 demonstrates that this will work. Lines disappeared, and anything one had the money to buy was on display in a variety that had not been seen in Poland for decades. Moreover, after a short spurt of inflation early in the process, within a year prices had stabilized.

Even if these policies are not enough to get inflation under control quickly, we should remember that there are economies that have lived with considerable inflation for extended periods of time. Indeed, many societies have survived hyperinflation. One scenario is to let inflation go completely out of control, and start over again with a new currency. The USSR itself did that in the twenties when the old ruble was replaced with a new one.

On the production side, a clear message of encouragement and wholesale removal of bureaucratic obstacles to local and private initiative will lead to new enterprise formation via numerous channels. Following through on the new law on leasing and selling land to people leaving the collective farms should help with the most urgent problem in keeping *perestroika* alive, i.e., more food production soon. It will not happen immediately,

---

3. The stock of money that people and firms want to hold (the demand for money) depends on the total spending they do, i.e., Σpxq. If prices rise, Σpxq grows, and people and firms become content to hold what was formerly an excessive stock of money.

but the USSR could see a response from resolute encouragement of leasing in agriculture within a couple of years. On the production side, in contrast to the demoralization in consumer-goods distribution, Soviet observers report that the atmosphere within the enterprise, where people function as *producers*, has changed significantly for the better. The main difficulty is that the law that promised enterprises greatly expanded rights (the law on the state enterprise) has been completely disregarded by the central administrative apparatus, which continues to operate in the old way. As (if) the bureaucratic superstructure gets cleared away, we will see managers in the state sector beginning to take responsibility, acting in a more enterprising way, and trying to elicit real effort from the workforce by paying for effort and penalizing shirkers.

By careful distinctions and prioritization between sectors and tasks, it should be possible to keep enough of the economy functioning under the old rules in crucial areas such as transport, basic industrial raw materials, and energy to avoid breakdown, to sustain exports for hard currency, and to enforce by directive such changes as a reorientation of the defense industry.

More pessimistic assessments see too many roadblocks and pitfalls along the path described. The leaders have initiated a process that is spinning out of their control. Communist societies do not seem to have developed a very robust social order that can cope with social strains. If the old methods of maintaining order and keeping production going are destroyed, there is little civic sense, no political tradition or political culture, no sense of self-reliance among the population as a whole, to guide a spontaneous process of self-renewal, or to support positive forces for the emergence of a more modern social and political structure. There is little understanding or acceptance of the impersonal forces that dominate a market economy.

For the USSR, it must be admitted, the record so far is certainly not encouraging. In the initial steps toward change, the reformers have made some terrible mistakes and have lost valuable time. One of the most interesting things that have emerged in the process of *perestroika* is how poorly the leaders understand their own system and their own society. The sociologist Tatiana Zaslavskaia has made that point eloquently, the revisionist historians tell the same story, and Gorbachev offered that excuse as one reason for the financial chaos which the leaders permitted to emerge.

The momentous question is whether the reform leaders and the new actors that *perestroika* has empowered are learning fast enough to hold these societies together.

A special threat for the USSR, but also relevant elsewhere, as in Yugoslavia and Czechoslovakia, is the danger of a collapse of national unity and the breakdown of the national economy into a set of regional economies. Surely a great deal more economic decentralization is a viable and desirable course, and even if erosion of the power of the center goes so far as to permit areas to leave the Soviet Union completely to become sovereign nations, this need not mean economic collapse of the new collection of semi-independent entities. It is often argued that the economies of these regions are so closely integrated with the Soviet economy as a whole, in the sense of both their production specialization and their financial relations, that they cannot disentangle themselves, pursue reform at a different pace, or operate as economically viable entities. Certainly in the early stages of the Baltic drive for independence some things happened that brought home the disruption that goes along with breaking long-established ties. At one point the Estonians raised the prices on consumer goods, in search of several objectives. This move was intended to help the budget deficit, to encourage production, to draw in greater supplies through the price differential between Estonia and the rest of the USSR, and to discourage purchases by people from outside the region. But the impact on other cities was too disruptive, and the Estonians were forced to rescind it. The Baltic separatists have been told that their small republics cannot go it alone, that they are dependent on materials, energy, and other essentials from the rest of the USSR. They are warned that they have an exchange relationship with the rest of the USSR that is more favorable than they can expect if they try to redirect their trade elsewhere. Although it is not clear just how much of an advantage they get from this relationship, it is quite clear that leaving the USSR will mean a large loss for them to absorb. (Of course, if the Soviet system as a whole is shifted to market principles and opened to the world market, the exchanges of the Baltic region with the USSR will be based on world-market prices anyway.) The counterargument is that this advantage in terms of trade is won at the cost of stultifying control and mismanagement from Moscow. If a republic can get free of that, it can quickly recoup any trading loss by the big productivity increases that will ensue. This argument may well make sense for the Baltic areas, given their location and their earlier cultural history.

But it is useful to distinguish economic viability and economic vulnerability. These smaller units are entangled with the Soviet economy, just as Hungary is entangled with the CMEA economies. Gorbachev, by unilaterally cutting off supplies of energy to Lithuania, has driven home the degree of its dependence on the rest of the USSR. The Lithuanian economy is so enmeshed with the rest of the Soviet economy that it is indeed vulnerable to economic pressure. But if we imagine a system in which the USSR seeks a normal relationship with a newly separated Lithuania, there is no reason it cannot be viable in the long run. The same argument applies to other parts of the USSR that have expressed their intention to seek independence. I would not, however, want to understate the practical difficulties of restructuring all these economic ties.

Another potential cleavage is that between the working class and the government. In Poland the labor interest as represented by Solidarity originally stood aside from reform, on the grounds that it was the communists who had created the mess and who should therefore bear the responsibility of cleaning it up. Only after the round-table talks and the formation of a new government was Solidarity co-opted into the reform process. In the USSR the coal miners have demonstrated a willingness to use for their own ends the bargaining power their control over a crucial input gives them. The railroad workers and the oil workers of West Siberia are talking along the same lines. If strikes become widespread, it would wreck whatever progress the reform program is making.

Another division is agricultural producers against the urban sector. This is an old division, and in none of these countries did industrialization go far enough to destroy agricultural producers as a powerful interest group. So far, this potential conflict has not become very open, though in Poland it has shown some signs of doing so.

There is something paradoxical in the way that a reforming leadership may be the victim of its own reform accomplishments. There is always a danger of raising unrealistic expectations, and even as the actions of the reformers begin to transform the old system, they may be unable to move fast enough to maintain the trust and forbearance of the population and will not be granted the time needed to make a reform program work. In the pessimistic view, none of the prerequisites of the optimistic scenario get fulfilled, and rather than generating improvement, the reform process will spiral down to stagnation and disintegration. Some have pointed to Argentina as one example of such an outcome. Argentina at the turn of the century had a GNP per capita on the same level as the U.S., and even at the beginning of the Second World War it was generating reasonable economic performance. But in the decades since, it has seemed incapable of developing a social contract that would support effective economic policies.

If *perestroika* does not work, what will happen? One possibility is the "Chinese solution" or the similar efforts on the part of old leaderships in Romania, Bulgaria, and North Korea. That involves a political decision to marshal the coercive power of the state while the regime is still in control to introduce repressive political policies, accepting that this means the end of economic progress. That seems an unrealistic prognosis for the USSR. The reform process has probably passed the point where it is possible to turn back to the classic Soviet model in either economics or politics, and even many conservatives in the USSR reject that course. The most powerful argument of the reformers is that going back is a dead end, and that there is no other way than to go forward with reform. Gorbachev has rejected as unacceptable the vision of socialism as just "a third world country with guns." This judgment is shared by the majority of the population who really do have a powerful aspiration for what they have come to describe as a normal, civilized life. They mean by that the kind of life they see or hear about in the West. This is probably even more true in Eastern Europe. It is far from clear whether the "Chinese solution" will be viable for very long even in China. When Deng dies, a new and younger leadership may emerge from the political scramble to resume the march toward economic and political reform and modernization. The reform of the Soviet-type economic-political-social order around the world has gone far enough that it is now probably not possible to restore a totally repressive order that could pull things together and consistently follow retrograde economic measures.

Our book must end on a properly tentative note. What is happening in the socialist world is a kind of economic transformation that has no historical precedent. The phenomenon of economic system change is thoroughly familiar. But all the other cases of creating a market economy have taken place over much longer historical periods than is the case here, and the cases of abrupt revolutionary system change have been mostly in the opposite direction, as when Soviet-type planning was installed in the first place. In laying out such stark alternatives as successful transition to a market economy versus failure that ends in breakdown and stagnation, we have surely understated the richness of possibility that exists. Only as the process moves forward can we begin to make more confident predictions about the ultimate outcome.

Suggestions for Further Reading

Covering as it does a very broad spectrum, this book has treated many issues cursorily. The purpose of this bibliography is to provide a highly selective list of sources that a reader can consult to follow up on individual countries, on particular aspects of the administrative-command model and the extensive development strategy. There is a huge literature on this multicountry, multiyear experience. In selecting a few works to supplement this text, I want to provide some that are fundamental, definitive, comprehensive, and widely accessible in libraries. The transformation of the system occurring today has also attracted enormous attention and spawned a huge volume of materials. Unfortunately much of this is tentative, somewhat superficial in its focus on immediate events, and not infused with any analytical underpinning that can provide long-lasting help in understanding the issues and prospects. But just because so much is written, it is all the more important to offer the reader some guidance to sources that *are* authoritative, and likely to be relevant to understanding the evolution even as it continues. The suggested readings that follow are organized by general topical headings, with their special qualities noted in brief annotations.

On the basic administrative-command model and its functioning, four general textbook treatments with rather divergent coverage and approaches are Michael Ellman, *Socialist Planning*, Second Edition, Cambridge: Cambridge University Press, 1989; Robert Campbell, *The Soviet-type Economies*, Third Edition, Boston: Houghton Mifflin, 1974; Alec Nove, *The Soviet Economic System*, Third Edition, Boston: Allen and Unwin, 1986; and Paul Gregory and Robert Stuart, *Soviet Economic Structure and Performance*, Fourth Edition, New York: Harper and Row, 1990. The last of these contains a fairly detailed bibliography, which an instructor wishing to supplement this text with material for an advanced course will find very useful. A classic work on some of the basic ideas of organization and administration is Herbert Simon, *Administrative Behavior*, New York: Free Press, 1976. Browsing the library shelf in the neighborhood of that work's call number (the HD31 section in the Library of Congress system) will provide a long list of works on organization and administration in numerous contexts.

For extended treatments of some of the specific sectoral and functional issues that have been touched on only lightly, the following are recommended. For Soviet agriculture in terms of both historical background and the evolution of Soviet policy, see Lazar Volin, *A Century of Russian Agriculture*, Cambridge: Harvard University Press, 1970. A survey of developments in the Soviet Union toward the end of the old system is D. Gale Johnson and Karen Brooks, *Prospects for Soviet Agriculture in the 1980s*, Bloomington: Indiana University Press, 1983. A thorough analysis of how private and collective interests were intermeshed in Soviet agriculture is Karl Wadekin, *The Private Sector in Soviet Agriculture*, Berkeley: University of California Press, 1973. The factors influencing technological progress, especially at the point of innovative activity within the enterprise, are covered in the definitive study Joseph Berliner, *The Innovation Decision in Soviet Industry*, Cambridge: MIT Press, 1976. A broader study of scientific research and development activity in the USSR as the system matured is Harvey Balzer, *Soviet Science on the Edge of Reform*, Boulder: Westview, 1989. For international trade, two excellent books are Frank Holzman, *International Trade under Communism—Politics and Economics*, New York: Basic Books, 1976, and Philip Hanson, *Trade and Technology in Soviet-Western Relations*, New York: Columbia University Press, 1981. For a fuller exposition of the ideas and applications of input-output, a useful text is Ronald E. Miller, *Input-Output Analysis*, Englewood Cliffs, N.J.: Prentice-Hall, 1985. Finance, as explained in the text, has not usually been given a great deal of attention in western research on the Soviet-type economies, but two fairly comprehensive works are P. T. Wanless, *Taxation in Centrally Planned Economies*, New York: St. Martin's, 1985, and George Garvy, *Money, Financial Flows, and Credit in the Soviet Union*, New York: National Bureau of Economic Research, 1977. The fullest exposition of the idea of the soft-budget constraint by its originator is Janos Kornai, *Economics of Shortage*, Amsterdam: North-Holland Publishing Co., 1980. For anyone who wants to follow up on detailed institutions, sectors, functions, and performance, there is a rich mine covering China, Eastern Europe, and the USSR in the series of studies published for the Joint Economic Committee of the U.S. Congress over a number of years. Titles for the most recent cycle are U.S. Congress, Joint Economic Committee (JEC), *Gorbachev's Economic Plans* (2 vols.), Washington, D.C.: USGPO, 1987; *East European Economic Assessment:*

Slow Growth in the 1980's (in 3 parts), Washington, D.C.: USGPO, 1985 and 1986; *Chinese Economy Post-Mao*, Washington, D.C.: USGPO, 1978.

For descriptions of the Chinese variant of the basic model, see Christopher Howe, *China's Economy*, New York: Basic Books, 1978, or Nicholas Lardy, *Economic Growth and Distribution in China*, Cambridge: Cambridge University Press, 1978.

On the record of *Soviet economic performance and the growth model*, Abram Bergson and Simon Kuznets, *Economic Trends in the Soviet Union*, Cambridge: Harvard University Press, 1963, is the starting point in western sovietological understanding of the growth record. That measurement effort was ultimately continued by the U.S. Central Intelligence Agency, and its findings for the period 1950–80 are exhaustively laid out in U.S. Congress, Joint Economic Committee, *USSR: Measures of Economic Growth and Development, 1950–1980*, Washington, D.C.: USGPO, 1982. The long-term record and the growth strategy are neatly summed up in Gur Ofer, *Soviet Economic Growth, 1926–1985*, Los Angeles: RAND/UCLA Center for the Study of International Behavior, 1988. A perspective on where the system was headed at the beginning of the eighties, along the same kind of analytical lines, is provided in Abram Bergson and Herbert Levine, *The Soviet Economy toward the Year 2000*, London: George Allen and Unwin, 1983.

On growth performance of China and the character and impact of the reforms on growth, a comprehensive source is Dwight Perkins, "Reforming China's Economic System," *Journal of Economic Literature*, June 1988, pp. 601–645. An informative source on China's development level and growth prospects at the beginning of the period of its great success in the mid-seventies may be found in a set of studies by the World Bank, *China: The Long Term Issues and Options*, Baltimore: Johns Hopkins University Press, 1985. This general survey is supported by a number of specialized sectoral studies, including *China: Agriculture to the Year 2000*; *China: Economic Structure in International Perspective*; *China: The Energy Sector*; and *China: The Transport Sector*. A general treatment of the Cuban variant on the Soviet model is Carmelo Mesa-Lago, *The Economy of Socialist Cuba: a Two-decade Appraisal*, Albuquerque: University of New Mexico Press, 1981.

On the breakdown of the traditional system in the seventies, Robert F. Byrnes, ed., *After Brezhnev*, Bloomington: Indiana University Press, 1983, gives a thorough analysis of the mature, precrisis stage of the Soviet system in all its dimensions and the need for reform. For the ideas of the major mover of this transformation, there is M. S. Gorbachev, *Perestroika: New Thinking for Our Country and the World*, New York: Harper and Row, 1987 (for anyone who wants practice in Russian, the original version is *Perestroika i novoe myshlenie dlia nashei strany i dlia vsego mira*, Moscow: Politizdat, 1988). For a narrower focus on the economic dimension of this same line of thought, see a treatment by one of the early critics of the economic system and a major advisor to Gorbachev, Abel Aganbegyan, *The Economic Challenge of Perestroika*, Bloomington: Indiana University Press, 1988. Ben Eklof, *Soviet Briefing: Gorbachev and the Reform Period*, Boulder: Westview Press, 1989, surveys the first stages of *perestroika* from a multidimensional point of view. Another excellent study of the connection of economic to other aspects of reform is Timothy Colton, *The Dilemma of Reform in the Soviet Union*, New York: Council on Foreign Relations, 1986. A useful collection of analyses by the Soviet sociologist Tatiana Zaslavskaia, mentioned in the text, including her famous memorandum to the Central Committee that posited the impossibility of continuing the old system, is *A Bold Voice for Reform*, White Plains, N.Y.: M. E. Sharpe, 1989. The theme of perestroika as a reform for social justice is developed in Zaslavskaya, *The Second Socialist Revolution: An Alternative Soviet Strategy*, Bloomington: Indiana University Press, 1990.

On the semi-reformed economy and the process of transformation, an insightful early treatment of the problem of a halfway-house reform and the approach of trying to steer the economy by economic regulators is given in Janusz Zielinski, *Economic Reforms in Polish Industry*, London: Oxford University Press, 1973. Four excellent treatments of reform in the Soviet system are Anders Aslund, *Gorbachev's Struggle for Economic Reform*, Ithaca: Cornell University Press, 1989; Ed A. Hewett, *Reforming the Soviet Economy*, Washington, D.C.: Brookings, 1988; Padma Desai, *Perestroika in Perspective*, Princeton: Princeton University Press, 1989; and John E. Tedstrom, ed., *Socialism, Perestroika, and the Dilemmas of Soviet Economic Reform*, Boulder, San Francisco, and Oxford: Westview, 1990. For Eastern Europe, two general treatments covering the pre-1990 reform era are Judy Batt, *Economic Reform and Political Change in Eastern Europe*, London: Macmillan Press, 1988, and Jan Adam, *Economic Reforms in the Soviet Union and Eastern Europe since the 1960's*, New York: St. Martin's Press, 1989. Josef C. Brada, Ed A. Hewett, and Thomas A. Wolf, eds., *Economic Adjustment and Reform in Eastern Europe and the Soviet Union*, Durham: Duke University Press, 1988, is a collection covering the pre-1990 turn in the socialist bloc, and includes much material on how international economic relations fit into its development. The Blue Ribbon Commission, *Action Program for Hungary in Transformation to Freedom and Prosperity*, Indianapolis: The Hudson Institute, 1990, is an analysis and set of recommendations by an international group of economic experts for reforming the Hungarian economy; it is distinguished by its comprehensiveness, thorough mastery of the details of the Hungarian economic situation, and deep concern for the practical aspects of actually implementing a reform program. Covering some of the same issues over a broader spectrum, including the USSR, is "Privatizing and Marketizing Socialism," special issue of *The Annals of the American Academy of Political and Social Science*, January 1990. For the history and results of economic reform in China, see the article by Dwight Perkins cited earlier.

Finally, to serve the needs of a narrower group of readers—students beginning their study of this area—it may be useful to list a few Russian examples that convey the flavor of the internal analysis by Soviet economists themselves of both the nature of the old system and the issues in reform. This is the best way to appreciate the confused but growing understanding of the indigenous critics of the system and to sample the flavor of the controversies about it. Oleg Antonov, *Dlia vsekh i dlia sebia*, Moscow: Ekonomika, 1965, already mentioned in the text, is a wonderfully insightful interpretation at an early stage of the debate on reforming the system of the distortions of the incentive structure. Two interesting *glasnost'*-inspired pioneer analyses of the weakness of the system and the falsity of the official view of it are Nikolai Shmelev, "Avansy i dolgi," *Novyi mir*, 1987:6, available in translation in Isaac Tarasulo, *Gorbachev and Glasnost'*, Wilmington, Del.: Scholarly Resources Books, 1989, and Vasilii Seliunin and Grigorii Khanin, "Lukavaia tsifra," *Novyi mir*, 1987:2. The deeper understanding of the fundamental incompatibility of the bureaucratized command system with rational performance is brilliantly described in E. Gaidar and V. Iaroshenko, "Nulevoi tsikl: k analizu mekhanizma vedomstvennoi ekspansii," *Kommunist*, 1988:8, pp. 74–86. A similar analysis of the R&D process is found in B. G. Saltykov, "Nauchnyi potentsial SSSR: perestroika struktury," *Ekonomika i matematicheskie metody*, vol. 26, no. 1, 1990, pp. 122–134. A thoroughgoing analysis of the impossibility of improving performance without a full shift to marketization, by two economists from the radical wing of the reform camp, is Nikolai Shmelev and Vladimir Popov, *Na perelome: ekonomicheskaia perestroika v SSSR*, Moscow: Novosti, 1989. The set of changes that would be needed to change the behavior of the old system in Soviet conditions were laid out by Leonid Abalkin at a large conference in Moscow at the end of 1989 (*Ekonomicheskaia Gazeta*, 1989:47). Although the leadership shrank back from taking resolute action on even the milder of its recommendations, this document outlines the considerations and alternatives in a way that continues to be valid.

Index

Abalkin, Leonid, 197, 234
Academy of Sciences of the USSR, 61
Academy system, 61
Accounting system, for CPE, 100–106
Adam, Jan, 232
Administration, theory of, 13, 19–20
Administrative-command model, 9; three
  pillars of, 166–167. *See also* Ellman;
  Campbell; Nove; Gregory and Stuart
Advantage of backwardness, 120, 129
Aganbegyan, Abel, 232
Aggregate demand, regulation of, 154, 161–
  162
Agriculture: administrative control of, 67,
  91; co-ops, 206; growth of, 125, 135; mar-
  ket, 67, 75–82; neglect of, 137; reform,
  Chinese, 7, 140; reform, Soviet, 81, 82,
  206. *See also* Volin; Johnson and Brooks
Alton, Thad P., 131
Analiz khoziaistvennoi deiatel'nosti, 17
Animals, slaughter of, 125
Annual plan, 16–17
Antonov, Oleg, 50, 233
Aslund, Anders, 232
Associations, 24
Auction, currency, 176; in USSR, 183–186
Autarky, 29, 86; Chinese, 140; in Eastern
  Europe, 137
Average-cost price, 201
Avtobank, 169

Balance sheet: of socialist firm, 204; of
  banks, 157
Balance-of-payments problems, 86–87, 173,
  177
Baltic republics, 189, 225
Balzer, Harvey, 230
Banking system, 147; reform of, 155–160
Banks: commercial, 155–156; cooperative,
  169
Batt, Judy, 232
Batteries, 46
Bergson, Abram, 123, 124, 128, 231
Berliner, Joseph, 230
Bilateral balancing, 88, 173

Black market, 69, 115, 116
Blast-furnace products, 47
Blue Ribbon Commission, 233
Bogdanov, A. A., 19
Bogomolov, Oleg, 197n
Bonds, state, 69, 115, 163, 223
Bonus function, 44–46, 48, 49–50, 107, 202
Brada, Josef C., 232
Brain drain, 191
Branch science, 61
Budget: deficit, USSR, 159; organs, 26
Buffer sectors, 36
Bukharinite policy, 80
Bulgaria: agriculture, 136; growth, 131,
  135, 136, 137; privatization, 203; reform,
  216; repression, 227
Bureaucracy, 18; need to dismantle, 167;
  structures of, 22–30
Byrnes, Robert F., 231

Campbell, Robert, 229
Capital: allocation of, 57; deepening, 130;
  intensity problem, 54–57; stock, growth
  of, 128, 136; supply of, 56
Ceausescu, Nicolae, 18
Central bank, creating, 159–160, 168–169
Central Committee, 23
Central Intelligence Agency, 125, 129, 231
Chief administrations, 24
China: agriculture, 67, 80; free economic
  zones, 188; growth, 3, 138–140; income
  distribution, 4; inflation, 159; reform,
  214, 227; repression, 227. *See also* Per-
  kins; Howe; Lardy
Chou En-lai, 139
Citizens' property, 194
Clearing: exchange rate, 185–186; markets,
  71, 72
CMEA (Council for Mutual Economic As-
  sistance), 59, 143, 172, 176–177, 178–
  179
Coal miners, bargaining power, 226
Collective farm, 78–80; as labor pool, 121;
  market, 12, 69, 115; privatizing, 206
Collective goods, 161

form, 158–159; collectivization, 67, 76, 78–80, 120, 125; foreign trade, 86, 182–183; growth, 119, 127, 134; independence of republics, 189, 218, 225; inflation, 69; ownership reform, 207–212; privatization, 194, 203; productivity, 127–129; reform programs, 3, 4, 143, 146, 171, 214, 218, 224; research and development, 61–64

Valovaia produktsiia or *val* (gross output), 47, 48
Velocity of circulation, 112
Vietnam, 172
Vodka, cuts in production of, 69, 223
Volin, Lazar, 230
von Mises, Ludwig, 198
Vseobshchaia organizatsionnaia nauka, 19–20
Vyborg, 188

Wadekin, Karl, 230
Wage levels, 72, 110
Wanless, P. T., 230
Waste, 29, 48, 50, 114, 122
Wolf, Thomas A., 232
Women in labor force, 136
Workers: leasing firms, 209; new consciousness of power, 221, 226; owning firms, 205, 207, 209–211. *See also* Labor
World Bank, 172, 231

Yugoslavia: cooperatives, 211; foreign trade, 172n; inflation, 4, 159; reform, 141, 143

Zaiavki (requisitions), 34
Zaslavskaia, Tatiana, 197n, 224, 232
Zatratnyi mekhanizm (expenditure mechanism), 48, 126n, 155
Zatraty obratnoi sviazi (inversely related outlays), 57, 142
Zielinski, Janusz, 232

ROBERT W. CAMPBELL is Distinguished Professor of Economics at Indiana University. In addition to general analyses of the Soviet economy, his publications concern energy policy, research and development, military affairs, and the telecommunications sector in the USSR.